# Systems Training for Emotional Predictability and Problem Solving for Borderline Personality Disorder

# Systems Training for Emotional Predictability and Problem Solving for Borderline Personality Disorder

*Implementing STEPPS Around the Globe*

**EDITED BY DONALD W. BLACK**

AND

**NANCEE S. BLUM**

OXFORD
UNIVERSITY PRESS

Oxford University Press is a department of the University of Oxford. It furthers
the University's objective of excellence in research, scholarship, and education
by publishing worldwide. Oxford is a registered trade mark of Oxford University
Press in the UK and certain other countries.

Published in the United States of America by Oxford University Press
198 Madison Avenue, New York, NY 10016, United States of America.

Library of Congress Cataloging-in-Publication Data
Names: Black, Donald W., 1956– editor. | Blum, Nancee S., editor.
Title: Systems training for emotional predictability and problem solving for borderline personality
disorder : implementing STEPPS around the globe / edited by Donald W. Black, Nancee S. Blum.
Description: Oxford ; New York : Oxford University Press, [2017] |
Includes bibliographical references and index.
Identifiers: LCCN 2016048022| ISBN 9780199384426 (alk. paper) | ISBN 9780199384433 (e-ISBN)
Subjects: | MESH: Borderline Personality Disorder—psychology | Borderline Personality Disorder—
therapy | Psychotherapy, Group—methods | Cognitive Therapy—methods | Ambulatory Care
Classification: LCC RC569.5.B67 | NLM WM 190.5.B5 | DDC 616.85/85206—dc23
LC record available at https://lccn.loc.gov/2016048022

9 8 7 6 5 4 3 2 1

Printed by Sheridan Books, Inc., United States of America

# CONTENTS

Over the last 25 years or so, the treatment of personality disorder has changed almost beyond recognition. Pervasive pessimism about the value of treating a condition that was considered enduring has been replaced by recognition that this is a treatable disorder that is far less persistent than originally thought. At the same time, a paucity of treatment methods has been replaced by an array of therapies with diverse conceptual origins that have been shown to be effective in randomized controlled trials. These are important advances. However, despite this progress, many problems and challenges still confront the treatment of personality disorder. Not the least of these is that most contemporary therapies are relatively long-term treatments extending for a year or more and many require extensive training. This seriously limits access to care. Most health care systems lack the resources to make these therapies available to all patients requiring treatment. Although it is difficult to be precise about prevalence given the arbitrary nature of diagnostic thresholds, it is clear that personality disorder is common enough that it is not feasible to provide specialized, longer-term therapy for the majority of patients. It is also clear that the specialized therapies are not as effective as we would like. Even after long-treatment, many patients still show considerable impairment. Although treatment leads to symptomatic improvement, decreased self-harming behavior, and reduced use of medical services, quality of life and social adjustment remain poor and the core interpersonal and self-identity problems, the defining features of personality disorder, remain relatively unchanged. Also, given the tendency for some cases of personality disorder to improve without treatment, it is not clear that all patients need such intensive treatment. However, as is often the case in the early stages of the development of a field or a new treatment, such problems and limitations do not prevent excessive claims from being made about the efficacy of some of these treatments, which tend to be advanced as definitive treatments for personality disorder or in some way not as comprehensive or evidence-based than others, although the evidence suggests that this is not the case.

The publication of Systems Training for Emotional Predictability and Problem Solving (STEPPS) was a refreshing addition to the mix. Rather than adopting the traditional approach of long-term treatment, STEPPS offers short-term treatment, and rather than seeking to offer comprehensive treatment for all aspects of personality pathology, it focuses on a specific but important problem—emotional dysregulation. As a result, STEPPS offers a much needed treatment option. Also, the authors are modest in how they see STEPPS being used—they suggest that it may often be used as an adjunct to other forms of therapy or as a stand-alone treatment. Originally designed to make treatment available to patients with emotional dysregulation who are living in rural areas where resources are thin and geographical distances great, it is essentially a distillate of primarily cognitive-therapy interventions designed to teach the skills needed to self-regulate emotional distress and its attendant problems. However, STEPPS is not a "lite" version of cognitive-behavioral therapy to be used when longer-term therapy is not available, but rather a carefully designed treatment package that focuses on different components of dysregulated emotions and co-occurring problems, either as a stand-alone treatment or as an adjunct to longer-term treatment.

However, I think the really appealing thing about STEPPS is the role it could play in an overall system of care for patients with personality disorder. Given the prevalence of personality disorder, probably the most viable way for mental health services to provide effective care is through some kind of stepped care system. Stepped care is a system of delivering and monitoring treatments in which effective but less resource intensive treatment is provided first and more "stepping up" intensive and specialized services are only used as required. A stepped approach to treating personality disorder suggests that treatment could be organized in modules and that not all patients would require each module. With such a system of care, STEPPS, with its primary focus on emotional dysregulation, would be an excellent choice as the first line treatment for most patients. With such patients, little is achieved until emotion regulation improves. STEPPS also meets the requirements of a first-line treatment. It is a carefully structured treatment designed to meet the needs of patients who struggle with intense, unstable emotions that has been shown to be effective in randomized controlled trials. Moreover, unlike some longer-term treatment options, therapists do not need extensive treating to deliver it effectively and the use of a group format means makes it relatively inexpensive to deliver. Following STEPPS, patients needing further help could be treated with additional modules that address their residual problems.

The other interesting feature about STEPPS is the preparedness of its authors to think outside the box in their efforts to provide readily accessible, cost-effective care that meets patients' needs. Besides rejecting the usual structure of long-term, comprehensive treatment package and delivery through weekly individual sessions with or without an associated group session, they had the audacity to opt instead for group treatment being delivered in a classroom format—and why not? The usual pattern of treatment delivery is largely based on tradition and practitioner convenience. Nevertheless, this innovation runs the risk of being dismissed as merely a form of psychoeducation. There of course is nothing wrong with psychoeducation—it is a necessary part of any treatment of personality disorder. However, as this manual clearly shows, STEPPS is something more, and the classroom format is a planned way to contain the emotional reactivity that is a challenge in managing these patients.

In sum, STEPPS makes a valuable contribution to the treatment of personality disorder, not only by offering a well-thought-out approach, but also by forcing us to rethink how we go about the task of treating this complex disorder and whether the traditional formats in use for decades are really necessary. We urgently need to find ways to make effective treatment more widely available. This treatment program is an important step in this direction.

John Livesley
Professor emeritus
Department of Psychiatry
University of British Columbia

Twenty years after the development of STEPPS, we thought the time was ripe to collect and publish the body of work that had accumulated on the program. In 1995, Nancee had been tasked by our Department head, Dr. George Winokur, a hard-nosed but eminently reasonable man, with developing a program for these challenging patients. They were orphan patients in the sense that no one claimed them. The only widely available program was dialectical behavior therapy, so the idea of developing a new program that would better fit with our needs and those of our patients was audacious. Nancee searched high and low and found a little known program being used at the DuPage County Health Department in Wheaton, Illinois. Its developers (Norm Bartels and Teresa Crotty) graciously agreed to allow her, along with several clinic colleagues (Don St. John and Bruce Pfohl), to modify the program. That was the beginning of STEPPS. The modified program was expanded in length, given a more detailed structure that resembles an educational curriculum reflective of Nancee's training as a teacher before she became a clinician, and was then implemented in our adult psychiatry outpatient clinic. Nancee and others started recruiting suitable patients for what was seen as a grand experiment. It worked like a charm. Over the next few years, the program was tweaked as its deficiencies were identified. Word-of-mouth and Nancee's many presentations to regional, national, and international colleagues led to the program's spread.

That's when I entered the picture. Nancee and I had been colleagues and friends for many years, and through our many discussions, I became impressed with the program. I made it clear that we needed to publish research data if we were to successfully disseminate the program. With great effort, we developed a grant application and were funded by the National Institute of Mental Health (NIMH) to compare the program to usual care. This work eventually led to what was then (when published) the largest randomized controlled trial in the literature for a psychotherapeutic treatment for borderline personality disorder patients. The study was a success, and we could now convincingly show that it was beneficial to "real world" patients.

In the meantime, colleagues in The Netherlands and the United Kingdom had become interested in STEPPS. Because those countries have nationalized medicine, it is relatively easy to widely disseminate programs, unlike in the United States, with its fragmented health care system. The story behind the adoption of STEPPS in these countries is recounted in the book. We also made connections with psychiatrists and psychotherapists in Italy and elsewhere. Close to home, we introduced the program to the Iowa correctional system in 2005 and have been collecting evaluative data since then. We have now shown that STEPPS can be easily transported to prisons and community corrections settings, and it works just as well as at an academic medical center, community-based mental health clinics, and private practice settings.

We are grateful to the many colleagues around the world who have embraced STEPPS, particularly those who have translated the program into other languages or modified the program to suit a special patient population. We have encouraged this type of collaboration. Our goal has always been to help patients overcome their symptoms and have a better quality of life, not to focus on developing a business model.

We are grateful to the many patients who have thanked us for our work and told us through letters and emails how the program has transformed their lives. Many have also brought new ideas with them that have been incorporated into the program, including illustrations, poetry, and essays. We have also incorporated new ideas from therapists who are group facilitators. One of Nancee's primary goals (along with that her STEPPS co-authors) was to provide a highly structured framework that allows room for patients and therapists to incorporate creativity to make abstract concepts more concrete.

Special thanks go to Dr. Bruce Pfohl, STEPPS co-developer, who was director of the University of Iowa Adult Psychiatry outpatient clinic in 1995. Without his whole-hearted support and encouragement, the program would not have taken shape. The program has also benefitted from the unequivocal support of Department Chair Dr. Robert Robinson and his successor Dr. James ("Jimmy") Potash. Last, we are grateful to the talented staff at Oxford University Press, including Andrea Zekus, Sarah Harrington, and others who shared our vision for the book and made it possible.

Donald W. Black, M.D.
Nancee S. Blum, M.S.W.
December 2015

ABOUT THE EDITORS

**Donald W. Black, M.D.,** is Professor of Psychiatry at the University of Iowa Roy J. and Lucille A. Carver College of Medicine in Iowa City, Iowa. He received his B.A. from Stanford University and M.D. from the University of Utah School of Medicine. He received his psychiatric training at the University of Iowa, where he serves as Director of Residency Training and Vice Chair for Education in the Department of Psychiatry. Dr. Black is an award-winning teacher and clinician and a leading authority on personality disorders and impulsive behavior. He has authored several books including *Introductory Textbook of Psychiatry, 6th Edition* (with Nancy C. Andreasen), the *DSM-5 Guidebook* (with Jon E. Grant), and *Bad Boys, Bad Men—Confronting Antisocial Personality Disorder (Sociopathy), Revised and Updated.* He is a Distinguished Fellow of the American Psychiatric Association and is President of the American Academy of Clinical Psychiatrists.

**Nancee S. Blum, M.S.W.,** is a psychotherapist and Adjunct Instructor of Psychiatry at the University of Iowa Roy J. and Lucille A. Carver College of Medicine in Iowa City, Iowa. She received her B.A. in education, her certification in aging studies, and her masters of social work at the University of Iowa. She was a medical editor and writer for several years before joining the Department of Psychiatry at the University of Iowa. She is coauthor of the *Structured Interview for DSM-IV Personality* (with Bruce Pfohl and Mark Zimmerman) and is the developer of the STEPPS Treatment Program and its derivative versions (with Norm Bartels, Don St. John, and Bruce Pfohl). She serves on the Scientific Advisory Board of TARA (Treatment and Research Advancements in Personality Disorders) and is a founding member (along with Dr. Black) of the North American Society for the Study of Personality Disorders (NASSPD). Nancee also serves as a consultant and provides consultation and training for the STEPPS program in the Iowa Department of Corrections.

**Roberta Alesiani, MSc**
Clinical Psychology and
   Psychotherapy
San Raffaele-Turro Hospital
Milano, Italy

**Jeff Allen, PhD**
Department of Psychiatry
University of Iowa Roy J.
   and Lucille A. Carver College
   of Medicine
Iowa City, IA, USA

**Donald W. Black, MD**
Department of Psychiatry
University of Iowa Roy J.
   and Lucille A. Carver College
   of Medicine
Iowa City, IA, USA

**Nancee S. Blum, MSW**
Department of Psychiatry
University of Iowa Roy J.
   and Lucille A. Carver College
   of Medicine
Iowa City, IA, USA

**Silvia Boccalon, MSc**
Clinical Psychology and
   Psychotherapy
San Raffaele-Turro Hospital
Milano, Italy

**Serena Borroni, PsyD**
Assistant Professor
San Raffaele-Turro Hospital
Milano, Italy
Vita-Salute San Raffaele University
Milano, Italy

**Diane Clare, MA, Diploma in
   Clinical Psychology, AFBPsS**
Mind Business Consultancy
Nelson, New Zealand

**Paul Emmelkamp, PhD**
Netherlands Institute for
   Advanced Study
Wassenaar, The Netherlands
The Center for Social and Humanities
   Research
King Abdulaziz University
Jeddah, Saudi Arabia

**Andrea Fossati, MD, PhD**
LUMSA University
Rome, Italy
San Raffaele-Turro Hospital
Milano, Italy

**Horusta Freije, MD**
Association of Cognitive
   and Behavioral Therapy
Dutch Psychotherapy Association
The Netherlands

**Laura Giarolli, MSc**
Clinical Psychology and
    Psychotherapy
San Raffaele-Turro Hospital
Milano, Italy

**Renee Harvey, MA**
Sussex Partnership
National Health Service
    Foundation Trust
United Kingdom

**Aldo Lombardo, MD**
Raymond Gledhill Residential Centre
    of Integrated Sociotherapy
Rome, Italy

**Maaike Nauta, PhD**
Department of Psychiatry
University Medical Center
Department of Clinical Psychology
University of Groningen
Groningen, The Netherlands

**Bruce Pfohl, MD**
Department of Psychiatry
University of Iowa Roy J.
    and Lucille A. Carver College
    of Medicine
Iowa City, IA, USA

**Marieke Schuppert, MD, PhD**
Department of Psychiatry
University of Groningen
Groningen, The Netherlands

**Antonella Somma, PhD**
LUMSA University
Rome, Italy

**Don St. John, PA**
Department of Psychiatry
University of Iowa Roy J.
    and Lucille A. Carver College
    of Medicine
Iowa City, IA, USA

Systems Training for Emotional
Predictability and Problem Solving
for Borderline Personality Disorder

# Overview of STEPPS

## History and Implementation

NANCEE S. BLUM, DON ST. JOHN, BRUCE PFOHL,
AND DONALD W. BLACK ■

This chapter provides an overview of the Systems Training for Emotional Predictability and Problem Solving (STEPPS) treatment program, a manualized, cognitive-behavioral, skills-based group treatment program, originally developed as an adjunctive treatment for adult patients/clients with borderline personality disorder (BPD) who are being treated in outpatient clinics (Blum, Bartels, St. John, & Pfohl, 2002a, 2009, 2012). The 20-week program combines psychoeducation about BPD, cognitive behavioral therapy, and skills training with a systems component. The *systems* component is unique to the program and refers to providing members of the client's support system (i.e., family members, friends, and key professionals) with an understanding of the STEPPS approach, a common language to communicate clearly about BPD, and how to reinforce the skills that patients are acquiring. Although STEPPS was originally developed in the mostly rural state of Iowa, it is now used by clinicians around the world. STEPPS is recognized as an evidence-based treatment by the United States Substance Abuse and Mental Health Administration and listed on the National Registry for Evidence-Based Practices (National Registry of Evidence-based Programs and Practices, 2012). A further discussion of the research evidence supporting STEPPS is detailed in Chapter 2.

Data show that STEPPS is effective and superior to treatment as usual in reducing symptoms related to BPD (Blum et al., 2008; van Wel et al., 2009; Bos, van Wel, Appelo, & Verbraak, 2010, 2011; Blum, Pfohl, St. John, Monahan, & Black, 2002b; Black et al., 2008; Freije, Dietz, & Appelo, 2002; Harvey, Black, & Blum, 2010; Boccalon et al., 2012; Alesiani et al., 2014). Surveys of patients and therapists showed high levels of acceptance (Blum et al., 2002b; Freije et al., 2002). The manual has been adapted for use in the United Kingdom (Blum et al., 2009), and the program (VERS, described in Chapter 3) is widely used in treatment facilities in The Netherlands (van Wel et al., 2006). Several adaptations of the VERS program have been developed for a variety of settings and populations (e.g., parenting groups, support groups, assertive community treatment teams), and these are also described in Chapter 3. German and Italian translations have been completed, as well as an adaptation for adolescents in the United Kingdom (Harvey et al., 2014), described in Chapter 4, and The Netherlands (Chapter 9). Since its inception, the program has been implemented successfully in a variety of settings, including partial hospital programs, residential treatment facilities, day treatment programs, and forensic settings (prisons and community corrections). Chapter 6 describes the use of STEPPS in a residential therapeutic community in Rome, Italy; Chapter 7 describes the use of STEPPS in an inpatient setting in Milan, Italy.

## THE DEVELOPMENT OF STEPPS AND ITS RATIONALE

The clinical management of borderline personality disorder is widely considered one of the most challenging tasks that mental health professionals face. Many view the treatment of BPD as so difficult, and the response so disappointing, that they prefer to avoid working with patients who have the diagnosis (Black et al., 2011). Yet the disorder is one of the most common in mental health settings, and most mental health workers will find themselves caring for patients with this disorder throughout their careers (Samuels et al., 2002; Torgerson, Kringlen, & Cramer, 2001; American Psychiatric Association, 2000). BPD is associated with impaired quality of life, disturbed interpersonal relationships, and impulsive and self-destructive behaviors. The degree of functional impairment in patients with BPD is similar to that in patients with schizophrenia and bipolar disorder and adversely affects education, employment, and family and other interpersonal relationships (Conklin & Westen, 2005; Stevenson, Meares, & Comerford, 2003; Zimmerman & Coryell, 1989). Though remission rates in longitudinal studies are high, significant functional impairment often remains (Zanarini et al., 2012; Skodol et al., 2005). Many patients have childhood histories of abuse and continue to be victims—and perpetrators—of domestic and other violence into adulthood (Silk et al., 1995; Zanarini, 2000; Zanarini et al., 2002). BPD is also associated with substantial medical and psychiatric comorbidity, resulting in high utilization of both medical and mental health care services (Zanarini, Frankenburg, Hennen, & Silk, 2004; Nakao et al., 1992; Zanarini et al., 1993; Frankenburg & Zanarini, 2004).

Early psychodynamic approaches focused on helping patients address past adversities and relationships. This approach was delivered through long-term (i.e., years) individual psychotherapy, often in residential and inpatient settings—an expensive and inefficient approach that did not appear to reduce patients frequency of deliberate self-harm, acting out behaviors, or hospitalization rates. Pharmacotherapy has been disappointing, and no specific medications have been approved by the United States Food and Drug Administration. In clinical practice, many drugs have been utilized, and many patients end up on multiple drugs with limited benefit, thus contributing to concerns about polypharmacy. Such efforts have resulted in feelings of frustration for patients, families, and prescribers.

In the mid-1990s, in response to the need for more effective as well as more cost-efficient treatment, a small group of clinicians at the University of Iowa who were interested in treating patients with BPD (including psychiatrists with research and academic interests in personality disorders, a social worker, a psychiatric nurse practitioner, and a physician assistant with additional training in family therapy), gathered to review the current treatment approaches and develop a group treatment approach that could be effective and user-friendly (to patients and clinicians). We were also responding to pressures from third-party payers to lower the cost of care, decrease length of inpatient treatment, and reduce rehospitalization rates. Because of a shortage of therapists trained to treat BPD at our center and around the state and the labor-intensive requirements of individual psychotherapy for BPD, we sought a time-limited group treatment to use in the outpatient setting. We also sought a treatment that could be readily learned by clinicians outside of the academic setting yet flexible enough to encourage implementation in a variety of settings. We also sought to incorporate members of the patient's non-professional support system and facilitate improved, ongoing interpersonal relationships after treatment ended (systems approach).

At the time, dialectical behavior therapy (DBT) was the only group treatment model with empirical support (Linehan et al., 1991; Linehan, Heard, & Armstrong, 1993; Linehan, Tupek, Heard, & Armstrong, 1994), but its implementation was considered too challenging at our center, as well as in outlying clinics. DBT required an extended time commitment (1 year) that was not feasible in a rural state with limited mental health resources, long distances between mental health facilities, and unpredictable weather that makes attendance particularly difficult during winter months. For that reason, we preferred a shorter program. Next, we believed the program could not be labor and resource-intensive; such a program would be difficult to implement in small clinics and in rural settings. DBT, for example, requires patients to meet both in a group setting and individually with DBT therapists each week and for DBT therapists themselves to meet weekly to discuss the therapy. Cost was also a concern, with DBT requiring a considerable outlay of funds for training and certification.

Since the development of STEPPS, Yeomans, Clarkin, and Kernberg (2002) have described a manualized approach that focuses on transference, but it was felt that this, too, would be difficult to implement in our setting and with our patient population. Bateman and Fonagy (1999, 2001, 2008) have reported positive results from their mentalization-based psychotherapy (MBT). As with DBT, the program is lengthy (18-month partial hospitalization with both individual and multiple group therapy meetings per week) and requires extensive therapist training, time, and resources. Schema focused therapy (SFT; Kellogg and Young, 2006; Farrell, Shaw, & Webber, 2009; Arntz, van Genderen, & Drost, 2009), which has been used in The Netherlands, is a 3-year program, a commitment that is difficult for patients to maintain, given the high dropout rate commonly reported in this population (Rüsch et al., 2008; Barnicot, Katsakou, Marougka, & Priebe, 2011; Wnuk et al., 2013). Davidson et al. (2006) also reported positive results in a trial of individual cognitive-behavioral therapy, but that, too, was not what we envisioned for our clinic and patients.

Common to these various approaches is a high degree of structure, an assertive therapist stance, and utilization of cognitive-behavioral techniques that are taught in most post-graduate therapy training programs, such as recognizing individual schemas, identifying and challenging distorted thoughts, engaging in structured problem-solving, and attending to behavioral management (e.g., sleep, diet, etc.). We believed those elements should also be incorporated into the model that eventually became STEPPS.

After an extensive review of the existing models, we chose to modify a little-known program developed by Bartels and Crotty (1992) in DuPage County, Illinois. The psychoeducational approach suited our training and interests, although we believed the length of the program and the manual required modification. Its *systems* approach was particularly appealing because it recognized the importance of the patient's current social system (e.g., family and friends, professional supports, etc.). In the context of STEPPS, the systems approach focuses not only on teaching emotion regulation and behavioral skills to patients to enable them to manage the symptoms of BPD, but also on teaching these skills to those in their system (i.e., persons with whom the patient regularly interacts and shares information about BPD). It was our experience that patients with BPD are involved with an extensive array of professional care providers, community support workers, and other agencies (e.g., vocational rehabilitation programs, substance abuse treatment, case managers, etc.). However, there was rarely evidence of regular, consistent communication among providers or between these providers and the patient. Family members frequently expressed frustration with a care system that seemed to blame them for the patient's disorder while avoiding interactions with them, even when the patient gave permission for providers to share information.

Based on these considerations, we developed STEPPS. Initially we developed a supplement to the original Bartels and Crotty manual; later, with permission from the authors, we created an entirely new manual that combined the original material and the supplement. The program was lengthened from 12 weeks to 20 (22 weeks if an optional screening/intake session and a lesson specific to managing holiday season stress are included), provided specific client agendas and weekly lesson packets that included an increased use of algorithmic worksheets for specific situations clients might encounter, and detailed weekly lesson guidelines for group facilitators. The program has two phases—the basic 20-week skills group referred to as STEPPS (one 2-hour group meeting per week), and a twice-monthly, 1-year advanced program called STAIRWAYS, which is described later in the chapter.

Another goal was to create a program that required little additional training for mental health professionals, already time-pressured to fulfill their responsibilities for clinical duties and productivity goals. We believed that STEPPS should employ general psychotherapy principles and techniques common to most graduate-level psychotherapy educational programs, so it could be used by therapists from a variety of educational and professional backgrounds without requiring an extended period of training prior to implementation. Finally, we sought to create a program that would potentially improve the efficiency and effectiveness of the patient's ongoing treatment regimen, which typically includes individual psychotherapy, pharmacotherapy, and case management. With DBT, the patient may need to drop his or her current therapist in order to adopt a DBT-trained therapist. We were concerned that this would be especially difficult for patients who have difficulty developing trust and who readily experience feelings of abandonment (Gunderson, 1996) when asked to cut ties with an important provider who may be viewed as the most important member of their existing support system.

STEPPS is intended to supplement (or augment) the patient's existing network of mental health treatment and providers already in place. For this reason, the program is considered adjunctive, not comprehensive. (DBT is an example of a comprehensive program.) Patients participating in STEPPS are encouraged to continue receiving care from their present team of mental health professionals and other programs, such as substance abuse treatment, vocational rehabilitation, and supported community living programs (Blum et al., 2008, 2012).

## THEORETICAL FOUNDATION OF STEPPS

STEPPS builds on cognitive-behavioral therapy (CBT) principles known to be effective in patients with BPD (Linehan et al., 1991; Davidson et al., 2006), and it includes identifying and challenging distorted thoughts and specific behavioral change, combined with elements of SFT (Young, 1994), problem-solving therapy (Mynors-Wallis, 2005), and acceptance and commitment therapy (Hayes, Stosahl, & Wilson, 1999; Hayes et al., 2006; Forman et al., 2007; Ruiz, 2010). The systems approach was integrated to include the patient's social and professional support system and to train both patients and those in their system to respond more consistently and effectively using the STEPPS "language." STEPPS is not intended to replace the client's ongoing treatment regimen, but rather to improve the effectiveness of those resources. When compared with other evidence-based treatments for BPD, the inclusion of a systems component is unique to STEPPS.

The systems approach derives from family systems theory, which assumes that changing a system involves the whole family because families tend to act in ways that maintain the status quo, even when it is dysfunctional. Minuchin (1974) developed structural family therapy to deal with dysfunctional family structures through education, behavioral techniques, and other directive approaches. STEPPS incorporates a workbook, materials to be shared with others in their support system, pocket-size skill cards, and other materials that function as learning tools for both the client and individuals in their support system. The manual is similar to a well-developed and detailed school curriculum with a combination of handouts, worksheets, and other resources such as art activities, poetry, and songs. The goal is to make abstract concepts as concrete and clear as possible and to use these materials with patients who may vary widely in their intellectual ability and functional status. The weekly lesson plans indicate what skill is being taught and how it will be covered during each session, as well as the materials needed for that lesson. This detail simplifies the training of group leaders and insures fidelity to the model in a variety of treatment settings.

The underlying assumption of STEPPS is that the core deficit in BPD is the individual's inability to regulate and manage emotional intensity. As a result, patients with BPD are frequently overwhelmed by abnormally intense emotional upheavals that drive them to seek relief, often through self-mutilation, impulsive and reckless behaviors, or substance misuse. The childhood history of individuals with BPD frequently includes inconsistent emotional support or even abuse by primary caregivers. This often leads therapists to focus treatment on identifying someone to "blame" for the disorder, an approach that is often unproductive. We reject the assumption that individuals with BPD consciously choose to have this disorder and, with rare exceptions, parents and other important caregivers do not consciously choose to create an abusive, inconsistent, and unsupportive child-hood environment (Blum et al., 2002a, 2012).

Providing education about BPD to reinforcement team members allows them to reinforce and support the patient's newly learned skills, thereby helping to avoid the tendency of persons with BPD to use "splitting" (i.e., externalizing their internal conflict by drawing others around them into taking sides against each other). Splitting, like other behaviors commonly described as part of BPD, is not viewed as an intentional act of aggression, but as a learned or automatic response to the emotional intensity. Patients learn to anticipate emotional intensity and replace dysfunctional responses with more appropriate and effective ones.

When patients enter treatment, they often view the term *borderline personality disorder* as pejorative and resist the diagnosis while readily acknowledging its symptoms. Bartels and Crotty (1992) used the term *emotional intensity disorder* (EID). EID may be easier for patients to acknowledge and accept, and provides a more accurate description of the way he or she experiences the criteria. In some settings where the word "disorder" may be undesirable (e.g., culturally unaccept-able, adolescent groups, and individuals with BPD traits but who do not meet the required number of criteria to make the diagnosis of BPD), EID is referred to as *emotional intensity difficulties*, and the title of the program is *Managing Emotional Intensity*. The versions for adolescents (STEPPS YP; Blum et al., 2014a) and for adults who do not meet the required number of diagnostic criteria (STEPPS EI; Blum et al., 2015) are described in Chapter 4. BPD and EID are used interchange-ably throughout the original versions of the treatment manual. Regardless of ter-minology, there are advantages to reframing the clients' understanding of BPD as a clinical disorder. Attention is removed from a diagnostic term (BPD), which clients cannot change, to a focus on problematic thoughts and behaviors that they can learn to change. We encourage patients to see themselves as driven by their dis-order to seek relief from painful emotions through desperate behaviors reinforced by negative and distorted thinking, both of which they can learn to challenge and replace. One of our patients wrote in response to learning about her diagnosis, "I no longer think of BPD as a crippling diagnosis. Rather, I get to see the world from a greater perspective of joy, a deeper sadness of pain, a stronger emotion of anger, and a deeper sense of compassion . . . Despite my many emotions about this illness, I can now see life as an adventure to be lived rather than just survived."

## THE SYSTEMS APPROACH TO STEPPS

The person entering therapy is often enmeshed in a system of unhealthy relationships that reinforce and support dysfunctional behavior even when friends and significant others are well intentioned. For example, the person experiencing a cognitive distortion that others dislike him or her may become irritated and behave in ways that turn the distortion into reality. This new reality serves to reinforce the cognitive distortions and maladaptive behaviors that follow.

Beginning with the first session, patients identify and utilize the previously described "reinforcement team," who agree to assist the patient in reinforcing the skills taught in STEPPS. Patients are strongly encouraged to enlist non-professionals, as well as professional care providers, and to help teach the skills by sharing appropriate materials provided for that purpose. It is common for some patients to initially express the belief that they have "no one" to list on the worksheet provided in their lesson packet. They are assured that the group leaders are willing and able to be part of their reinforcement team, and they are encouraged to list additional names and contact information over the subsequent weeks as they become more comfortable sharing information about the STEPPS program and the skills they are learning. After there is sufficient time for fellow group members to become comfortable in the group (usually 4–6 weeks into the program), they may volunteer to be members of one another's reinforcement team (with review of the group guidelines to maintain appropriate boundaries). Including a reinforcement team reduces the tendency for individuals with BPD to focus on one person (e.g., their individual therapist), who runs the risk of being alternately overidealized and devalued. For patients engaged in individual therapy, we ask the therapist to support the program by reviewing the workbook materials provided to the patient each week. Patients are reminded that it is their responsibility to take their workbook materials to their individual therapy sessions.

Patients are expected to become STEPPS experts and to teach their reinforcement team how to respond appropriately to them by using the STEPPS "language." They are encouraged to share what they learn in group and to share appropriate handouts. Patients receive "Reinforcement Team" cards that list specific instructions for team members about how to respond when contacted by the patient. The cards provide a common language and more consistent interaction between the patient and his/her support system. Hearing the same responses calmly repeated by members in their system reminds patients of what they are learning and does not give them another confusing language to process during a time of emotional intensity.

A 2-hour evening meeting is held for reinforcement team members, usually between weeks 4 and 8. The group members also attend this meeting to avoid any concerns that the session is merely an opportunity for reinforcement team members to "vent" frustrations and complaints about their family member or friends. During this educational session, the criteria (and clinical symptoms) of BPD are shared, and the STEPPS language and group format are discussed. In some settings, group facilitators have involved the group members in delivering the information by making up posters that summarize the material. Reinforcement team members are instructed that their role is to reinforce and support the use of the skills taught in STEPPS. However, non-professional reinforcement team members are also reassured that they are not expected to assume the therapist role. Including members of the patient's system and providing specific guidelines empowers reinforcement team members to make more consistent and neutral responses and helps avoid the temptation to solve problems for, or provide therapy to, the patient. The central message is that the primary goal in the immediate moment is on the *process* of helping the client reduce emotional intensity, not responding to the client's perception (usually distorted by the level of emotional reactivity) of the *content*. They are instructed in how to use the cards which list the skills taught in STEPPS and specific questions to ask when contacted by the participant:

- Where are you on emotional intensity continuum?
- Have you used your notebook?
- What skill can you use in this situation?
- How will you use it?

If the patient cannot think of a skill, the reinforcement team member is instructed to calmly read each one listed on the card. Hearing the same response from all members of the reinforcement team (using exactly the same language) often decreases patients' emotional intensity. Family members and other non-professionals often report that responding in the same language each time makes it less likely that they will respond with increased emotional intensity and further escalate the intensity of the person with BPD.

In a community setting where patients and reinforcement team members do not have to travel a significant distance, it may be desirable to expand this component of the program. One example of this expanded component is described by Renee Harvey in Chapter 4. The United Kingdom adaptation of STEPPS for adolescents includes a concurrent group for parents/caregivers.

## MAJOR COMPONENTS OF STEPPS

STEPPS has three major components: (1) awareness of illness, (2) emotion management skills training, and (3) behavior management skills training. See Box 1.1 for a brief description of the 20 sessions.

Box 1.1.

SESSION BY SESSION DESCRIPTION OF THE PROGRAM

Session 1:
- Introduction of participants and co-facilitators.
- Completion, scoring, and recording of BEST scale.
- Review guidelines for participating in STEPPS program.
- Review concept of BPD, including DSM-IV criteria and introduction of Emotional Intensity Disorder (EID) as an alternate "diagnostic" label.
- Identification of reinforcement team (members of support system with whom they choose to share information about BPD, the skills they are learning, and how the team can reinforce).
- Each group member identifies his/her specific goals.

Session 2:
- Completion of schema questionnaire and education about schemas in BPD.
- Completion of the BEST. (From this point on, participants complete the BEST prior to each subsequent session.)

Session 3:
- Description of *distancing* from emotional intensity, and relaxation breathing; each subsequent session begins with a different relaxation exercise.

Sessions 4 & 5:
- Introduction to the EIC. These two sessions also teach the *communication* of feelings, filters, and thoughts more accurately.
- Beginning with session 5, the relaxation exercise is followed by a review of each participant's use of the EIC and specific STEPPS skills.

Sessions 6–8:
- Teach the *challenging* of maladaptive filters and identifying of common cognitive distortions; participants learn to replace cognitive distortions with alternative thoughts.

Sessions 9 & 10:
- Teach distracting behaviors and positive affirmations to reduce emotional intensity.

Sessions 11 & 12:
- Teach the *managing of problems* using specific problem-solving paradigms.

**Session 13:**
- Identify *problematic life-style behaviors* (eating, sleeping, exercise, etc.) and discuss the need for balance. Participants complete a questionnaire to identify areas of difficulty. A specific problematic behavior is identified for each participant.

**Session 14:**
- Goals are set for the previously identified problematic behaviors, which are worked on in the remaining weeks.

**Session 15:**
- Healthy eating and sleep behaviors are reviewed.

**Session 16:**
- Healthy exercise, leisure, and physical health behaviors are reviewed.

**Session 17:**
- Skills to reduce self-harm behaviors are taught.

**Sessions 18 & 19:**
- Relationship boundaries and interpersonal effectiveness are reviewed.

**Session 20:**
- Comparison of initial and termination schema questionnaire.
- Evaluation of the group's progress and use of skills.
- Celebration of completion.

---

## Awareness of Illness

This component occurs in weeks 1 and 2. In the first weekly session, the content focuses on replacing misconceptions about the BPD label with an awareness of the thought patterns, feelings, and behaviors that define the disorder, that is, labeling these as *symptoms* of BPD/EID. Thoughts and behaviors can be changed; feelings can be tolerated and managed. Individuals often begin with the belief that they are fatally flawed (for which they may alternately blame themselves or others) and that they deserve to suffer. The ability to seriously consider that BPD is a legitimate disorder and that the individual can learn specific skills to manage the symptoms is an important precursor to developing the capacity for change. If patients believe their disorder will improve only if others around them change, they may not be suitable for the program. Alternatively, persons who believe they cannot learn these skills (even in the absence of intellectual limitations) may not be ready to benefit from this approach. Group members are given a printed handout listing the DSM criteria for BPD, and time and encouragement are provided to acknowledge examples of the criteria in their own behavior ("owning" the disorder).

The second week's lesson introduces the concept of cognitive filters. Therapists may recognize the similarity to the concept of schemas described by Young (1994). Young's Schema Questionnaire was adapted (with permission) to allow group members to identify their early maladaptive filters and to see the relationship between these filters, the DSM criteria, and their subsequent patterns of feelings, thoughts, and behaviors.

## Emotion Management Skills Training

This component teaches five basic skills (distancing, communicating, challenging, distracting, and managing problems) that help the person with BPD manage both the cognitive and emotional symptoms of the disorder. These skills assist participants to predict the pattern of an emotional episode, anticipate stressful situations that may lead to increased emotional intensity with impulsive and/or self-destructive behaviors, and assist them to develop confidence in their ability to manage the disorder. These five emotion management skills form the basic vocabulary for responding to the emotional intensity episodes; the skills are described briefly as follows:

*Distancing* (week 3) involves noticing and acknowledging the increasing emotional intensity and describing its components (feelings, thoughts, and behaviors), and then "taking a step back." This can be done with a physical action (e.g., moving to a different room) or a mental action (e.g., choosing to focus on a calming image or object, or deep breathing). In the session on distancing, a specific activity involves creating a collage from pleasant images cut from magazines that can be carried in their STEPPS binder or folder or put up on the wall where it is easily accessible. Beginning with lesson 3, each session begins with a relaxation exercise, such as progressive muscle relaxation, visualization, and a variety of focusing activities, each exercise starting with mindfulness breathing (a list of suggested relaxation exercises is included in the guidelines for the group leaders).

*Communicating* (weeks 4 and 5) can be described as "putting words on" the emotions being experienced and also expanding the participants' vocabulary to describe feelings. Clients often have a limited vocabulary, such as "sad, mad, glad." One of the worksheets in this lesson asks the client to describe emotions in a variety of ways such as using a different word, a color, a sound, a physical sensation, an experience, and/or an action urge. The group setting is very helpful in stimulating responses for individuals who might have difficulty responding without helpful ideas from others in the group. The *Emotional Intensity Continuum (EIC)* is introduced as part of this skill and is described later in this chapter.

*Challenging* (weeks 6, 7, 8) teaches the STEPPS participant to recognize distorted and negative thoughts and, through the worksheets and homework assignments, replace them with more rational and neutral or positive ones that are less likely to generate emotional intensity. As this skill develops, clients move away from their typical "all or nothing" perception of other people and situations.

*Distracting* (weeks 9 and 10) gives individuals an opportunity to create a list of distracting activities to use during times of emotional intensity to allow time to pass until that intensity decreases. Group members work on prioritizing the list, and the five easiest or most accessible activities are written on a small card to be carried with the individual, thus making the skills "portable." Clients often have the expectation that someone outside of them (e.g., their therapist) will "rescue" them or direct them in how to respond to a situation. The ultimate goal of STEPPS is for individuals with BPD/EID to recognize increasing emotional intensity and use the skills to manage the intensity on their own (or with only an occasional reminder from a member of their reinforcement team).

*Managing Problems* (weeks 11 and 12) allows the client to more clearly state the problem and desired solution. This skill requires practice in generating alternative responses and evaluating the potential consequences of each response. An event/episode management worksheet guides clients through the process, and they are given additional worksheets to use for the remainder of the lessons.

It should be noted that several of the emotion management skills require more than one session to complete. In the behavior management section, some skills are combined into one session (e.g., eating and sleeping; exercise, leisure, and physical health). This allows the program to be completed in 20 weekly sessions, although there may be settings where the length and frequency of the individual sessions are adjusted to the intellectual and/or functional level of group participants or to fit with the schedule for a particular facility (e.g., residential treatment, forensic settings). There are two optional sessions that may be used at the discretion of the group leaders. The *Introductory/Intake Session* is useful as a screening session to assess a prospective group member's ability to participate appropriately in a group setting. The other optional session (designed specifically for those groups that meet prior to or during the winter holidays) addresses stress related to holiday celebrations (e.g., Thanksgiving, Christmas, etc.) that typically involve significant interpersonal interactions with families and others with whom the person may have had a difficult relationship.

## Behavior Management Skills Training

With BPD, disruptive interplay often occurs between emotionally intense episodes and the individual's social environment, which becomes increasingly nonempathic and unresponsive, leading many of these functional areas to break down. Learning and relearning patterns of managing these functional areas helps the client with BPD keep these areas under control during emotionally intense episodes. This component focuses on eight behavioral skills (goal-setting, eating, sleeping, exercise, leisure, physical health, abuse avoidance, and interpersonal relationships). Behavior management (week 13) begins with clients completing a behavior questionnaire to assess and rank the severity of their problems in the previously listed areas.

*Goal-setting* (week 14) outlines the process of clearly articulating a primary goal based on one of the behavioral areas, using worksheets to guide group members in breaking that goal into smaller ones, identifying resources needed and potential obstacles to achieving their goal, and providing worksheets to monitor their progress.

*Eating and sleeping* (week 15). The eating behaviors section of this week provides information to distinguish healthy eating behaviors from disordered ones. Clients complete a daily food journal to increase their awareness of eating behaviors and the relationship of unhealthy ones to their level of emotional intensity. The sleeping behaviors section emphasizes good sleep hygiene and provides a sleep diary to filled be out. This helps clients become more aware of the relationship between poor sleep habits and their emotional intensity.

*Exercise, leisure, and physical health* (week 16). This training encourages participation in regular exercise and committing to an exercise partner (which can include another group member) and provides worksheets to monitor activity. The leisure section encourages clients to expand their repertoire of leisure activities. The physical health section describes skills to help clients improve their relationships with health care providers, as well as encouraging better adherence to medication use, where appropriate.

*Abuse avoidance* (week 17) includes a wide variety of self-damaging and self-destructive behaviors such as self-harm (cutting, burning, etc.), suicide attempts, substance abuse, and money mismanagement, and criminal behaviors such as shoplifting. Clients use the Emotional Intensity Continuum to "get a picture" of what their feelings, thoughts, filters, action urges, and actual behaviors are at each level of intensity. Worksheets allow the client to add additional "clues" about the behavior and to identify STEPPS skills and resources to avoid those behaviors.

*Interpersonal relationships* (weeks 18 and 19). This training focuses on increasing interpersonal effectiveness, discussing the warning signs of abusive relationships, learning how to inform others about BPD/EID, improving problem solving in interpersonal relationships, and establishing appropriate boundaries. The homework assignment prior to the ending of the group the following week asks participants to complete another filter (schema) questionnaire and compare it to the one they filled out in week 2.

*Wrapping it up* (week 20) is a "celebration" of completing the program. Group members typically bring food to share, and each member receives a certificate of completion. Most of the session is spent reviewing the progress group members have made and asking them to give feedback about the group process. At approximately week 17, patients may express concern and anxiety about the STEPPS program ending and losing the weekly support of peers and group leaders. Group leaders work to minimize the impact of this by encouraging the patients to continue using their reinforcement team. From the beginning, patients are encouraged to view STEPPS as a time-limited program to help them use their existing support system more effectively, rather than as a replacement for that system.

Patients receive information about options after STEPPS, which may include continuing their current treatment (e.g., individual psychotherapy, pharmacotherapy, case management), repeating STEPPS, or joining STAIRWAYS (described later in the chapter). During STEPPS, some patients may resist completing homework assignments, but eventually realize the benefits of practicing the skills (through homework or encouragement from other group members) as they notice the improvement in other patients. Those who continue to have difficulty understanding or applying the skills may be encouraged (by the group leaders or another professional care-provider) to repeat STEPPS. This is reframed as an opportunity to go through the program "at a higher level," to avoid the perception of having "failed" the group. Some individuals will ask to repeat a STEPPS group immediately. Others may request to join a group months to years later, to improve or refresh their skills, especially if they had not been practicing them and were beginning to relapse.

## THE FORMAT OF STEPPS

The recommended format in outpatient settings is a weekly 2-hour classroom experience with two therapists and from 6 to 10 patients. Session length may be decreased and the frequency increased in some settings (e.g., 1 hour twice weekly), depending on the functional abilities of group members and/or the facility's schedule. Patients receive a binder for their materials which they are asked to bring to each session. They are encouraged to share the binder and the lesson materials with others in their system. The binders are considered resources to turn to in difficult times.

Sessions have the feeling and look of a seminar or classroom with group members sitting at a table facing a board. Lesson concepts are facilitated by poetry, song recordings, art activities, and relaxation exercises. Suggested auxiliary materials and resources are listed in the facilitator guidelines for each lesson. Participants are encouraged to bring in materials, poems, or artwork they have created to reinforce the themes of the particular lesson. Examples of these from past STEPPS participants are incorporated into the STEPPS manual(s).

Sessions begin by completing the 15-item Borderline Evaluation of Severity over Time (BEST) self-report scale to rate the intensity of their thoughts, feelings, and behaviors over the past week (a copy is included in the Appendix). This instrument was developed as a companion to the STEPPS program to rate symptoms specific to BPD (Blum et al., 2002; Pfohl et al., 2009). In graphing their weekly scores, patients observe the variation in symptom severity over time. They may also observe that during the course of 20 weeks, the increased use of their skills leads to a decrease in the frequency and intensity of their emotional episodes along with a gradual decrease in their scores. The graph visually reinforces their progress. BEST data allow patients to monitor fluctuations in suicidal feelings, self-harm urges and behaviors, as well as emotional intensity, negative behaviors (e.g., substance abuse, abnormal eating behavior), and positive behaviors (e.g., choosing a positive activity, keeping appointments).

In the first few weeks, patients typically notice that their BEST scores are erratic, and sometimes express concern that they are not improving. In our experience, the peaks and valleys on their graph are much briefer and their scores start to decrease noticeably between weeks 8–12 (Blum et al., 2008). For most patients, scores are markedly decreased by the end of 20 weeks. After completing the BEST, a brief relaxation exercise follows. A variety of techniques are used so clients can find the ones that work best for them.

The EIC scale, which all patients are asked to fill out during the week, is reviewed. This is a five-point Likert-like scale, which rates emotional intensity from 1 to 5 (1, feeling calm and relaxed; 5, feeling out of control). Patients are asked to complete the EIC daily, and to summarize the amount of time spent at each level during the previous week. The EIC Recording Sheet allows patients to enter the percentage of time at each level for each of the 20 weeks and to note a gradual decrease in the percentage of time at the higher levels (4 and 5) and increased amounts at levels 1, 2, and 3. Patients achieve a more balanced view of themselves through this self-rating, and they are often surprised to observe substantial periods of time when they are not at a level 5. They use the EIC to identify thoughts, feelings, maladaptive cognitive filters (schemas), physical sensations, action urges, and behaviors at each level of intensity. A copy of the EIC is included in the Appendix.

By using the EIC consistently, patients become more adept at predicting the course of an emotional episode and anticipating stressful situations that lead to destructive responses. The original metaphor for the EIC worksheet used weather symbols (1, sun shining; 2, partly cloudy; 3, cloud with rain; 4, dark cloud with thunder and lightning; 5, tornado). As STEPPS was disseminated to different geographic areas, we learned the tornado was not a universal metaphor. A volcano was suggested by another group. One STEPPS participant observed that she "had no more control over the weather than over her emotional intensity," and suggested pots on a stove (1, no heat under the pot; 2, some heat; 3, water starting to boil; 4, boiling harder; 5, boiling over). This metaphor was well received by the group and became the suggested worksheet for subsequent groups, although all three designs are included in the manual. We suggest that group leaders make multiple copies of each. Patients may then choose the one they prefer (or draw their own).

A skills-monitoring card asks patients to indicate which skills were used in the previous week. The previous week's homework assignment is reviewed and the remainder of the session is devoted to the material for the current lesson.

With few exceptions, our patients respond well to this structured approach. On one occasion when a group leader was delayed unexpectedly for 20 minutes, she arrived to discover the group had appointed one of the members to act as leader and the group was well into reviewing the EIC for each participant. We now regularly ask for a volunteer to review the EICs, beginning 4 or 5 weeks after a STEPPS group begins. Patients often request permission to lead this portion for the following week. At other times, patients volunteer to teach a new relaxation exercise such as some gentle yoga stretches.

During a session, patients may try to reframe their emotional experience in the context of or as the result of a personal or interpersonal problem. Although there are opportunities to respond to and share experiences relevant to the skills being taught, the structure of the STEPPS model does not allow the group to spend long periods focusing on a given group member who is experiencing a crisis. One effect of this structure is to model how to acknowledge problems and offer support yet impose reasonable limits on the scope of the interaction. Group facilitators are trained to reframe problems in the context of the disorder and its filters. Patients are reminded to "focus on the disorder, not the content."

One of our patients, a 19-year-old woman, reported the benefits she had gained from STEPPS: "STEPPS has made so many positive changes in my life. For the first time, I'm starting to figure out who I am. The biggest thing is that I am not angry all the time. I'm learning to deal with the big things in life and let the little trivial things slide, instead of everything making me angry. Before STEPPS I did not know there were trivial things. I'm learning to live all over again with a new set of rules for myself. Sometimes it's hard because the others had been in place for so long, but the new rules make my life a lot easier."

## USING STEPPS IN OTHER TREATMENT SETTINGS

This approach to treatment for BPD has been adapted successfully for a variety of treatment settings that include inpatient units, partial hospital, day treatment programs, residential facilities, substance abuse treatment, and correctional settings, including prisons and community corrections (Black et al., 2008, 2011, 2013). On inpatient units where the typical length of stay is only a few days, the awareness of BPD component may be used to assess the client's suitability for the full STEPPS program and to prepare the client to enter such a program. Boccalon et al. (2012) and Alesiani et al. (2014) describe the implementation of STEPPS on an Italian inpatient unit with continuation in the outpatient setting.

## SELECTION OF STEPPS PARTICIPANTS

Some patients learn about STEPPS from previous participants and request admission to a treatment group, but we recommend a formal professional referral that can serve as a screening tool. Although patients need not meet full criteria for BPD to enter a group, Bos et al. (2011) reported that persons with borderline traits who do not meet full syndromal criteria were more likely to drop out. Once 20 to 30 potential participants have been identified, they are invited to attend the next group. Our experience has been that one-quarter to one-third of potential participants respond to the invitation, and one or two will not show. Patients are told at the introductory/intake session that if they miss three consecutive sessions for reasons other than illness or bad weather, they will be asked to drop out of the group (a letter is mailed giving patients other treatment options, including the dates of future groups). It is not uncommon for one or two persons in each group to have attended a prior STEPPS group (and who wish to consolidate their skills).

This is helpful to newcomers in demonstrating hope and providing early leadership and encouragement in the group.

It may be helpful for mental health professionals to screen potential STEPPS participants with formal structured assessments. We encourage clinicians to review information from referral sources. Highly narcissistic individuals may not be suitable. It is essential for patients to share time with other group members, and limit discussion of their own problems to those elements that serve the goals of STEPPS. The person's capacity for these attributes can often be gauged by his or her ability to allow the facilitator to direct discussion during the introductory screening. Those who cannot maintain their focus on issues introduced by the facilitator (or accept redirection constructively) may not be appropriate. Each group member must have some capacity to appreciate that others have problems that they view as equally serious or disturbing, even though the person may see those problems as different from or less challenging than his or her own. A key requirement is the individual's ability to consider that another person's perception may be different from his or her own, but nevertheless has some validity.

Ongoing substance misuse is viewed as counterproductive to treatment goals and patients are encouraged to seek appropriate substance use disorder treatment either before attending STEPPS or concurrently. This recommendation for either a prior or concurrent treatment program also applies to those with severe eating disorder behaviors. Patients are instructed to inform those providers of their participation in STEPPS and are encouraged to share their STEPPS materials with those providers.

Individuals who deal with conflict by physical threats or intimidation are potential threats to the integrity of a group and may not be suitable for STEPPS. This might be observed in patients with marked antisocial traits. That said, many STEPPS participants with mild antisocial traits have been able to benefit from the program, and their traits did not lead to any disruption of the group process (Blum et al., 2008).

An aggressive man may be threatening to women in the group, because some women with BPD have been abused by men in the past. Some settings maintain separate groups for men and women. In a mixed gender group, having at least two men increases the chance they will have sufficient common experiences to provide support for one another. Including more than one man in a group may also reduce the perception that a single man represents the opinions and feelings of all men. Members are cautiously encouraged to use one another as reinforcement team members between sessions, once they feel safe in the group. They are instructed to use the suggested responses on the skill card they give to their reinforcement team members.

## GROUP FACILITATORS

We recommend that groups be led by two co-facilitators, both for practical reasons (if one facilitator is gone, the group does not have to be cancelled) and to reduce the tendency of persons with BPD to alternately overidealize and then devalue a single individual. Group leaders should have graduate level training in the social sciences and psychotherapy experience that includes training in cognitive-behavioral techniques. Where possible, having a man and a woman as group leaders allows the modeling of relationship behaviors between genders, projecting a healthy male role model, and providing support for male participants, who are in the minority in most mixed gender groups. However, there are numerous STEPPS groups with two female facilitators for an all-male group or two male facilitators for an all-female group. Facilitators do not sit at the table with participants and maintain clear professional boundaries.

Initially the role of the facilitators is active and directive; this decreases over time as patients gradually assume increasing leadership (e.g., writing on the board, leading brief reviews of homework assignments). Facilitators should treat all participants equally and not give some members preferential treatment. It is preferable for facilitators to avoid seeing a group member for individual therapy, unless there is a preexisting therapeutic relationship. However, in small clinics with limited personnel, this may not be possible. Group members are instructed (as part of the printed guidelines for the group) that if they are in a therapeutic relationship with one of the group leaders, that issues discussed in their individual sessions will not be discussed in the group.

The primary tasks of facilitators are to maintain a psychoeducational format and adhere to the facilitator guidelines. Facilitators should avoid being drawn into the issues and past traumas of a particular participant and should focus on teaching new skills, not "putting out fires." It is essential to maintain focus on skills acquisition rather than content, encourage group cohesiveness, and facilitate the participants' change of perspective from victims of BPD/EID to experts on managing their BPD symptoms.

Facilitators should avoid focusing on a particular patient's problems without generalizing it to the group and asking the group for assistance. The group should be involved in helping the patient use the skills being taught and avoid the therapist being "the expert" who is expected to resolve all issues. Facilitators must curb their tendency to respond to the expressed problems (i.e., content), rather than focusing on the symptoms of the disorder and the cognitive filters (schemas) that drive the emotional responses of the client with BPD.

Crises are common in patients with BPD (e.g., suicidal threats, flashbacks) and can easily derail the group process if not attended to appropriately. Crises are acknowledged and, if necessary, managed within the group by focusing attention on using the skills (e.g., using a crisis as an example for applying the skill being taught in that or a previous session). Patients should be referred to their individual therapist to deal with more long-standing personal issues.

Crises that cannot be managed in the group should lead to an urgent referral to an emergency department, for example, individuals in imminent danger of self-harm or who are suicidal. In our experience, this is rare. The referral should be made quickly to avoid disrupting the group and the perception of special treatment. Otherwise self-harm thoughts or behaviors are treated as unhelpful behaviors to be addressed by using the EIC to examine the situation and where those thoughts or behaviors occurred; the group can be involved in helping to identify what skills might be helpful, or giving feedback on what skills have been helpful when they have experienced similar thoughts or behaviors.

As a group facilitator observed after working with group members in this approach, "I now look at patients with BPD differently and interact in a different way. I feel more competent to help them when they are in a crisis. My main response now is to listen, talk with them about how intense their feelings are, and ask what skills they can (and will) use to decrease the intensity."

## FACILITATOR TRAINING

Facilitators are generally trained during a 1- or 2-day onsite workshop with a provision for further web-based (e.g., Skype) consultation or supervision, if desired. Further consultation is strongly recommended if one-day training is chosen. The training format includes an overview of personality disorders, discussion of BPD, and a detailed discussion on cognitions and behaviors typical for the disorder. Other treatment models are described, followed by a thorough discussion of STEPPS and how it complements other treatments the client may be receiving. We are available by telephone or e-mail to "trouble-shoot" with therapists using STEPPS, or to provide more extensive web-based consultation, as previously described. We require therapists training at our home department to attend an entire 20-week therapy program and act as co-therapists after the first three or four sessions. We recommend that facilitators have at least a master's degree (or higher) in one of the social sciences and experience in counseling clients with personality disorders.

Although only a limited number of clinicians in a given setting may be identified as potential facilitators, we recommend inviting other professionals who regularly interact with clients with BPD to attend the initial day of training to become familiar with the basics of STEPPS. This applies to professionals in other parts of the system (e.g., substance abuse services, vocational rehabilitation, community supported living services, hospital inpatient services, etc.). This makes it more likely that those members of the professional care provider system will reinforce what participants are being taught in the STEPPS program. Further information about training may be obtained from one of the authors (NB).

The *Adherence Rating Scale* was developed to ensure therapist fidelity to the STEPPS model. This is a Likert-like scale consisting of 28 items rated by a trained rater(s), usually done via video recording of sessions or in person. Level of adherence is rated as follows: 1, poor; 2, barely adequate; 3, satisfactory; 4, good; and 5, excellent; not applicable is indicated for a particular item not included in the lesson plan for that session. A copy of this scale is included in the Appendix.

## CASE VIGNETTE

"Marilyn" was a divorced woman in her early 40s, referred for psychotherapy after discharge from the hospital; the hospitalization occurred after she expressed suicidality during an appointment in another department. This was her first hospitalization at our hospital, but she had a long history of prior psychiatric treatment and more than 25 hospitalizations, beginning in late adolescence. She carried numerous past diagnoses, including attention deficit/hyperactivity disorder (ADHD) at age 10; additional diagnoses were added at various hospitalizations, including bipolar disorder (sometimes Type I, other times Type II), alcohol dependence and abuse, and pathological gambling. Despite multiple examples of behavior patterns that met more than the required number of criteria for BPD, there was no mention of this in her records or by self-report, except for a notation of "borderline traits" from a recent hospitalization. Marilyn estimated that she spent a third of each year in the hospital since age 17.

Marilyn was the youngest of four children. She reached normal developmental milestones and entered school at age 4, a year earlier than most children. Her mother described her as "different from the other siblings, extremely active from the time she could walk." The family moved frequently and the patient did not attend the same school for two consecutive years until age 11. She believed the frequent moves fueled feelings of abandonment that later became a recurrent theme in her adult life. Her father was described as drinking heavily after a serious accident, and was "falling down and mean" when he was drunk. Her mother had severe postpartum depression, a sister had seasonal depression, and Marilyn believes her father and one of his sisters had hypomanic episodes. Another sibling had emotional volatility similar to the patient's. Her father died in his 80s, and her mother was still living independently at age 90. Marilyn was married twice, the first time to someone she described as alcoholic; the second marriage was physically and emotionally abusive and ended in divorce.

Marilyn dates the onset of her problems to age 7 or 8 years, when she exhibited problems with anger control, such as putting her foot through a wall and bullying other children. She was disruptive in the classroom, and had learning problems related to vision and distinguishing sounds. At age 10 she was seen by a psychologist who diagnosed ADHD, although her mother disputed the diagnosis, explaining that at home Marilyn could read for long periods at a time, put an entire picture puzzle together, etc. Marilyn's physician prescribed methylphenidate, and Marilyn said she learned, "that solutions to my problems would come from outside myself," including medication and health professionals. She believes this eventually led to her alcoholism, which was another "solution."

At age 10 she overdosed on the methylphenidate, the first of more than two dozen subsequent attempts. She thought that many of her attempts could be described as gestures, but at least 6 were serious attempts. One resulted in numerous fractures which continue to cause chronic pain and difficulty walking many years later. Another involved an overdose that left her comatose for three months. In her early 20s, she used cutting to, "feel if I was alive."

Marilyn described life-long problems with anger control. During one hospitalization an anger outburst was triggered by not receiving a salad with dinner. This was accompanied by yelling, overturning tables in the dining area, throwing items off the tables, and breaking glass. During another hospitalization, she was discharged to another facility after assaulting staff members. She was jailed twice for assaults outside the hospital, one of them after another person cut ahead of her in a line.

Her alcohol use began at age 12, and she was drinking daily by age 14; this continued into her 20s, when she was jailed for public intoxication; following this, she joined Alcoholics Anonymous, and at the time of our last contact, she had not used alcohol for nearly 40 years. She had a history of week-long binge eating every 2–3 months, beginning in high school. She engaged in periodic gambling episodes, sometimes spending as much as $400–$500 per day, 3–5 times per month, which she could not afford and that led to illegal behaviors including embezzlement, writing bad checks, and stealing money from a significant other. She described relationships as stormy and unstable. She admitted to initially seeing the person as flawless and, just as quickly, becoming completely disillusioned. She would frequently end a relationship prematurely because she believed the other person was preparing to leave her.

Marilyn was hospitalized for episodes of depression once or twice a year, during which she experienced low mood, oversleeping, decreased energy and appetite, loss of motivation, and increased risk for suicide attempts. Sometime in her 20s, she began to have periodic episodes characterized by racing thoughts, excessive energy, poor concentration, rapid and excessive speech, increased irritability, and reckless driving. She was not usually hospitalized for these episodes. Outside of these specific episodes, she experienced frequent, intense mood swings and suicidal thoughts on a daily basis.

She had a very limited response to a variety of medications. Antidepressants reportedly improved her energy but also increased the risk of acting on suicidal thoughts. Mood stabilizers seemed to temper the hypomanic episodes, but she still had multiple daily mood swings.

Marilyn's sensitivity to abandonment, stormy relationships, impulsivity, suicide gestures, affective instability, and anger dyscontrol easily meet criteria for BPD. She also had symptoms suggesting additional diagnoses of major depression, bipolar disorder Type II, intermittent explosive disorder, alcohol dependence, pathological gambling, ADHD, and antisocial personality disorder. However, BPD was seen as the primary diagnosis.

Following discharge from the inpatient unit, Marilyn was initially referred for individual therapy (with NB), and subsequently enrolled in the STEPPS program. Her medication management was done by one of the other authors (DSJ). The initial focus of individual therapy educated Marilyn about BPD, because this was the first time she had received the diagnosis. Her response was, "This is the first diagnosis that really seems to fit." Her STEPPS-based therapy focused on accepting the reality of her symptoms and learning specific emotion management and behavior skills for dealing with them. This allowed a cognitive shift that directed her away from looking for a source to "blame" for her disorder, and encouraged her to accept responsibility for using the skills to manage her symptoms. This was facilitated by using the analogy of managing the symptoms of her diabetes (rather than blaming someone or something) and this made sense to her.

Marilyn was seen for individual therapy approximately every 2 weeks to reinforce the STEPPS material to apply the skills to her daily life. She filled out an EIC on a daily basis to monitor her symptom severity. This tool increased her awareness of thoughts, feelings, cognitive filters, physical signs, urges, and behaviors that correlated with each level of severity. She could also begin to see a recurrent pattern in each level of severity, regardless of the content of whatever she identified as the trigger. She could then apply her skills more effectively to decrease the time spent at levels 4 and 5, the levels where self-destructive behaviors and damage to relationships were most likely to occur. She realized that physical pain from the aforementioned fractures was one of the most frequent triggers for her emotional intensity, as well as financial stressors.

Marilyn worked on her anger control and impulsivity by using the *distancing* skill to notice the increase in emotional intensity and then "stepping back" by talking to a reinforcement team member, going to another room, or taking a drive. She became more adept at *communicating* to accurately convey her feelings and thoughts, was more open to hearing feedback from others, and then used *challenging* to replace her distorted thoughts with more rational ones. She had several *distracting* activities (baking, craft activities, and drawing) that were helpful in decreasing her emotional intensity. At a lower level of emotional intensity, she was able to better define the problem, the desired solution, consider a wider range of alternative responses, and then thoughtfully evaluate the likely consequences of each response (*managing problems* skill).

She credited the *eating behavior skills* for helping to stop binge eating episodes. Marilyn continued to attend weekly AA meetings, and also attended a weekly gambling treatment group in her local community. She identified the facilitator of that group as a member of her reinforcement team and stated, "I brought her my materials and taught her what I was learning, because she was unfamiliar with the program." Marilyn was in a stable relationship with a man whom she described as a reinforcement team member "to a certain extent;" she was able to accept that his limited ability was due to his own health problems, and to have more realistic expectations of what he and others could provide in terms of emotional support.

Periodically Marilyn discontinued her medications, sometimes due to financial difficulties, but other times because she was angry with her physician or other treating professionals. As she progressed through the behavioral lessons in the STEPPS program, she identified one of her goals as being more adherent to her medication regimen; she was asked to consider possible actions to make it more likely that she would increase her consistency in taking her medications. She accomplished this by making a weekly chart to give herself a "gold star" sticker each day that she took her medications. She then brought her weekly charts to her individual therapy session, and also shared them with the STEPPS group which gave her positive feedback; another group member with a similar goal adopted a similar strategy. The *physical health skills* section helped her achieve a more realistic view of the role of her health care providers and medications. She observed, "I now realize that my medications are like my crutches. They help, but they are not the fix-it answer." She achieved better control of her diabetes, and improved her relationships with health care providers.

Following STEPPS, Marilyn completed the STAIRWAYS program. Individual sessions decreased to once a month or fewer, but she would email periodically between appointments to "check in," and to share some of the new activities she added to her life (teaching a Sunday school class at her church and volunteering at a women's shelter, where she also shared some of the STEPPS materials with clients who were experiencing emotional intensity).

Marilyn continued to attend AA meetings at least once a week or more, and became a sponsor for another person. She stopped attending the gambling support group and her gambling behaviors were limited to buying one lottery ticket per week.

Marilyn's hospitalizations decreased from 3 to 4 months a year to a total of 21 days in the following 5 years after starting STEPPS. She saw an individual therapist once a month or less in her local community after STAIRWAYS. When the therapist moved away, Marilyn sent an email which said, "I will miss her, but I know she is not abandoning me, and I am not devastated." She has not been hospitalized for the past 16 years. She continues to periodically experience suicidal thoughts, but states, "Now I know it's my disorder talking and not how I really feel or want to react."

Marilyn has not been in regular treatment for more than 12 years. About two times a year, she will email or call to let us know how she is doing. During her last follow-up interview, she reported using no psychotropic medications for more than 12 years. She still experiences some symptoms of major depression and hypomania, but feels they are manageable by using the emotion management and behavior skills she learned in STEPPS. Marilyn has a part-time job driving older adults to appointments, recreational activities, etc. One of those activities involves taking them to a nearby gambling casino; when I asked if it was difficult for her to resist the temptation to gamble, given her history of pathological gambling, she assured me that she spends the waiting time drinking coffee with the security guards during their breaks. Marilyn gave us permission to speak with her mother who said, "Marilyn is a totally different person since STEPPS. She is now responsible and accountable, and she is no longer impulsive."

## SUMMARY

### Stairways

A year-long program has been developed for participants who have completed STEPPS. The group meets twice a month. The program consists of stand-alone modules that are designed to consolidate and expand the patients' repertoire of skills. STAIRWAYS is an acronym for Setting goals, Trying new things (oriented toward long-term goals, such as furthering education, employment, etc.), Anger management, Impulsivity control, Relationship management (emphasis on conflict-management), Writing a script (preparing for future stressors), Assertiveness training, Your choices (making healthy choices), and Staying on track (maintaining recovery and relapse prevention). STAIRWAYS follows a format similar to STEPPS, with a detailed manual, classroom setting, and homework assignments. Participants maintain contact with the STEPPS model by repeated use of previously learned skills to facilitate learning and applying new ones.

Once a STEPPS group begins, no additional patients are allowed to join because each skill builds on the previously learned ones. In STAIRWAYS, each module (some modules take 2 or 3 sessions to complete) is discrete; clients who complete STEPPS and join STAIRWAYS receive an introductory packet of materials and then join the STAIRWAYS program at the beginning of any new module and stay in the program until they complete all the modules. In some settings, patients may attend repeated cycles of STAIRWAYS as an "after-care" program or request permission to repeat a particular skill when it is being offered. We encourage each clinic or agency to determine its own policies with regard to repeating either STEPPS or STAIRWAYS.

## Future Directions for STEPPS

STEPPS has been adapted for other populations and settings as described in subsequent chapters, that is, correctional settings, adolescents, inpatient units, therapeutic community, parenting groups, and private practice. The adolescent version (Blum et al., 2014a), has been implemented in the United Kingdom. A 13-week adaptation for adults considered to have subsyndromal BPD has been developed for delivery in the primary care system in the United Kingdom (Blum et al., 2014b). In both the adolescent version and the adaptation for use in the primary care system, the titles use Managing Emotional Intensity, rather than referring to BPD. Additional adaptations, not described in this book, include patients with mild intellectual developmental disabilities, substance abuse, and in-school counseling programs. Others have offered more frequent reinforcement team meetings and proposed family support groups. We are piloting an 8-week refresher program that focuses on the emotion management skills for those who have completed the 20-week outpatient program. Dismantling research may be helpful in identifying the effective components.

## DISCLOSURES

Ms. Blum receives royalties from Level One Publishing LLC, publisher of STEPPS, STEPPS UK, STEPPS YP, and STAIRWAYS, Psychiatrie Verlag, publisher of the German translation, Sussex Partnership NHS Foundation, Aldo Lombardo, publisher of the Italian translation, and from the American Psychiatric Press, Inc., and Oxford University Press. Mr. St. John receives royalties from Level One Publishing LLC. Dr. Black receives research support from AstraZeneca, and royalties from American Psychiatric Publishing, Oxford University Press, and UpToDate.

## REFERENCES

Alesiani, R., Boccalon, S., Giarolli, L., Blum, N., & Fossati, A. (2014). Systems Training for Emotional Predictability and Problem Solving (STEPPS): Program efficacy and personality features as predictors of drop-out—an Italian study. *Comprehensive Psychiatry, 55*, 920–927.

American Psychiatric Association (2001). Practice guideline for the treatment of patients with borderline personality disorder. *American Journal of Psychiatry, 158* (suppl.), 1–52.

Arntz, A., van Genderen, H., & Drost, J. (2009). *Schema therapy for borderline personality disorder.* Hoboken, NJ: Wiley.

Bartels, N., & Crotty, T. (1992). *A systems approach to treatment: The Borderline personality disorder skill training manual.* Winfield, IL: EID Treatment Systems.

Barnicot, K., Katsakou, C., Marougka, S., & Priebe, S. (2011). Treatment completion in psychotherapy for borderline personality disorder: A systematic review and meta-analysis. *Acta Psychiatrica Scandinavica, 123*, 327–328.

Bateman, A., & Fonagy, P. (1999). Effectiveness of partial hospitalization in the treatment of borderline personality disorder: A randomized controlled trial. *American Journal of Psychiatry, 15*, 1563–1569.

Bateman, A., & Fonagy, P. (2001). Treatment of borderline personality disorder with psychoanalytically oriented partial hospitalization: An 18-month follow-up. *American Journal of Psychiatry, 158*, 36–42.

Bateman, A., & Fonagy, P. (2008). Eight-year follow-up of clients treated for borderline personality disorder: Mentalization-based treatment versus treatment as usual. *American Journal of Psychiatry, 165*, 631–638.

Black, D. W., Blum, N., Eichinger, L., McCormick, B., Allen, J., & Sieleni, B. (2008). STEPPS: Systems Training for Emotional Predictability and Problem Solving in women offenders with borderline personality disorder in prison—a pilot study. *CNS Spectrums, 13*, 881–886.

Black, D. W., Blum, N., & Allen, J. (2013). STEPPS treatment in borderline offenders. *Journal of Nervous and Mental Diseases, 201*, 1–6.

Black, D. W., Pfohl, B., Blum, N., McCormick, B., Allen, J., North, C. S., . . . Zimmerman, M. (2011). Attitudes toward borderline personality disorder: A survey of 706 mental health clinicians. *CNS Spectrums, 16*, 67–74.

Blum, N. S., Bartels, N. E., St. John, D., & Pfohl, B. (2002a). *Systems Training for Emotional Predictability and Problem Solving group treatment program for borderline personality disorder.* Coralville, IA: Level One Publishing, www.steppsforbpd.com.

Blum, N., Pfohl, B., St. John, D., Monahan, P., & Black, D. W. (2002b). STEPPS: A cognitive-behavioral systems-based group treatment for outpatient clients with borderline personality disorder—a preliminary report. *Comprehensive Psychiatry, 43*, 301–310.

Blum, N., St. John, D., Pfohl, B., Stuart, S., McCormick, B., Allen, J., . . . Black, D.W. (2008). Systems Training for Emotional Predictability and Problem Solving (STEPPS) for outpatient clients with borderline personality disorder: A randomized controlled trial and 1-year follow-up. *American Journal of Psychiatry, 165*, 468–478.

Blum, N. S., Bartels, N. E., St. John, D., & Pfohl, B. (2009). *Systems Training for Emotional Predictability and Problem Solving (STEPPS UK): Group treatment program for borderline personality disorder.* Iowa City, IA: Level One Publishing, www.steppsforbpd.com.

Blum, N. S., Bartels, N. E., St. John, D., & Pfohl, B. (2012). *Systems Training for Emotional Predictability and Problem Solving (Second Edition): Group treatment program for borderline personality disorder.* Iowa City, IA: Level One Publishing, www.steppsforbpd.com.

Blum, N. S., Bartels, N. E., St. John, D., & Pfohl, B. (with Harvey, R., Henley-Cragg, P., Burgess, J., & Parrott, M. (2014a). *Managing emotional intensity: A STEPPS resource for younger people.* Iowa City, IA: Level One Publishing, www.steppsforbpd.com.

Blum, N. S., Bartels, N. E., St. John, D., & Pfohl, B. (with Harvey, R.) (2014b). *STEPPS ei group programme for managing emotional intensity—Early intervention.* Iowa City, IA: Level One Publishing, www.steppsforbpd.com.

Boccalon, S., Alesiani, R., Giarolli, L., Franchini, L., Colombo, C., Blum, N., & Fossati, A. (2012). Systems Training for Emotional Predictability and Problem Solving (STEPPS): Theoretical model, clinical application, and preliminary efficacy data in a sample of inpatients with personality disorders in comorbidity with mood disorders. *Journal of Psychopathology, 18*, 335–343.

Bos, E. H., van Wel, B., Appelo, M. T., & Verbraak, M. J. P. M. (2010). A randomized controlled trial of a Dutch version of Systems Training for Emotional Predictability and Problem Solving for borderline personality disorder. *Journal of Nervous and Mental Disease, 198*, 299–304.

Bos, E. H., van Wel, B., Appelo, M. T., & Verbraak, M. J. P. M. (2011). Effectiveness of Systems Training for Emotional Predictability and Problem Solving for borderline personality disorder in a real world sample: Moderation by diagnosis or severity? *Psychotherapy and Psychosomatics, 80*, 173–181.

Conklin, C. Z., & Westen, D. (2005). Borderline personality disorder in clinical practice. *American Journal of Psychiatry, 162*, 867–875.

Davidson, K., Norrie, J., Tyrer, P., Gumley, A., Tata, P., Murray, H., & Palmer, S. (2006). The Effectiveness of cognitive behavior therapy for borderline personality disorder: Results from the Borderline Personality Disorder Study of Cognitive Therapy (BOSCOT) trial. *Journal of Personality Disorders, 20*, 450–465.

Farrell, J. M., Shaw, I. A., & Webber, M. A. (2009). A schema-focused approach to group psychotherapy for outpatients with borderline personality disorder: A randomized controlled trial. *Journal of Behaviour Therapy and Experimental Psychiatry, 40*, 317–328.

Forman, E. M., Herbert, J. D., Moitra, E., Yeomans, P. D., & Geller, P. A. (2007). A randomized controlled effectiveness trial of acceptance and commitment therapy and cognitive therapy for anxiety and depression. *Behavior Modification, 31*(6), 772–799.

Freije, H., Dietz, B., & Appelo, M. (2002). Behandeling van de borderline persoonlijkheidsstoornis met de Vers: de Vaardigheidstraining emotionele regulatiestoornis. *Directive Therapies, 4*, 367–378.

Gunderson J. (1996). The borderline client's intolerance of aloneness: Insecure attachments, and therapist availability. *American Journal of Psychiatry, 153*, 752–758.

Harvey, R., Black, D. W., & Blum, N. (2010). Systems Training for Emotional Predictability and Problem Solving (STEPPS) in the United Kingdom: A preliminary report. *Journal of Contemporary Psychotherapy, 40,* 225–232.

Harvey, R., Blum, N., Black, D. W., Burgess, J., & Henley-Cragg (2014). Systems Training for Emotional Predictability and Problem Solving (STEPPS). In C. Sharp & J. Tackett (eds.), *Handbook of borderline personality disorder in children and adolescents* (pp. 415–429). New York, NY: Springer.

Hayes, S. C., Luoma, J. B., Bond, F. W., Masuda, A., & Lillis, J. (2006). Acceptance and commitment therapy: Model, processes and outcomes. *Behaviour Research and Therapy, 44*(1), 1–25.

Hayes, S. C., Stosahl, K. D., & Wilson, K. G. (1999). Acceptance and commitment therapy: An experiential approach to behavior change. New York, NY: The Guilford Press.

Kellogg, S. H., & Young, J. E. (2006). Schema therapy for borderline personality disorder. *Journal of Clinical Psychology, 62,* 445–458.

Linehan, M. M., Armstrong, A. G., Suarez, A., Allmon, D., & Heard, H. S. (1991). Cognitive-behavioral treatment of chronically parasuicidal borderline clients. *Archives of General Psychiatry, 48,* 1060–1064.

Linehan, M. M., Heard, H. L., & Armstrong, H. E. (1993). Naturalistic follow-up of a behavioral treatment of chronically parasuicidal borderline clients. *Archives of General Psychiatry, 50,* 1971–1974.

Linehan, M. M., Tupek, D. A., Heard, H. L., & Armstrong, H. E. (1994). Interpersonal outcome of cognitive-behavioral treatment for chronically suicidal borderline clients. *American Journal of Psychiatry, 151,* 1771–1776.

Mynors-Wallis, L. (2005). *Problem-solving Treatment for Anxiety and Depression.* New York, NY: Oxford University Press.

Minuchin, S. (1974). *Families and family therapy.* Cambridge, MA: Harvard University Press.

Nakao, K., Gunderson, J. G., Phillips, K. A., Tanaka, N., Yorifuji, K., Takaishi, J., & Nishimura, T. (1992). Functional impairment in personality disorders. *Journal of Personality Disorders, 6,* 24–33.

National Registry of Evidence-based Programs and Practices (NREPP). Systems Training for Emotional Predictability and Problem Solving (STEPPS), http://nrepp. samsha.gov. Downloaded from the http://nrepp.samsha.gov website on June 3, 2014.

Pfohl, B., Blum, N., McCormick, B., St. John, D., & Black, D. W. (2009). Reliability and validity of the Borderline Evaluation of Severity over Time: A new scale to measure severity and change in borderline personality disorder. *Journal of Personality Disorders, 23,* 281–293.

Ruiz, F. J. (2010). A review of acceptance and commitment therapy (ACT) empirical evidence: Correlational, experimental psychopathology, component and outcome studies. *International Journal of Psychology and Psychological Therapy, 10,* 125–162.

Rüsch, N., Schiel, S., Corrigan, P. W., Leihener, F., Jacob, G. A., Olschewski, M., . . . Bohus, M. (2008). Predictors of dropout from inpatient dialectical behavior therapy among women with borderline personality disorder. *Journal of Behavior Therapy and Experimental Psychiatry, 39,* 497–503.

Samuels, J., Eaton, W. W., Bienvenu J., Clayton, P., Brown, H., Costa, P. T., & Nestadt, G. (2002). Prevalence and correlates of personality disorder in a community setting. *British Journal of Psychiatry, 180,* 536–542.

Silk, K. R., Lee, S., Hill, E. M., & Lohr, N. E. (1995). BPD symptoms and severity of sexual abuse. *American Journal of Psychiatry, 152,* 1059–1064.

Skodol, A. E., Gunderson, J. G., Shea, M. T., McGlashan, T. H., Morey, L.C., Sanisolow, C. A., . . . Stout, R. L (2005). Collaborative longitudinal personality disorders study. *Journal of Personality Disorders, 19,* 487–504.

Stevenson, J., Meares, R., & Comerford, A. (2003). Diminished impulsivity in older patients with borderline personality disorder. *American Journal of Psychiatry, 160,* 165–166.

Torgerson, S., Kringlen, E., & Cramer, V. (2001). The prevalence of personality disorders in a community setting. *Archives of General Psychiatry, 58,* 590–596.

Van Wel, B., Kockmann, I., Blum, N., Pfohl, B., Heesterman, W., & Black, D. W. (2006). STEPPS group treatment for borderline personality disorder in The Netherlands. *Annals of Clinical Psychiatry, 18,* 63–67.

Van Wel, B., Bos, E. H., Appelo, M. T., Berendsen, E. M., Willgeroth, F. C., & Verbraak, M. J. P. M. (2009). De effectiviteit van de vaardigheidstraining Emotieregulatiestoornis (VERS) in de behandeling van de Borderlinepersoonlijkheidsstoornis; een gerandomiseerd onderzoek. *Tijdschrift voor psychiatrie, 51,* 291–301.

Wnuk, S., McMain, S., Links, P. S., Habinski, L., Murray, J., & Guimond, T. (2013). Factors related to dropout from treatment in two outpatient treatments for borderline personality disorder. *Journal of Personality Disorders 27,* 716–726, Epub 2013 May 29.

Yeomans, F. E., Clarkin, J. F., & Kernberg, O. F. (2002). *A Primer for transference focused psychotherapy for the borderline patient.* Northvale, NJ: Jason Aronson Inc.

Young, J. E. (1994). *Cognitive Therapy for Personality Disorders: A Schema-Focused Approach,* rev. ed. Sarasota, FL: Professional Resource Press.

Zanarini, M. C. (2000). Childhood experiences associated with the development of BPD. *Psychiatric Clinics of North America, 23,* 89–101.

Zanarini, M. C., Frankenburg, F. R., Dubo, E. D., Sickel, A. E., Trikha, A., Levin, A., & Reynolds, V. (1993). Axis I comorbidity of BPD. *American Journal of Psychiatry, 151,* 733–1739.

Zanarini, M. C., Frankenburg, F. R., Reich, D. B., & Fitzmaurice, G. (2012). Attainment and stability of sustained remission and recovery among patients with borderline personality disorder and Axis II comparison subjects: A 16-year prospective follow-up study. *American Journal of Psychiatry, 169,* 476–483.

Zanarini, M. C., Frankenburg, F.R., Hennen, J., & Silk, K. R. (2004). Mental health service utilization by borderline personality disorder patients and axis II comparison subjects followed prospectively for 6 years. *Journal of Clinical Psychiatry, 65,* 28–36.

Zanarini, M.C., Yong, L., Frankenburg, F. R., Hennen, J., Reich, D. B., Marino, M. F., & Vujanovic, A. A. (2002). Severity of reported childhood sexual abuse and its relationship to severity of borderline psychopathology and psychosocial impairment among borderline patients. *Journal of Nervous and Mental Diseases, 190,* 381–387.

Zimmerman M., & Coryell, W. (1989). DSM-III personality disorder diagnosis in a non-patient sample: Demographic correlates and comorbidity. *Archives of General Psychiatry, 46,* 682–689.

# 2

# Research Evidence
# Supportive of STEPPS

DONALD W. BLACK, NANCEE S. BLUM, AND JEFF ALLEN ■

This chapter reviews the evidence base supportive of the Systems Training for Emotional Predictability and Problem Solving (STEPPS) group treatment program. As described in chapter 1, the program was developed in 1995 in response to clinical needs at the University of Iowa. While the treatment of patients with borderline personality disorder (BPD) has always been challenging, there were very few published treatment programs to choose from at the time. Linehan's dialectical behavior therapy was available, but we sought a shorter and less intensive program. We found those qualities in a program developed by Bartels and Crotty (1992), and with their encouragement and permission, the program was adapted to create STEPPS. The new program satisfied our clinical needs and was accomplished without external funding.

A range of psychotherapies has since been developed and several programs have garnered empirical support. In addition to dialectical behavior therapy, they include mentalization-based therapy, cognitive behavioral therapy, schema-focused therapy, transference-focused therapy, and general psychiatric management (Bateman and Fonagy, 1999; 2008; Clarkin, Levy, Lenzenweger, & Kernberg, 2007; Linehan et al., 1991; 1993; 2006; Giesen-Bloo et al., 2006; McMain et al., 2012; Yeomans et al., 2002). Each program has a place in the treatment armamentarium for BPD, but research has provided little guidance about which program is best suited to a particular patient.

As described in chapter 1, STEPPS successfully combines cognitive behavioral elements with skills training. The program consists of 20 weekly group sessions led by two co-facilitators. A unique aspect of STEPPS is its systems component designed for individuals with whom a patient regularly interacts (both professionals and non-professionals), an element influenced by family systems theory

(Minuchin, 1974). We believe the program is easily learned by therapists of varying educational and professional backgrounds. Importantly, the program supplements a patient's ongoing treatment, but does not replace it. For that reason the program is considered *adjunctive* rather than comprehensive. With this in mind, we review the data supportive of STEPPS and evidence for the reliability and validity of the Borderline Evaluation of Severity over Time (BEST), a self-report scale to rate symptomatic severity and clinical improvement in BPD patients.

## RESEARCH EVIDENCE

STEPPS has accumulated considerable empirical support that consists of eight uncontrolled studies or chart reviews and three randomized controlled trials (RCTs). This provides one of the world's largest bodies of data supportive of *any* group treatment for persons with BPD, exceeded only by that for dialectical behavior therapy. The data are remarkably consistent in showing that patients have measureable improvements in mood, impulsiveness, and symptoms specific to BPD such as mood instability, cognitive problems (e.g., overvalued ideas, depersonalization, and nonpsychotic paranoia), identity issues, and disturbed relationships (Blum et al., 2008; van Wel et al., 2009; Bos et al., 2010; Blum et al., 2002; Black et al., 2008; Freije, Dietz, & Appelo, 2002; Harvey, Black, & Blum, 2010; Boccalon et al., 2012). Patients also have a reduction in health care seeking and self-harm behaviors and, in the correctional setting, a decrease in disruptive behaviors. Further, data show that STEPPS is well accepted by patients and therapists. On the strength of this research evidence, STEPPS has been designated by the United States Substance Abuse and Mental Health Administration as an evidence-based treatment and is listed on the National Registry for Evidence-Based Practices (NREPP, 2014).

## UNCONTROLLED STUDIES/CHART REVIEWS

This section reviews data from uncontrolled studies and retrospective chart reviews and includes studies from the United States, The Netherlands, Italy, and the United Kingdom. The studies are described in chronological order and are summarized in Table 2.1.

### Blum et al. (2002)

Blum and coworkers (2002) conducted a study to review the experience of 52 patients (49 women, 3 men) who had participated in STEPPS groups between July 1997 and November 1998. The groups took place either at the University of Iowa or at one of several off-campus sites and were conducted by trained therapists. The

*Table 2.1.* RESULTS OF UNCONTROLLED STUDIES OF STEPPS IN SUBJECTS
WITH BORDERLINE PERSONALITY DISORDER

| Author | Year | Location | No. Subjects | Female (%) | Mean Age, Years | Results: STEPPS associated with |
|---|---|---|---|---|---|---|
| Blum et al. | 2002 | Iowa | 52 | 94 | 33 | ↓ BDI, ↓ BEST, ↓ PANAS-NA Scale |
| Freije et al. | 2002 | Netherlands | 85 | 91 | 32 | ↓ SCL-90 Subscales (D, A, IP) and General Symptom Index, and ↓ BEST |
| Black et al. | 2008 | Iowa | 12 | 100 | 35 | ↓ BDI, ↓ BEST, ↓ PANAS-NA Scale |
| Harvey et al. | 2010 | Sussex, UK | 38 | 84 | 37 | ↓ BDI, ↓ BEST, ↓ PANAS-NA Scale; ↓ Suicidal behaviors |
| Bocallon et al. | 2012 | Milan, Italy | 20 | 85 | 47 | ↓ Suicidal attempts; ↓ Hospitalizations |
| Black et al. | 2013 | Iowa | 77 | 31 | 82 | ↓ BDI, ↓ BEST, ↓ PANAS-NA Scale; ↓ Disciplinary infractions, ↓ Suicidal behaviors |
| Alesiani et al. | 2014 | Milan, Italy | 32 |  |  | ↓ Suicidal attempts; ↓ Hospitalizations |

BDI = Beck Depression Inventory; BEST = Borderline Estimate of Severity over Time; PANAS = Positive and Negative Affectivity Scale; NA = Negative Affectivity; SCL-90 = Symptom Checklist-90; D = Depression; A = Anxiety; IP = Interpersonal Sensitivity.

patients were all participating in individual psychotherapy and took psychotropic medication, mostly antidepressants, mood stabilizers, or antipsychotics, as is typical for patients with BPD (Black et al., 2011). The patients had a mean age of 33 years with a range from 18 to 51 years. Each person met DSM-IV (American Psychiatric Association, 1994) criteria for BPD, confirmed through a clinical interview and a review of the patient's case notes.

The Borderline Evaluation of Severity Over Time (BEST; Blum et al., 2002), the Positive and Negative Affectivity Scale (PANAS; Watson & Clark, 1983), and the Beck Depression Inventory (BDI; Beck, 1978) were used to assess the efficacy of STEPPS. The BEST, a self-report scale developed to assess patients with BPD, and its psychometric properties, is described later in the chapter. Subscales include negative thoughts and feelings, positive behaviors and negative behaviors. The PANAS is a self-rated 60-item questionnaire that taps both positive and negative affect states considered to be important dimensions of emotional experience

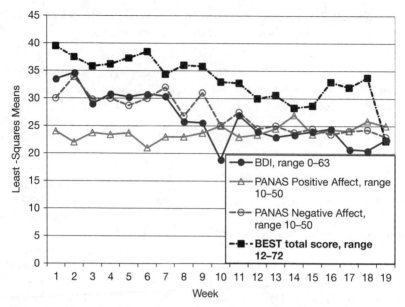

**Figure 2.1** Generalized Least-Squares Means for Outcome Measures by Week

SOURCE: Reprinted with permission from Blum, N., Pfohl, B., St. John, D., Monahan, P., & Black, D.W. (2002). STEPPS: A cognitive behavioral systems based group treatment for outpatients with borderline personality disorder-A preliminary report. *Comprehensive Psychiatry*, 43, 301–310.

(Watson & Clark, 1994). The BDI is a widely used 20-item self-report measure that assesses cognitions and behaviors typical of depression.

Patients experienced a significant decrease in borderline symptoms assessed with the BEST ($P = 0.01$), the largest effect occurring in the decrease of negative behaviors. This is noteworthy because these behaviors often lead to treatment-seeking (e.g., self-harm, substance abuse, destruction of property, physical fights). Of 29 patients with data at Week 10, 41% were rated as responders (defined as a ≥25% decrease in BEST total score). There was a significant drop in BDI scores, with scores dropping significantly (34%) from 30 at intake to 20 by Week 13 ($P = 0.009$). There was also a significant decrease in the PANAS negative affectivity scores ($P = 0.0004$), although positive affect scores were mostly unchanged ($P = 0.67$). Thus, the data suggest that STEPPS is associated with a greater reduction in negative behaviors than it is with an increase in positive behaviors. These changes are shown in Figure 2.1. The results indicated a large effect size for the change in the BEST total score (–1.35), two BEST subscales (thoughts and feelings; –1.32; negative behaviors, –1.10), and a moderate effect size for the BDI (–0.78).

## Freije et al. (2002)

Freije et al. (2002) described the experience of 85 patients (77 women, 8 men) who had enrolled in STEPPS groups in Groningen, The Netherlands, following the program's introduction to that country in 1998. The patients had a mean age of 32 years. They were assessed pre- and post-treatment using the Symptom

Checklist-90 (SCL-90; Derogatis, 1983), a scale used to rate a range of psychiatric symptoms, as well as a Dutch version of the BEST. Significant improvement was seen on all SCL-90 subscales, particularly those rating anxiety, depression, and interpersonal sensitivity. Scores on the BEST were also significantly improved. The authors point out that 85 subjects had entered the study and 56 completed, yielding a 34% drop out rate, a problem that affects nearly all studies of BPD.

## Black et al. (2008)

In a report on 12 incarcerated women, Black and coworkers (2008) concluded that STEPPS produced measureable improvements in mood and behavior and was well accepted by staff and offenders. The women ranged in age from 19 to 49 with a mean of 35 years; 10 were Caucasian and two were African-American. Eleven women (92%) were prescribed a mean (SD) of 2.5 (1.4) psychotropic medications; 10 took an antidepressant, seven a sedative/hypnotic, four a mood stabilizer, four an anxiolytic, and two an antipsychotic. One woman dropped out after the baseline assessment and another dropped out after week 12 because both were discharged from prison. All other women completed the program with perfect attendance (i.e., attended all 20 sessions). It is worth noting that attendance was voluntary.

Significant improvements were seen for borderline-related symptoms, depression, and negative affectivity by comparing means at baseline to those in subsequent weeks using a linear mixed-effects model. The BEST total score dropped from 28.0 to 16.9 at week 20, yielding a nearly 40% drop that was highly significant ($P = 0.009$). Other significant improvements were seen on all three BEST subscores, the PANAS negative affectivity scale, and the BDI. Significant effect sizes ranged from 0.41 for the PANAS negative affectivity scale to 0.86 for the BDI. We concluded from this pilot study that STEPPS could be successfully integrated into the prison setting.

## Harvey et al. (2010)

A study from the United Kingdom (Harvey et al., 2010) reported improvements in 38 patients (32 women, 2 men) who had participated in STEPPS groups conducted in West Sussex. The subjects had a mean age of 37 years with a range from 20 to 58 years. The patients experienced improvements in borderline symptoms, negative affectivity, and suicidal behavior. Efficacy was assessed with the BEST, the BDI; the PANAS; the Zanarini Rating Scale for Borderline Personality Disorder (ZAN-BPD; Zanarini et al., 2003); and the Clinical Outcomes in Routine Evaluation-OM (CORE-OM; Connell et al., 2007). The ZAN-BPD is a clinician rated 5-point scale that measures change in borderline psychopathology. Subscales measure affective disturbance, cognitive symptoms, impulsivity, and relationship difficulties. The CORE-OM is a 34-item questionnaire that measures psychological distress, including well-being, symptoms, day-to-day functioning, and risk to self or others. The instrument is used to assess general functioning.

The BEST total score fell from 45.5 at baseline to 35.1 at week 20 ($P < 0.001$). Overall improvement is also indicated by statistically significant improvements on the ZAN-BPD total score and its four subscales, the BDI, the two PANAS scales, and the CORE-OM. A subscore analysis showed a significant change on ZAN-BPD question #7, which relates to incidents of self-harm and suicide attempts.

The CORE-OM also yielded data on end of therapy assessments by clinicians. In all ten categories, a higher percentage of patients were rated as "improved" by clinicians. The greatest improvement was for gains in personal insight and understanding; 94% of patients were rated as improved. Patients were generally rated as more able to express and explore feelings (87%) and to better use coping strategies or techniques (81%). Clinicians thought that only 55% of participants had shown improvement in their personal relationships. Day-to-day functioning and subjective well-being were also rated as improved in 71%. Eighty-one percent of patients had not changed their medication.

Based on feedback from patients and therapists, the introduction of STEPPS was welcomed and highly valued. The authors concluded that STEPPS can be transported to other countries and adapted to suit the local population.

## Boccalon et al. (2012)

Boccalon et al. (2012) reported data from 20 inpatients in Milan, Italy who had either full-blown BPD or prominent BPD features plus comorbid mood disorders. Outcome measures included the number of self-destructive acts and hospitalizations during the treatment and 6 months after the end of therapy. The patients completed a self-report questionnaire to identify distorted thoughts before starting therapy, at the end of treatment, and at a 6-month follow-up. The number of self-destructive behaviors and the number of hospitalizations during STEPPS treatment and at a 6-month follow-up were used as outcome criteria. Outcome measures also included the self-report Filters Questionnaire developed for the STEPPS program to assess distorted cognitive schemas (e.g., emotional distrust, abandonment) and adapted from the work of Young (1994), and the Emotional Intensity Continuum (EIC), a visual analogue assessing the intensity of emotional states developed as a daily measure of functioning for patients enrolled in STEPPS (Black, Blum, Pfohl, & St. John, 2004).

Nine of 20 patients (45%) completed the program. On average, the non-completers showed a significantly higher number of histrionic ($P < 0.01$) and passive-aggressive ($P < 0.05$) traits than completers. Patients who completed the program showed a significant and progressive decrease in the number of self-destructive behaviors ($P < 0.01$) and hospitalizations ($P < 0.001$). The cognitive filters of distrust and abandonment correlated with the number of BPD traits, and there was a significant decrease in the distrust filter at the 6-month follow-up. EIC scores significantly decreased during the course of the program ($P < 0.005$).

The authors concluded that STEPPS was effective in reducing the number of self-destructive acts and hospitalizations, and that the results were stable over the 6-month follow-up. Further, the authors suggested that the decrease in the cognitive filter of distrust at the 6-month follow-up indicates that STEPPS reduces pessimistic expectations about self and others, and mobilizes resources and skills patients can later rely on. The reduction in the Emotional Intensity Continuum scores shows that STEPPS reduces self-rated emotional intensity, a prominent feature of the disorder.

## Black et al. (2013)

In another report on their experience in the Iowa correctional system, Black et al. (2013) reviewed the experience of 77 offenders (14 men, 63 women) enrolled in STEPPS groups, including the 12 subjects whose experience was described earlier (Black et al., 2008). Sixty-seven subjects were enrolled in one of 7 prison-based groups; 10 were probationers enrolled in a group in a community corrections setting.

The offenders ranged in age from 19 to 50 years with a mean of 31 years. Forty subjects (89%) took some form of psychotropic medication, 36 (80%) an antidepressant, 10 (22%) a sedative/hypnotic, 20 (44%) a mood stabilizer, 11 (24%) an anxiolytic, 18 (45%) an antipsychotic, 17 (38%) a benzodiazepine, and 15 (33%) a pain medication. They took a mean of 3.0 psychotropic medications. Forty-one offenders (53%) completed the 20 week program.

Significant improvements were seen for measures of borderline symptoms, mood, and negative affectivity. The BEST total score and all three subscales, the PANAS negative affectivity scale, and the BDI scores were all significantly improved. Effect sizes ranged from 0.69 for the PANAS negative affectivity score to 1.30 for the BEST total score. Significant reductions in suicidal behaviors and disciplinary infractions were observed ($P = 0.029$ and $P = 0.043$ for suicidal behaviors and disciplinary infractions, respectively). At baseline, 14% of the offenders had reported at least one suicidal behavior in the past four weeks; 26% were reported to have had at least one disciplinary infraction. At week 20, 5% of the sample had at least one suicidal behavior in the past four weeks and 17% had one or more disciplinary infractions.

We concluded that STEPPS can be easily transported to prison and community corrections settings, and that the program leads to clinically significant improvement in men and women offenders. The data also show a significant reduction in the number of suicide/self-harm behaviors and disciplinary infractions occurring in prison. From a practical standpoint, in addition to being less depressed by the end of the 20 week program, the offenders were less likely to report extreme moodiness or anger dyscontrol, or to have fewer thoughts of being abandoned by important persons in their lives. The decrease in negative affectivity suggests that they felt less hopeless and had fewer negative self-impressions. Offenders also had an *increase* in positive behaviors such as following through with therapy plans.

All of these changes reflect the emphasis of STEPPS to teach people skills to help self-regulate their intense emotions and maladaptive behaviors.

## Alesiani et al. (2014)

Alesiani et al. (2014) present a follow-up to the report by Boccalon et al. (2012). Their sample has now increased to 32 inpatients with either full-blown BPD or who had prominent BPD features along with a comorbid mood disorder, and the follow-up has been extended to 12 months. Another goal was to identify predictors of drop-out in order to better understand characteristics that make a person suitable for STEPPS. Outcome measures included the number of hospitalizations related to self-harm acts; the number of suicide attempts; self-reported EIC scores; and cognitive filter scores at the 12-month follow-up using the Filter Questionnaire. Subjects had a mean age of 44 years with a range of 26 to 63 years. Half of the subjects had comorbid major depression; the others had a bipolar disorder. All had been previously hospitalized (mean = 3.71) and had multiple prior suicide attempts (mean = 2.28).

Seventeen (53%) patients completed the treatment. Patients who completed the program had a significant decrease in the number of hospitalizations ($P = .000$), both at the end of the treatment and at the 12-month follow-up. There was a measureable and significant drop in suicide attempts during and after STEPPS and at the 12-month follow-up ($P = .001$). EIC scores also dropped significantly. Improvement in the EIC scores occurred after an initial unstable trend, but continued downward from Week 12 forward. The patients who dropped out differed significantly from completers in having higher levels of histrionic personality traits and magical thinking. The authors concluded that those with "infantile, suggestible, inauthentic, and attention-seeking personalities" are not good candidates for STEPPS (p. 925).

## RANDOMIZED CONTROLLED STUDIES

This section reviews three randomized controlled trials of STEPPS conducted in the United States and Holland. They are discussed in chronological order. They are summarized in Table 2.2.

## Blum et al. (2008)

Blum et al. (2008) randomized 165 patients to STEPPS plus treatment as usual (TAU) or to TAU alone. TAU included individual psychotherapy, non-STEPPS group treatments, psychotropic medication, and case management. TAU was not

*Table 2.2.* RESULTS OF CONTROLLED STUDIES OF STEPPS IN SUBJECTS
WITH BORDERLINE PERSONALITY DISORDER

| Author | Year | Location | No. Subjects/ randomized | Female (%) | Mean Age, Years | Results: STEPPS > TAU |
|---|---|---|---|---|---|---|
| Blum et al. | 2008 | Iowa | 165 | 83 | 31.5 | ↓ ZAN-BPD total, affective, cognitive, impulsivity subscales; ↑ CGI improvement; ↓ CGI severity; ↑ GAS; ↓ BEST thoughts and feelings; ↓ PANAS Negative Affectivity; ↓ BDI; ↓ BIS' ↓ SCL-90-R general severity; ↓ Emergency visits |
| Van Wel et al.; Bos et al. | 2009; 2010 | Netherlands | 79 | 86 | 32.4 | ↓ BPD-40; ↓ SCL-90-R general severity; ↑ WHOQOL-Bref overall, physical health, psychological health |
| Schuppert et al. | 2008 | Netherlands | 43 | 88 | 16.1 | ↑ Internal locus of control |

controlled by the research team. The patients were assessed with the Structured Clinical Interview for DSM-IV Axis I Disorders (Spitzer, Williams, & Gibbon, 1994) and the Structured Interview for DSM-IV Personality (Pfohl, Blum, & Zimmerman, 1997) to assess Axes I and II. Outcome measures included the BEST, the BDI, the PANAS, and the ZAN-BPD. The ZAN-BPD total score was considered the primary outcome variable. Social and interpersonal functioning, adjunctive medication usage, suicidal behaviors, deliberate self-harm, and health care utilization data were also collected.

One-hundred twenty-five patients received the allocated interventions, and data from 124 were analyzed. The groups were balanced on baseline demographic and clinical variables (Table 2.2), except that avoidant personality disorder was more frequent in the TAU alone group (66% vs. 45%; $P = 0.016$). Forty-five (69%) subjects assigned to STEPPS plus TAU and 51 (86%) subjects assigned to TAU alone completed the week 20 assessment ($P = .022$). STEPPS plus TAU recipients attended a mean (SD) of 12.9 (5.4) sessions.

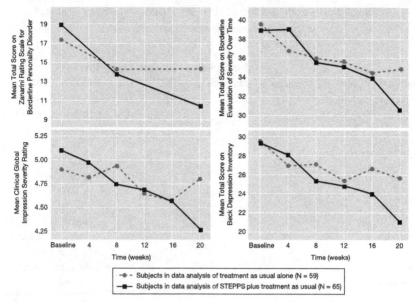

**Figure 2.2** Mean Primary and Secondary Outcome Measure Scores

NOTE: The Zanarini Rating Scale for Borderline Personality Disorder was obtained at baseline, week 8, and week 20. The Borderline Evaluation of Severity over Time, CGI ratings, and Beck Depression Inventory were obtained at baseline and weeks 4, 8, 12, 16, and 20.

SOURCE: Reprinted with permission from Blum, N., St. John, D., Pfohl, B., Stuart, S., McCormick, B., Allen, J., Arndt, S., Black, D.W. (2008). Systems Training for Emotional Predictability and Problem Solving (STEPPS) for outpatients with borderline personality disorder: a randomized controlled trial and 1-year follow-up. *American Journal of Psychiatry*, 165, 468–478.

Patients assigned to STEPPS plus TAU improved from baseline through week 20 on primary and secondary outcome measures (see Figure 2.2). The mean rate of change for the STEPPS plus TAU group was significantly greater than that for the treatment as usual alone group for the ZAN-BPD total score and all four subscales, the Clinical Global Impression Severity and Improvement Scales, the Global Assessment Scale score, the BEST Thoughts/Feelings subscale, the Barratt Impulsiveness Scale total score, the PANAS Negative Affectivity subscale, the BDI score, the SCL-90-R depression, psychoticism, and global severity subscales, and the Social Adjustment Scale social/leisure subscale and total scores. For other outcomes, improvement observed in the STEPPS plus TAU group was greater than the TAU alone group, but differences were not statistically significant. A 1-year follow-up showed that the improvements were mostly maintained, thus suggesting that patients learned new skills that were used beyond the treatment period to enhance their quality of life.

Effect sizes at 20 weeks represent group differences in mean improvement divided by the pooled standard deviations at baseline. For the ZAN-BPD total score, the estimated effect size was 0.84, indicating a large effect of the STEPPS program. For secondary outcome measures, effect size estimates ranged from 0.12 to 1.09. Generally, those of 0.50 and greater were statistically significant.

Patients assigned to STEPPS plus TAU had a greater change in Clinical Global Impression Severity and Improvement scale scores than those randomized to

TAU alone. Using each subject's last observation within the treatment period, those randomized to STEPPS plus TAU were more likely to be rated "very much" or "much" improved (40.0% vs. 5.1%, $P < 0.001$); the patients' own global self-ratings showed similar results, with 58.5% of STEPPS plus TAU recipients rating themselves as "very much" or "much" improved, compared to 22.0% for those assigned to TAU alone ($P < 0.001$). STEPPS plus TAU recipients were more likely to reach the clinically relevant Global Assessment Scale cutoff (>60; 18.5% vs. 5.1%, $P = 0.023$).

Figure 2.2 shows estimated means over the treatment period for the primary and selected secondary outcomes. Improvements for the STEPPS plus TAU group appear to be monotonic and roughly linear. Improvements for the TAU alone group appear mostly confined to the first half of the treatment period.

Ninety percent of subjects reported at least one psychotropic medication at baseline. Antidepressants were reported by 42 (65%) of the STEPPS plus TAU recipients and 33 (56%) of the TAU alone group ($P = 0.323$). Psychotropic usage significantly decreased during the 20-week treatment period for both groups (from 2.9 to 1.3 medications per subject), but there was no group difference in level of change ($P = 0.782$). Thus, medication usage did not confound study results. Additionally, 63% of STEPPS plus TAU patients and 54% of TAU alone patients were engaged in individual psychotherapy at baseline. These percentages remained relatively constant during the 20-week treatment period.

Patients were asked to report crisis care utilization within the last month. Overall, 35 (28.2%) patients had at least one hospitalization during treatment period or follow-up. Those randomized to STEPPS plus TAU averaged 1.13 months per year during which hospitalization occurred and subjects randomized to TAU alone averaged 1.24, but the difference was not significant. In addition, 43 (34.7%) patients had at least one emergency department visit during the treatment or follow-up. Those randomized to STEPPS plus TAU averaged 0.97 months per year with at least one emergency department visit and those randomized to TAU alone averaged 1.52; the difference was significant (P = 0.040). Finally, 60 (48.4%) patients made at least one crisis call during the treatment or follow-up. Those randomized to STEPPS plus TAU averaged 2.49 months per year during which at least one crisis call was made and subjects randomized to TAU alone averaged 2.31, but the difference was not significant.

Suicide attempt and self-harm data were available for 108 of the 124 patients. Suicide attempts were reported by 24 patients (22.2%), and self-harm acts were reported by 56 (45.2%) during treatment and follow-up. Nearly all who attempted suicide (88%) also reported self-harm acts. Among those who attempted suicide, the median number of attempts was 1.75 per year and the mean was 2.60. Among those who reported acts of deliberate self-harm, the median number of acts was 9.8 per year and the mean was 16.6. Using the Cox Proportional Hazards Model, treatment group was not associated with time to first suicide attempt ($P = .994$) or first self-harm act ($P = 0.902$).

We concluded that STEPPS leads to broad-based improvements in the affective, cognitive, impulsive, and disturbed relationship domains, and that the treatment has a robust antidepressant effect. These changes reflect the emphasis of the program, in that patients are taught to regulate their intense emotions and maladaptive behaviors. Improvements were mostly maintained during the 1-year follow-up. This suggests that people assigned to STEPPS learned new skills that they used beyond the treatment period to enhance their quality of life.

In a secondary analysis, we (Black et al., 2009) examined the predictors of response for those participating in the study. Improvement in the ZAN-BPD total score was associated with greater global severity (CGI Severity), greater severity of BPD-related symptoms (all ZAN-BPD subscales), the presence of additional personality disorders, being randomized to STEPPS plus TAU, having attempted to harm oneself in the past, and having paranoid personality disorder. Improvement in BEST total score was associated with greater severity of BPD-related symptoms (BEST total), being randomized to STEPPS plus TAU, and having a lifetime substance use disorder. Improvement in GAS score was associated with greater global severity (i.e., worse GAS score) at intake and being randomized to STEPPS plus TAU. Thus, higher baseline severity was associated with greater improvement in global functioning and BPD-related symptoms, while higher levels of impulsivity were predictive of dropping out. In another substudy, we concluded that optimal improvement was associated with attending ≥15 sessions.

In conclusion, we concluded that subjects most likely to improve had more severe borderline symptoms at baseline, that high levels of impulsivity were associated with early discontinuation, and attending ≥15 sessions was associated with improved outcome.

The Dutch study design was similar to that employed in the US trial. Seventy-nine patients with BPD were randomized to STEPPS plus TAU or to TAU alone (van Wel et al., 2009; Bos, van Wel, Appelo, & Verbraak, 2011). They were recruited at one of two non-academic mental health clinics in Groningen and Deventer, Netherlands. The presence of BPD was confirmed using a Dutch translation of the Structured Clinical Interview for DSM-IV Personality Disorders (SCID-II; Weertman et al., 2003). The Dutch version of STEPPS uses the acronym VERS ("Vaardigheidstraining Emotie Regulatie Stoornis") and involves 18 weekly sessions but is otherwise identical in content and approach to the US version. TAU could include individual therapy or medication, and was available to all participants. All patients were engaged in individual psychotherapy, but other family or group experiences were not allowed.

The main outcome measures included general psychiatric and BPD specific measures including the SCL-90-R total score (Derogatis, 1983) and the Borderline Personality Disorder Checklist-40 (BPD-40; Arntz & Dreesen, 1992). The latter is a 40-item self-report questionnaire covering the DSM-IV BPD criteria that assesses severity in the last month; scores can range from 40 to 200. Secondary measures included impulsive and suicidal behaviors assessed using subscales of the BPD Severity Index (BPDSI; Arntz et al., 2003). This is a semistructured interview that assesses the frequency of borderline symptoms in the previous 3 months. Quality of life was assessed with the World Health Organizations

Quality of Life Assessment (WHOQOL-Bref; Trompenaars et al., 2005). Patients were assessed at baseline (T1), at the end of the program (T2), and at a 6-month follow-up (T3). Of the 79 patients, 13 (16.5%) dropped out prior to the post-treatment assessment.

One-hundred ninety-eight patients were assessed and 83 were randomized, with 4 withdrawing after randomization, yielding a final sample of 79 (42 STEPPS plus TAU, 37 TAU alone). Scores on the main outcome measures (SCL-90-R, BPD-40) decreased from T1 to T3, more so In the STEPPS plus TAU recipients ($P < 0.001$). Quality of life measures improved from T1 to T3 particularly for overall quality of life and general health, physical health, and psychological health. There were no measurable improvements for impulsivity and parasuicide subscales of the BPDSI-IV.

Effect sizes were calculated for the differences in the treatment groups between T1 and T2: SCL-90-R, 0.68; psychological health, 0.53; at T3, effect sizes were: SCL-90-R, 0.56; BPD-40, 0.53; overall quality of life and general health, .61; physical health, 0.56; and social relationships, 0.61. Next, the research team looked at whether the subjects showed "reliable improvement," using a method described by Jacobson and Truax (1991). By these calculations, 58.3% of STEPPS plus TAU recipients and 29.2% of TAU alone recipients met the definition of reliable change at T2 ($P = 0.042$); at T3, the figures were 70.0% and 46.5%, respectively ($P = 0.069$). The number of patients rated as "deteriorated" using this method was smaller in the STEPPS plus TAU group.

The research team concluded that STEPPS plus TAU was more effective than TAU alone with regard to general and borderline specific symptoms and general quality of life, and that the changes persisted over a 6-month follow-up. The findings appear to replicate those reported in the study by Blum et al. (2008) though the Dutch study had much better patient retention.

Another communication from this research team (Bos et al., 2011) describes the experience of patients with subsyndromal BPD who participated in the study (Bos et al., 2010). These patients did not meet criteria for full-blown BPD, but had received a clinical diagnosis of BPD from their treating psychiatrist. Rather, they appeared to have subsyndromal BPD as assessed using the SCID-II (First et al., 1996) and the Personality Diagnostic Questionnaire (Hyler et al., 1989; PDQ+4), and were embedded with the larger group described earlier. The 168 subjects (85 with BPD and 83 with subsyndromal BPD) were randomly assigned to STEPPS plus TAU or to TAU alone, and assessments took place before (T1), post-treatment (T2), and at a 6-month follow-up (T3). The protocol and outcome measures are as described previously. The analysis investigated the impact of the diagnosis (BPD/subsyndromal BPD) and found no differences in outcome between groups. STEPPS plus TAU was effective in both groups of patients, and outperformed TAU alone on all outcomes and all time points (except the BPD-40 at T3 for subsyndromal BPD). Differential effectiveness was found based on initial severity regardless of diagnostic group. STEPPS plus TAU was superior to TAU alone, particularly in patients with high baseline severity.

## Schuppert et al. (2009)

Emotion Regulation Training (ERT) was developed for adolescents with symptoms of BPD and emotion dysregulation, but not the full disorder. ERT is an
adaptation of STEPPS, and its focus is on skills training and cognitive behavioral therapy. Problems with emotion regulation and the development of a more
internal locus of control were selected as the primary goals of the treatment. ERT
involves 17 weekly sessions with two booster sessions at 6 and 12 weeks post-
treatment. The adaptation is described in Chapter 8.

The effectiveness of ERT was examined in a randomized controlled study of
adolescents between age 14 and 19 years in five mental health clinics in Holland.
They had been referred for treatment of emotion dysregulation problems or
symptoms of BPD. They were required to have mood instability as described in
DSM-IV, plus at least one of the following: impulsivity, recurrent suicidal behavior, or anger dyscontrol. Forty-six patients entered the study, but three withdrew;
43 were randomized to receive ERT plus TAU or TAU alone. The mean age of the
subjects was 16.1 years, and 88% were female. Assessments included the BPDSI-
IV (Arntz et al., 2003) to assess frequency and severity of BPD symptoms, the
Youth Self Report (Achenbach, 1991) to assess internalizing and externalizing
symptoms, and a modification of the Multidimensional Health Locus of Control
scale (Wallston, 2005) was administered to measure locus of control. The patients
were assessed before and after random assignment to ERT plus TAU ($n = 23$) or
to TAU alone ($n = 20$).

Both groups showed equal reductions in BPD symptoms over time. The group
receiving ERT plus TAU had a significant increase in internal locus of control
($P < 0.006$). ERT participants reported more sense of control over their own mood
swings, and attributed changes in mood swings not only to external factors. The
study was complicated by high attrition (39%).

The researchers concluded that ERT is a relatively brief and adjunctive program
that could be implemented as part of a first step in a stepped care model, but note
that the results were less powerful than hoped. This could be due to the adolescent
population itself.

## DATA ON ACCEPTANCE BY PARTICIPANTS AND THERAPISTS

Data show that the STEPPS program achieves high levels of acceptance by participants and therapists, a finding that has been reproduced in several studies. These
results are described below.

The first study to show high levels of acceptance was reported by us (Blum et al.,
2002), described earlier in the chapter. Two brief mail surveys were developed to
assess patient and therapist attitudes toward the program. The survey was mailed
to 49 patients and 18 forms were returned. The survey of therapists was mailed to
28 persons and 13 forms were returned. Although response rates for the surveys
were suboptimal, they show that STEPPS has high levels of acceptance for efficacy

(i.e., self-harm) and process (i.e., amount of materials, length of session) variables. Further, the mostly qualitative results suggest that STEPPS is viewed by therapists as relatively easy to learn and complements other treatments the patient may be receiving. In a similar report from Holland, Freije et al. (2002), provided qualitative data from STEPPS attendees regarding their experience with the program. Typical statements included the following: "I understand my emotional fluctuations better." "I can talk and think about my BPD without drowning in it." Overall, these two studies were consistent in showing that patients and therapists reported high levels of acceptance for the treatment.

In our randomized trial (Blum et al., 2008), the Client Satisfaction Questionnaire-8 (Attkinson and Greenfield, 1999) was used to assess patient satisfaction with the program. The scale was developed as a multidimensional rating of client satisfaction with mental health services and yields scores that range from 8 to 32. The total scores were significantly higher for the STEPPS plus TAU group relative to the TAU alone group ($P < 0.001$), with means of 28.2 and 22.6, respectively. The ratings were obtained from patients who completed the trial at week 20.

In additional demonstrations of overall satisfaction with the program, we showed (Black et al., 2008, 2013) that offenders give the program high marks. In our first uncontrolled study (Black et al., 2008), the 10 women offenders reported high levels of satisfaction based on their mean CSQ-8 score of 27. In our second, and larger study (Black et al., 2013), 37 of 41 offenders who completed the 20 week program (including both men and women) again used the CSQ-8; the offenders' mean score was 28.5. These findings compare favorably to scores reported by STEPPS plus TAU recipients in the randomized trial; 27% achieved the scale maximum of 32.

Data from Harvey et al. (2010) are mostly qualitative, but also indicate high levels of satisfaction from therapists and patients. The researchers used a questionnaire of their own design that consisted of open- and closed-ended questions. Subjects reported that they were generally happy with the length of the program and the breaks. Negative comments were either that the program was too long or too short. The majority felt their understanding of BPD was better (73%), and that they were better able to cope with their difficulties (90%). They also believed that others thought they were better able to cope (77%). They also found the materials useful (77%). There was greater ambivalence around a specific tool, the reinforcement team skill cards (27% positive, 40% negative). This may relate to the way these were introduced into the teams, and this issue will be discussed further below. Similarly, there was a wider spread of responses regarding how well their individual therapists agreed with the materials.

## Validity of the BEST

The Borderline Estimate of Severity over Time (BEST) was developed as a companion to the STEPPS program (Blum et al., 2002; Pfohl et al., 2009). Data confirm that the instrument is reliable and valid in assessing people with BPD and has the advantage over other instruments for being self-administered. Further, the BEST shows evidence for good internal consistency and for both face and content validity, because the items were constructed to assess behaviors relevant to BPD. The scale also is sensitive to clinical change.

When STEPPS was initially developed, it was clear that patients needed a quick, self-rated, symptom-based measure that could be filled out at the beginning of each session to yield a "snapshot" of the individual's current status, for example:

- Since the last session has the patient been more emotionally stable, less impulsive, or less likely to have hurt him- or herself?
- Was the person more likely to have put into practice skills taught in the STEPPS program?

The scale has 15 items and three subscales: Subscale A ("Thoughts and Feelings") has 8 items that involve assessments of mood reactivity, identity disturbance, unstable relationships, paranoia, emptiness, and suicidal thinking; subscale B ("Behaviors-negative") has 4 items that rate negative actions such as injuring oneself (items on these subscales are rated from 1, "none/slight," to 5, "extreme"); subscale C ("Behaviors-positive") has 3 items that rate actions such as following through on therapy plans, and are rated from 5, "almost always," to 1, "almost never."

Subscales A and B map directly to the DSM-IV BPD criteria. The subscales recognize that "thoughts and feelings" (A) are different from the "negative behaviors" (B) typical of the disorder. As the STEPPS program developed, it was thought that negative behaviors (B) would improve more rapidly than thoughts and feelings (A), and that the use of the newly taught behavioral skills would be reinforced when subjects noted the improvement in their subscale B score. Section C was added to acknowledge the acquisition of positive behaviors, as well as to reinforce the use of new skills before seeing improvement in A and B, because scores in subscale C were expected to improve first. It was thought that seeing this change (i.e., improvement in C) reinforces the continued use of new skills, which eventually would become evident from improvement in B, and then A. Patients might become discouraged if their expected use of new skills failed to produce *some* observable improvement. Thus, seeing improvement in C encourages patients to keep using the skills despite noticeable lack of improvement in A and B.

To score the BEST, the total for each subscale is determined. The scores of subscales A and B are then added together and the total from subscale C is subtracted. A correction factor of 15 is added to yield the final score which can range from 12 (best) to 72 (worst). The BEST was designed to measure severity in an ill population, and was not designed as a diagnostic instrument. The scale is included in the Appendix.

There are two studies which show the instrument is reliable and valid, essential features for any scale, and that it is sensitive to change, and these are described below.

In our initial uncontrolled study (Blum et al., 2002), the clinical change experienced by the subjects was itself considered evidence for score validity. To provide a measure of internal validation, Pearson correlation coefficients were calculated between BEST total and subscale scores and other outcome measures (PANAS, BDI). As expected, BEST total, negative thoughts and feelings, and negative behavior scores were all moderately to strongly correlated with BDI and PANAS negative affect scores (median $r = 0.63$, 2.079). BEST positive behavior scores were also moderately positively correlated with PANAS positive affect scores (mean $r = .58$), and moderately negatively correlated with BDI scores (median $r = -0.48$). The magnitude of correlations between the three negative BEST scale scores and the PANAS positive affect scores were low, although in the right direction (median $r = -0.14$ to $-0.29$). Also, the correlation between the BEST positive behavior cores and the PANAS negative affect scores was low, but in the right direction (median $r = -0.21$). After reversing scoring items 13, 14, and 15 on the positive behavior scale, the median of the weekly Cronbach $\alpha$ coefficients was 0.90 for the BEST total score, indicating good internal consistency. Median item-total correlations were all above 0.50, except for item 15, which assesses therapy compliance ($- = 0.32$).

Our randomized controlled trial (Blum et al., 2008) provided a further opportunity to examine the BEST's reliability and validity and build on the preliminary data reported earlier. The results (Pfohl et al., 2009) show that the instrument has good test-retest reliability. Internal consistency was excellent, as shown by the moderate to high Cronbach's $\alpha$ coefficients across study visits, which provides evidence of construct validity. The scale also demonstrates excellent discriminant validity and is sensitive to clinical change occurring as early as week 4 of the study. BEST scores were robust indicators of illness severity for subjects with BPD.

The BEST total score significantly separated BPD and comparison subjects according to baseline severity ($P < .001$). The items that best discriminated the groups were items #3 ("extreme changes in how you see yourself"), #4 ("severe mood swings"), and #12 ("temper outbursts"). For item #4, 30 of 133 (23%) subjects with BPD exhibited "extreme" difficulty with the item compared to 0 of 28 (0%) comparison subjects; 22 of 28 (79%) comparison subjects showed "none/slight" difficulty compared to 7 of 133 (5%) subjects with BPD.

To examine internal consistency, Cronbach's $\alpha$ coefficients at baseline for subjects with BPD and comparison subjects were calculated; at 0.86 and 0.90, respectively, the scores show that test homogeneity was relatively high. When subjects with BPD were combined with comparison subjects, the test homogeneity of the baseline scores remained high ($\alpha = 0.92$). Cronbach's $\alpha$ coefficient for the borderline subjects was 0.89 after the first month of treatment, and remained high (0.90 to 0.92) during the 20 week treatment period. Item-total correlations and the corresponding overall measure of internal consistency, Cronbach's $\alpha$ coefficient, from these visits indicate that all items are measuring the same dimension.

To examine test-retest reliability, we assessed the correlation between baseline and screening BEST total scores which was moderate ($r = 0.62$, $n = 130$, $P < 0.001$). A mean of 53.1 days passed between screening and baseline assessments.

As a test for convergent and discriminant validity, the BEST total score at screening correlated strongly with the ZAN-BPD score, the SCL-90-R total score, the SAS total score, the CGI severity score, and both the GAS and BDI scores. At each time point throughout the study (baseline through week 20), each instrument score remained significantly correlated to the BEST total score, yet the relationship between the BEST and the BDI scores produced the highest coefficients (0.67–0.80), while the relationship with the CGI severity score and the SAS total score produced the lowest (0.33–0.59, and 0.41–0.59, respectively).

The BEST total score was sensitive to clinical change that occurred among all subjects with BPD who participated in the trial. Using a repeated measures model, the BEST total score decreased from a mean of 38.7 at baseline to a mean of 32.9 at week 20. The overall time effect for visits at baseline through week 20 was significant ($P < 0.001$). The CGI severity scale, the patient-rated global improvement scale, and the BDI were also sensitive to clinical change by week 20 ($P < 0.001$). However, follow-up contrast tests which compared each weekly visit to the screening visit showed that the CGI severity scores were not significantly different at week 4 from screening scores, and did not become significant until week 12 ($P = 0.002$). BEST scores, on the other hand, showed an average decrease of 3.5 from screening to week 4 ($P = 0.001$), indicating that the BEST was sensitive to clinical change that occurred early. The BDI also showed a significant difference by week 4, and changes in both the BDI and ZAN-BPD were significant by week 8.

Thus, data confirm that the BEST has good test-retest reliability. Internal consistency is excellent, as shown by the moderate to high Cronbach's α coefficients across study visits, which argues strongly for construct validity. The scale demonstrates excellent discriminant validity and is sensitive to clinical change occurring as early as week 4 of the study. Lastly, data show that BEST scores were the most robust indicators of illness severity for subjects with BPD.


## SUMMARY

STEPPS is a program that developed for treatment of patients with BPD and has accumulated a large evidence base. The treatment is efficacious, and has the advantage over other programs of being briefer and less time consuming, and therefore potentially more cost-effective. STEPPS is adjunctive and used to augment what the patient is already receiving. Data from controlled and uncontrolled studies show that STEPPS is associated with improvement in overall psychological functioning and in BPD specific symptoms. Further, the treatment appears to reduce self-harm behaviors, hospitalizations, and emergency visits; among offenders STEPPS is associated with a decrease in disciplinary infractions. Data also show that STEPPS is well accepted by clients and therapists, and effectively treats a wide range of symptoms experienced by patients with BPD. The BEST self-rated scale is a reliable and valid scale that can be used to rate severity and change in subjects with BPD.

# REFERENCES

Achenbach, T. M. (1991). *Manual for the child behavior checklist 4-18, YSR, and TRF profiles.* Burlington, VT: Department of Psychiatry, University of Vermont.

Alesiani, R., Boccalon, S., Giarolli, L., Blum, N., & Fossati, A. (2014). Systems Training for Emotional Predictability and Problem Solving (STEPPS): Program efficacy and personality features as predictors of drop-out—an Italian study. *Comprehensive Psychiatry, 55,* 920–927.

American Psychiatric Association. (1994). Diagnostic and Statistical Manual of Mental Disorders, Fourth Edition (DSM-IV). American Psychiatric Publishing, Inc., Washington, DC.

Arntz, A., & Dreesen, L. (1992). *Borderline personality disorder checklist.* Maastricht, The Netherlands: Rijksuniversitait Limburg.

Arntz, A., van den Horn, M., Cornelius, J., Verheul, R., van den Bosch, W. M., & de Bie, A. J. (2003). Reliability and validity of the Borderline Personality Severity Index. *Journal of Personality Disorders, 17,* 562–567.

Attkisson, C. C., & Greenfield, T. K. (1999). The UCSF client satisfaction questionnaire (csq) scales: the client satisfaction questionnaire-8. In M. Maruish (Ed.), *Psychological testing: Treatment planning and outcome assessment,* 2nd ed. Hillsdale, NJ: Earlbaum.

Bartels, N., & Crotty, T. (1992). *A systems approach to treatment: The borderline personality disorder skill training manual.* Winfield, IL: EID Treatment Systems.

Bateman, A., & Fonagy, P. (1999). Effectiveness of partial hospitalization in the treatment of borderline personality disorder: A randomized controlled trial. *American Journal of Psychiatry, 156,* 1563–1569.

Bateman, A., & Fonagy, P. (2008). 8-year follow-up of patients treated for borderline personality disorder: Mentalization-based treatment versus treatment as usual. *American Journal of Psychiatry, 165,* 631–638.

Beck, A. T. (1978). *Depression inventory.* Philadelphia, PA: Philadelphia Center for Cognitive Therapy.

Black, D. W., Blum, N., Pfohl, B., & St. John, D. (2004). The STEPPS group treatment program for outpatients with borderline personality disorder. *Journal of Contemporary Psychotherapy, 34,* 193–210.

Black, D. W., Allen, J., McCormick, B., & Blum, N. (2011). Treatment received by persons with BPD participating in a randomized clinical trial of the Systems Training for Emotional Predictability and Problem Solving programme. *Personality and Mental Health, 5,* 159–168.

Black, D. W., Blum, N., McCormick, B., & Allen, J. (2013). STEPPS group treatment program for borderline offenders. *Journal of Nervous and Mental Disease, 201,* 124–129.

Black, D. W., Blum, N., Eichinger, L., McCormick, B., Allen, J., & Sieleni, B. (2008). Systems Training for Emotional Predictability and Problem Solving (STEPPS) in women offenders with borderline personality disorder in prison: A pilot study. *CNS Spectrums, 13,* 881–886.

Black, D. W., Blum, N., Pfohl, B., St John, D., McCormick, B., & Allen, J. (2009). Predictors of response to Systems Training to Emotional Predictability and Problem Solving (STEPPS) for borderline personality disorder: An exploratory study. *Acta Psychiatrica Scandinavica, 120,* 53–61.

Blum, N., Pfohl, B., St. John, D., Monahan, P., & Black, D. W. (2002). STEPPS: A cognitive behavioral systems based group treatment for outpatients with borderline personality disorder—A preliminary report. *Comprehensive Psychiatry*, *43*, 301–310.

Blum, N., St. John, D., Pfohl, B., Stuart, S., McCormick, B., Allen, J., ... Black, D. W. (2008). Systems Training for Emotional Predictability and Problem Solving (STEPPS) for outpatients with borderline personality disorder: A randomized controlled trial and 1-year follow-up. *American Journal of Psychiatry*, *165*, 468–478.

Boccalon, S., Alesiana, R., Giarolli, L., Franchini, L., Colombo, C., Blum, N., & Fossati, A. (2012). Systems Training for Emotional Predictability and Problem Solving (STEPPS): Theoretical model, clinical application, and preliminary efficacy data in a sample of inpatients with personality disorders in comorbidity with mood disorders. *Journal of Psychopathology*, *18*, 335–343.

Bos, E. H., van Wel, B, Appelo, M. T., & Verbraak, M. J. P. M. (2010). A randomized controlled trial of a Dutch version of Systems Training for Emotional Predictability and Problem Solving for borderline personality disorder. *Journal of Nervous and Mental Disease*, *198*, 299–304.

Bos, E. H., van Wel, B., Appelo, M. T., & Verbraak, M. J. P. M. (2011). Effectiveness of Systems Training for Emotional Predictability and Problem Solving for borderline personality disorder in a real world sample: Moderation by diagnosis or severity? *Psychotherapy and Psychosomatics*, *80*, 173–181.

Clarkin, J. F., Levy, K. N., Lenzenweger, M. F., & Kernberg, O. F. (2007). Evaluating three treatments for borderline personality disorder: A multiwave study. *American Journal of Psychiatry*, *164*, 922–928.

Connell, J., & Barkham, M. (2007). Core-10 User Manual, Version 1.1. Core System Trust & Core Information Management Systems Ltd.

Derogatis, L. R. (1983). *SCL-90-R administration, scoring, and procedures manual II.* Towson, MD: Clinical Psychometric Research.

First, M. B., Gibbon, M., Spitzer, R. L., & Williams, J. B. W. (1996). *Structured Clinical Interview for DSM-IV Axis II Personality Disorders (SCID-II): User's Guide.* American Psychiatric Press, Washington, DC.

Freije, H., Dietz, B., & Appelo, M. (2002). Behandling van de borderline persoonlijkheidsstoornis met de VERS: de Vaardigheidstraining emotionele regulatiestoornis. *Directive Therapies*, *4*, 367–378.

Giesen-Bloo, J., van Dyck, R., Spinhoven P., van Tilburg, W., Dirksen, C., van Asselt, T., et al. (2006). Outpatient psychotherapy for borderline personality disorder-randomized trial of schema-focused therapy vs. transference-focused therapy. *Archives of General Psychiatry*, *63*, 649–658.

Harvey, R., Black, D. W., & Blum, N. (2010). Systems Training for Emotional Predictability and Problem Solving (STEPPS) in the United Kingdom: A preliminary report. *Journal of Contemporary Psychotherapy*, *40*, 225–232.

Hyler, S. E., Rieder, R. O., & Spitzer, R. L. (1989). *Personality diagnostic questionnaire, revised.* New York, NY: New York State Psychiatric Institute.

Jacobson, N. S., & Truax, P. (1991). Clinical significance: a statistical approach to defining meaningful change in psychotherapy research. *Journal of Consulting and Clinical Psychology*, *59*, 12–19.

Linehan, M. M., Armstrong, A. G., Suarez, A., Allmon, D., & Heard, H. S. (1991). Cognitive-behavioral treatment of chronically parasuicidal borderline clients. *Archives of General Psychiatry, 48,* 1060–1064.

Linehan, M. M., Heard, H. L., & Armstrong, H. E. (1993). Naturalistic follow-up of a behavioral treatment of chronically parasuicidal borderline clients. *Archives of General Psychiatry, 50,* 1971–1974.

Linehan, M. M., Comtois, K. A., Murray, A. M., Brown, M. Z., Gallop, R. J., Heard, H. L., et al. (2006). Two year randomized controlled trial and follow up of dialectical behavior therapy vs. therapy by experts for suicidal behaviors and borderline personality disorder. *Archives of General Psychiatry, 63,* 757–766.

McMain, S. F., Guimone, T., Streiner, D. L., Cardish, R. J., & Links, P. S. (2012). A randomized trial of dialectical behavior therapy compared with general psychiatric management for borderline personality disorder: Clinical outcomes and functioning over a 2-year follow-up. *American Journal of Psychiatry, 169,* 650–661.

Minuchin, S. (1974). *Families and family therapy.* Cambridge, MA: Harvard University Press.

National Registry of Evidence-based Programs and Practices (NREPP). Systems Training for Emotional Predictability and Problem Solving (STEPPS). Downloaded from the http://nrepp.samsha.gov website on June 3, 2014.

Pfohl, B., Blum, N., & Zimmerman, M. (1997). *Structured interview for DSM-IV personality disorders (SIDP-IV).* Washington, DC: American Psychiatric Press.

Pfohl, B., Blum, N., McCormick, B., St. John, D., Allen, J., & Black, D. W. (2009). Reliability and validity of the borderline evaluation of severity over time: A new scale to measure severity and change in borderline personality disorder. *Journal of Personality Disorders, 23,* 281–293.

Schuppert, H. M., Giesen-Bloo, J., van Gemert, T. G., Wiersema, H. M., Minderaa, R. B., Emmelkamp, P. M., & Nauta, M. H. (2009). Effectiveness of an emotion regulation group training for adolescents: A randomized controlled pilot study. *Clinical Psychology and Psychotherapy, 16,* 467–478.

Silk, K. (2008). Augmenting psychotherapy for borderline personality disorder: The STEPPS program. *American Journal of Psychiatry, 165,* 413–415.

Spitzer, R. L., Williams, J. B. W., & Gibbon, M. (1994). *Structured clinical interview for DSM-IV.* New York: New York State Psychiatric Institute, Biometrics Research.

Trompenaars, F. J., Masthoff, E. D., Van Heck, G. L., Hodiamont, P. P., & De Vries, J. (2005). Content validity, construct validity and reliability of the WHOQOL-BREF in a population of Dutch adult psychiatric outpatients. *Quality of Life Research, 14,* 151–160.

Van Wel, B., Kockmann, I., Blum, N., Pfohl, B., Heesterman, W., & Black, D. W. (2006). STEPPS group treatment for borderline personality disorder in The Netherlands. *Annals of Clinical Psychiatry, 18,* 63–67.

Van Wel, B., Bos, E. H., Appelo, M. T., Berendsen, E. M., Willgeroth, F. C., & Verbraak, M. J. P. M. & (2009). De effectiviteit van de vaardigheidstraining Emotieregulatiestoornis (VERS) in de behandeling van de Borderlinepersoonlijkheidsstoornis; een gerandomiseerd onderzoek. *Tijdschrift voor psychiatrie, 51,* 291–301.

Wallston, K. A. (2005). The validity of the Multidimensional Health Locus of Control scales. *Journal of Health Psychology, 10,* 623–631.

Watson, D., & Clark, L. A. (1994). *The PANAS-manual for the positive and negative affect schedule: Expanded form.* Iowa City, IA: University of Iowa.

Weertman, A., Arnoud, A., Dreesen, L., van Velzen, C., & Vertommen S. (2003). Short interval test-retest interrater reliability of the Dutch version of the structured clinical interview for DSM-IV personality disorders (SCID-II). *Journal of Personality Disorders, 17,* 562–567.

Yeomans, F. E., Clarkin, J. F., & Kernberg, O. F. (2002). *A primer for transference focused psychotherapy for the borderline patient.* Northvale, NJ: Jason Aronson, Inc.

Young, J. (1994). *Cognitive therapy for personality disorders: A schema-focused approach.* Sarasota, FL: Professional Resource Press.

Zanarini, M. C., Vujanovic, A. A., Parachini, E. A., Boulanger, J. L., Frankenberg, F. R., & Hennen, J. (2003). Zanarini rating scale for borderline personality disorder (ZAN-BPD): A continuous measure of DSM-IV borderline psychopathology. *Journal of Personality Disorders, 17,* 233–242.

# 3

# STEPPS in The Netherlands

HORUSTA FREIJE ■

There were few structured treatments for borderline personality disorder (BPD) in The Netherlands in the late 1990s. At times, the care of these patients strained resources, thus leading mental health experts to reconsider treatment options for these challenging patients.

In June 1997, Geerhard Schaap and Roelof ten Doesschate attended the International Society for the Study of Personality Disorders (ISSPD) conference in Vancouver, Canada. These psychiatrists were directors of different Dutch mental health agencies—Schaap at the Groningen Mental Health Care Agency (now called Lentis), and Ten Doesschate at the Psychiatric facility Brinkgreven/St. Elizabeths Gasthuis (now called Dimence). They were seeking new approaches for patients with BPD that they hoped would reduce the frequency and length of hospitalizations. At the conference, they heard Nancee Blum of the University of Iowa describe Systems Training for Emotional Predictability and Problem Solving, or STEPPS. Schaap and Ten Doesschate were immediately attracted to STEPPS. They liked the simplicity of its language, for example the analogy of emotional intensity to pots on the stove. Training in the model appeared straightforward, as was its implementation. They liked the fact that STEPPS is readily combined with other supportive or psychotherapeutic treatments. Its applicability in all kinds of settings—outpatient or inpatient—was also appealing. The three components of STEPPS—psychoeducation, emotion regulation skills, and behavior regulation skills—had an inherent logic. Schaap and Ten Doesschate found the systems component (i.e., involving patients' families and significant others) a valuable and unique feature among the various programs in use at the time.

## IMPLEMENTATION OF STEPPS IN THE NETHERLANDS

As a first step, Schaap and Ten Doesschate invited Blum to The Netherlands in January 1998. The purpose of the visit was to introduce STEPPS to mental health professionals at their facilities. Blum presented a four-day workshop to enthusiastic trainees. Six therapists from each facility were invited and, if the training was successful, the goal was to implement STEPPS nationwide. Following the training, Schaap and Ten Doesschate formed a working group with these therapists, who met twice a year under their supervision. This was the platform from which new developments regarding the program were driven.

The next step was to translate the STEPPS manual into the Dutch language, which was then edited by members of the working group. The Dutch version of STEPPS is the acronym VERS, which stands for *Vaardigheidstraining* (skills training) *Emotie* (emotion) *Regulatie* (regulation) *Stoornis* (disorder). The Dutch word *vers* means fresh. This name has appealed to a broad audience. The Dutch translation was bound in a four-ring binder with an image of the ocean on the cover. A binder might reinforce the sense that the patient is actively using the workbook and it makes it easy to add and remove pages used in homework assignments.

Blum's suggested two-hour weekly patient session was extended by a half hour with a 15-minute break (because of the amount of material that needed to be covered). A VERS folder was made for patients and anyone who might refer patients to VERS. VERS trainers (i.e., therapists) provided information to colleagues at their own institutions so they could refer patients who might benefit. Providing therapists with information about VERS also enabled them to function as a patient's individual therapist, while the patient was simultaneously participating in VERS. The program was received enthusiastically and implemented by both agencies.

In contrast to Blum's method of having an introductory group session, our patients had an individual intake session. Intake could vary from a brief motivational and introduction interview to a structured diagnostic assessment, depending on the clinician's vision of this process.

Long waiting lists developed for VERS because therapists, patients, and their families all wanted to start as soon as possible. There was great excitement regarding STEPPS and the hope that any new treatment brings. This hope later prompted research on the effectiveness of VERS.

When participating in the working group, the VERS trainers exchanged their experience with the program. In some cases, this led to heated discussions about different concerns, such as how to structure the intake process, whether VERS should emphasize psycho-education over cognitive behavioral therapy, and even whether trainers should check the patient's homework assignments. Other topics included the trainers' competencies and personal style, and whether trainers should maintain contact with a patient's individual therapist. These issues are discussed later in the chapter.

An evaluation of the efficacy of the training program began early (Freije et. al., 2002). This was followed by a randomized control trial (Van Wel et al., 2009) that included an ancillary study (Horsselenberg, 2006).

Over the course of time the manual was revised in response to feedback from trainers. The qualitative preliminary study conducted by van Wel and coworkers (2003) contributed to the revision by Heesterman et al. (2004).

A website was launched in 2007 (www.verstraining.nl). The website includes information about the program; patients and trainers can download individual lessons, place orders, and ask questions of the experts. For families and significant others, referring parties, and therapists, Freije (2008) compiled a file of summaries of the different lessons and forms used in VERS.

STEPPS and VERS are described in the Multidisciplinary Guidelines for Personality Disorders (2008) as "a considerably effective and cost-efficient group skills training program that is offered as a module of a treatment package, often in combination with individual therapy, pharmacotherapy, and system sessions, whereby the facets of the treatment package have to correspond with each other. The treatment can also be offered in a clinical setting (day clinic) if more support is deemed necessary."

Freije (2012) authored a chapter on the theoretical and practical aspects of VERS for the *Manual for Borderline Personality Disorders*, which can also be used for the VERS training program for trainers and therapists.

A turnover of participants took place in the working group in 2008. Schaap and Ten Doesschate retired, and Houkje Tamsma and Bas van Wel were their successors as supervisors of the working group. Van Wel and Tamsma considered transferring the rights to a foundation or publisher to ensure survival of VERS. The rights to VERS I (STEPPS, basic skills group program) were transferred in 2014 to the Trimbos Institute (a major center of expertise on mental health and addiction) to safeguard the program for the future.

Members of the working group remained affiliated as a feedback group. It was decided that VERS I in the Netherlands should closely mirror Blum's STEPPS program so that research in the United States would also apply to the Dutch version. The second edition of the STEPPS manual (Blum et al., 2012) was translated by the Trimbos Institute in 2014. At the time of this writing the working group is making several adjustments before the final version is released. The Trimbos Institute will also arrange the "train the trainers" sessions, encourage further research, and investigate the possibilities for incorporating VERS into e-Health. Initially the Trimbos Institute only took over the rights to VERS I. It has already published a course for the patients' family and social environment using elements of VERS (Siegert & Krook, 2006).

## IMPLEMENTATION OF STAIRWAYS AT LENTIS, DIMENCE, AND NATIONWIDE

When the STEPPS follow-up program called STAIRWAYS appeared, the name of the first skills training program became STEPPS, Basic Skills Group Program. Both programs together are called STEPPS. STAIRWAYS (Blum & St. John, 2008) expands on intrapersonal and interpersonal skills, while important life domains are brought more into balance by setting goals. Patients, trainers, and therapists have reported that these satisfy the treatment needs. Follow-up groups have often formed because people wanted to continue working with the acquired knowledge.

STAIRWAYS was translated into Dutch in 2004, and was introduced as a follow-up to VERS called VERS II. With the introduction of VERS II, the name VERS was changed to VERS I. Blum trained the working group in STAIRWAYS in 2005.

## NATIONWIDE IMPLEMENTATION

As soon as both agencies had implemented VERS, a training program was developed with the goal of implementing VERS nationwide. This was a two-day training session followed by a one-day refresher course a year later. This training program has been offered since 2000, after which VERS spread quickly throughout Holland because of the enormous interest it generated among therapists from the community psychiatric institutions. Therapists from other clinical settings have attended, including those working in forensic settings, addiction clinics, and youth institutions.

Van Gemert and Wiersma (2007) later developed Emotion Regulation Training (ERT) for adolescents, a program similar to STEPPS/VERS, but omitting the diagnostic component. At first, some agencies delivered VERS alongside dialectical behavioral therapy. Because VERS was easier to implement and had greater appeal for therapists, an estimated 80% of mental health clinics and hospitals now have staff members trained to deliver VERS. As of this writing, there are 960 people trained to deliver VERS I and 182 trained to deliver VERS II.

Members of the working group have made presentations at numerous conferences to further disseminate VERS. An education television broadcaster, Teleac (now called NTR), made a documentary about VERS. Patients and families also participated in the series to receive information about mental disorders. This 30-minute documentary also served as a psychoeducation tool for therapists, future trainers, patients, and their support groups.

In October 2005, a symposium was held in the Netherlands where Blum and colleague Donald Black made presentations on research findings in the United States for the VERS trainers (400 at the time) and other interested parties. This symposium addressed the experiences acquired in the previous years with VERS I. The patients' experiences were also included. STAIRWAYS was officially introduced at this symposium. The members of the working group had received training by Blum in VERS II prior to the symposium.

In 2008, another conference took place with Blum and Black in attendance ("*10 jaar VERS in Nederland* [10 years of VERS in the Netherlands]"). All agencies that offered the program were invited. The morning session included speakers from abroad. Blum and Black made presentations about STEPPS in the United States; there were also presentations on STEPPS in the United Kingdom and in Norway. The afternoon session was dedicated to discussing the various training programs derived from VERS, including new information on "The BOOG (*BPS Opvoedings Ondersteuning Groep* [BPS Parenting support group, a version of VERS for parents]"). Lastly, there was a presentation on VERS and addiction treatment.

## REVISIONS, ADJUSTMENTS, AND TRAINING PROGRAMS BASED ON VERS

Diverse training programs based on VERS have been developed in the Netherlands. These are as follows.

### Revisions to STEPPS

Freije (2008) published a revision to make the first chapters more accessible. Learning goals, biopsychosocial theory, explanation of relaxation exercises, and theoretical explanations were added to offer trainers and patients more explanations about the work sheets and exercises. The Emotional Intensity Continuum (EIC) was constructed so that patients would be able to record aspects of their emotions as they developed. The revised EIC expanded the initial task of simply marking the intensity of emotions three times a day to include requesting the patient also describe the intensity with regard to situation, thoughts, feelings, behaviors, and consequences. Finally, there was a format where they could simply mark again and note the trigger.

The *thought patterns* and *challenges* were placed in one block with a clearer structure for challenging the dysfunctional thought patterns. The order of the behavioral skills was altered so that interpersonal skills were the first behavioral skill addressed. Behavioral goals were formulated and successes were written down on a one-page format. Summaries of each chapter were prepared, and worksheets for each lesson were placed next to that lesson in the binder. User-friendliness was increased. This version was used in diverse places in advance of its publication. The revision later shaped the Basic VERS/short version of VERS.

In 2003 Van Wel began his PhD research with a qualitative study of VERS, which served as the basis for a new revision that became the first revision (Heesterman et al., 2004) and was called VERS I. The filters and dysfunctional patterns appeared later in the binder with a sequence of lessons on challenging patterns and distorted thinking. The filters used were fewer but more detailed. An emotion management plan was an improvement; the "situation pan" (continuum working sheet) was added, which was elaborated upon by dealing with the situation, thoughts, feelings, behavior, and consequences through implementing the skills learned up to that point. A second support group was also added. A CD with relaxation exercises was created and added to the binder. The *Vroeger en Verder* (Earlier and Further: a stabilization course after sexual or physical abuse) training program of Dorrepaal et al. (2008) incorporated parts of VERS I.

## Dealing with Borderline: Psycho-Educational Course for Patients' Social Environment

Using the Landelijke Steunfunctie Preventie (an organization dedicated to preventative interventions for people with mental illness), Siegert and Krook (2006) developed a training program for patients' social environment: "Dealing with Borderline: Psycho-Educational Training Course for Patients' Social Environment." This corresponds to VERS and is intended to support patients' social environment and strengthen their ability to deal with the borderline personality disorder of a family member, partner, friend, or significant other. The Trimbos Institute refers to this as best practice, and it is used nationwide in the Netherlands.

Siegert and Krook compared diverse training programs and compiled a binder with 10 two-hour lessons for a maximum of 12 participants. The training program is preferably conducted by a prevention worker and a therapist. The greater the number of members of a patient's social environment who participate, the greater the base of support there is for changes in the family. People can participate whether or not they have been definitely diagnosed with Emotional Intensity Disorder (EID) or are in treatment for EID.

The binder is divided into four parts:

1. Design and background information of the course
2. Protocol manual for the course sessions
3. Participant workbook
4. Course reader

The goal is to reduce the distress of people immediately involved with the borderline patient. The experiences, options, and questions these people have are a key focus. The fundamental assumption is that patient peers can learn from each other. The objectives are to increase competence (to be better equipped with information), deal with one's own emotions differently, deal with borderline behavior differently, and realize one's own goals and needs.

The sequence of topics that appear in the 10 lessons are

1. Getting acquainted with each other and the training program
2. Borderline in the family and relationship
3. How does BPD develop?
4. Dealing with borderline behavior
5. Dealing with volatile emotions
6. Communication
7. Dealing with yourself; empowerment
8. Children and other family members
9. Social support and dealing with mental health services
10. Steps and evaluation

There is a format for follow-up sessions. The Trimbos Institute also provides the one-day training for trainers.

## Emotion Regulation Training Program for Adolescents

Van Gemert and Wiersema (2007) have developed a training program for adolescents called Emotion Regulation Training (ERT), inspired by VERS. This training program, which has 17 weekly sessions, is described by Marieke Schuppert in Chapter 10.

## THE BASIC VERS

The Basic VERS (Freije, 2008) comprises 10 two-and-a-half-hour weekly lessons, with a reinforcement group session. There is also a "train the trainers" program that can be customized according to the participants' knowledge and experience with VERS. The training program usually takes a half day if the participants are familiar with VERS; otherwise a whole day is needed.

Therapists have frequently asked for a simplified version of VERS. The Basic VERS, also known as the Shortened VERS, comprises the five emotion management skills along with the introduction and awareness of illness. In comparison to VERS, the Basic VERS is written in simpler language that is easier to use. Each chapter is summarized, and worksheets are included in each lesson, which makes it more comprehensible. Informative PowerPoint presentations are used during the lessons and the reinforcement group evening. These presentations are included in a digital package with other supportive material including the CD with relaxation exercises, an information folder, an intake format, and a practical and theoretical handbook.

Horssenberg's Master's thesis (2006) includes information about patients' evaluations on what they found to be the most effective part of VERS. They rated the trainers, psychoeducation, and patient-peer contact as very effective. The process of gaining understanding of their own situation seems to be important. They prioritize the importance of the three sections of the binder as follows: General aspects (contact with therapists and patient peers, and psychoeducation), emotion regulation skills, and behavioral skills. That patients find the general aspects of treatment important is in agreement with other studies such as Livesley (2007), Perkins (2001), and Hooley and Hoffman (1999). The importance they place on cognitive skills corresponds with Dietz (2001), and that patients mainly have difficulty in regulating emotions is in accordance with Linehan (1987). Horssenberg recommends developing abbreviated versions of VERS consisting of emotion regulation skills and other general aspects and to compare those with the complete VERS, along with other interventions, in order to determine their value.

Many participants benefit and learn from the long-term contact with VERS therapists and patient peers. This was the reason that a customized VERS training program was created a few years ago for the specialized mobile community mental health team. It included an introductory course, the Basic VERS if needed, VERS I, and VERS II. The turnaround of patients who started and their progression occurs collectively as a group. This program is operating very well. The trainers' positive attitude towards the program and the patients seems to be partially responsible for the fact that few patients drop out.

Participants can enter the Basic VERS before VERS I. This is beneficial for those who have learning difficulties, have not participated in any type of learning situation for a long time, have had distressing experiences in learning situations and feel insecure, or have found courses difficult. Other reasons that participants could benefit by choosing to take the Basic VERS as their first step (or as their only step, in some cases) in the VERS program could be a lack of self-motivation, anxiety in group settings, difficulties with basic skills such as attendance, being on time, doing homework, or because they cannot speak in a group without dominating the conversation. The Basic VERS can be used as a way to stabilize patients in order to engage in other psychotherapies.

The Basic VERS is also suitable for those whose lives are in reasonably good order and who do not need the behavior management skills, but may struggle with emotion regulation. This program may be implemented in individual therapy if a group setting is too difficult or not suitable. It becomes apparent for some participants during the group setting that they would be more successful by completing the training on an individual basis in parallel with the group. A participant can sometimes be more positively reinforced during the Basic VERS as a stepping stone to VERS I, rather than starting with VERS I.

Trainers are instructed to convey an involved, warm, and positive attitude. They learn to react enthusiastically to a patient's achievements, which is important to people who have faced many disappointments. Patients may act as if they are disinterested or angry, but this only reflects the emotional intensity and is a way to protect themselves from vulnerability. They may need to learn simple things like being on time and how to participate appropriately in a group. Everything possible is done to keep them in the group. Trainers often mention in the group that it is a pathway walked and stumbled on together, which continues after this group. Homework is always reviewed. A further discussion of this attitude for trainers is elaborated on later in this chapter.

The lessons are successive (the same structure as VERS I):

1. Introductions, support group, emotion intensity scale, and Skill Monitoring Card
2. Relaxation exercises and awareness of illness
3. Distancing
4. Emotion Management Plan, part I
5. Communicating
6. Distracting

7. Challenging
8. Managing problems
9. Emotion Management Plan, part II
10. Closing

It helps if participants have already attended a short orientation for BPD. They will have experienced what it is like to function as a pupil in a group and to be addressed regarding their healthy capacity to learn and manage problems instead of isolating themselves.

The FACT (assertive community treatment for patients with psychotic disorders and comorbid personality problems) also uses the Basic VERS, as do forensic facilities and addiction clinics in Holland. It has also been implemented in basic community mental health agencies, and it has even been adapted for the needs of people with intellectual disabilities, although a specific version derived from the Basic VERS still needs to be developed. The Basic VERS has been used in a number of Dutch community mental health agencies and is quickly being disseminated throughout the Netherlands.

## VERS AND PARENTING

The VERS and Parenting course was formerly known as the BOOG–an acronym for BPD Opvoedings (parenting) Ondersteunings (support) Groep (group). VERS and Parenting was developed by Van den Berg (2009) for patients with BPD who have children. It is a training program with 13 two-and-a-half-hour sessions every other week. The first six sessions occur weekly whenever possible. Many parents who participate in the VERS program had problems and questions regarding parenting.

Intense emotions often occur when dealing with children. These emotions can trigger all sorts of negative dynamics. These patients commonly have been traumatized and have emotional shortcomings that can lead to history repeating itself. They usually have not been educated about what a child needs to develop properly. They learn this during the training program, where they can practice using these acquired skills.

The training program is preferably delivered by someone from the adult department, accompanied by someone from the youth department. In actual practice, the latter has proven difficult to implement. As a prerequisite, patients should have attended the first part of VERS I (the emotion regulation skills). There is one support group session (or more if needed) for the social environment and co-parents.

The VERS scale has been adapted to behaviors associated with interacting with children. The structure is the same as VERS I. The Skill Monitoring Card has also been adapted to the skills associated with interacting with children. The focus is placed on parenting in the EIC worksheet and in the emotion management plan. The support group helps the patient come up with ideas for a safe place where the child can go if necessary during intense emotional episodes. Patients learn how to inform their social environments about their emotional episodes, and ways to speak to children about their emotion regulation problems in language appropriate to the child's age.

The training program addresses the following topics successively in 13 lessons:

1. Reinforcement group/safe place for your child during emotional episodes, awareness of illness, observe your child's behavior that you like and dislike
2. EIC and filter/schema questionnaire (dysfunctional schemas with regard to parenthood)
3. Sufficient parenthood—challenge thoughts about being a perfect parent
4. Information about what a parent's psychiatric problems can mean for a child and about an emotion management plan in relation to children
5. Attachment and developmental tasks and what children need (according to Young)
6. Attachment promoting skills, learning to mentalize through mirroring and signaling
7. Attachment promotion through healthy communication with your child
8. Learning to ask for social support, analyzing and informing your network and your child's network about the problem, and also discussing an emergency plan or childcare plan with them to implement during episodes
9. Give positive attention and reward (how to do that)
10. Setting limits part 1. Assess limits, as are they now and setting limits; thoughts that hinder this, ignoring, saying no and prohibiting (how to do that)
11. Setting limits part 2, punishment and separation (how to do that and why)
12. Talking with children
13. Closing and evaluation

The VERS and Parenting has not been used extensively at this time, but patients who have completed it and trainers who have given the training program are very enthusiastic. Future revisions can include placing more attention on helping parents develop enjoyable activities together with the children, "reinforcing the happy child," as schema therapy describes it, and also doing these activities during the sessions. Videos and images can support the training program. It may be useful to examine where VERS terminology and mentalization terminology are similar, and then determine which is preferable.

## EXPERIENCES WITH VERS

Trainers, patients, and primary individual therapists all found the training program valuable right from the start. The training program is easy to use and provides a good learning environment with the binder containing 18 lessons, with the same structure; patients value the constant and familiar repetition of the material presented. Adjusting some global aspects of the binder to increase user friendliness was a recurring issue.

All the parties involved (trainers, patients, members from the patient's social environment, and main individual therapists) collaborated openly and participated in an atmosphere where an exchange of knowledge and learning new skills together were key. The metaphor of pots on a burner worked as intended. A communal language developed that people were able to use to examine volatile emotions and discuss them easily and clearly instead of withdrawing or rejecting the patient. The intensity was not experienced as personal.

When VERS started, the cognitive behavioral therapy component was new for many trainers and needed extra attention. This has become more common knowledge in recent years.

Some institutions performed better than others in keeping the program alive and moving forward. An effective strategy was to have a working group in the institution that met a few times a year to schedule groups and manage problems and desired developments. This offered time to reflect together and be proactive.

VERS seemed to make all parties involved more creative. New developments seem to occur naturally, provided the program receives enough attention.

## TOPICS THAT RAISED DISCUSSION

Many topics raised in the working group caused intense discussions. An example was agreeing on what the *intake* process for VERS should entail. Freije recommended that the referring party electronically provide information on the patient's diagnosis and symptoms, past medical history, family history, and treatment history (and how that might differ during the VERS program). The referring party should also provide the reason for referral, as well as information regarding the patient's patterns/schemas, and the goals for VERS.

The use of DSM-IV BPD criteria was discussed. Working group members suggested that each item be assessed on a 0–3 scale (0, not present; 3, often present). The patient's current functioning should be assessed, including housing, daily activities, and social relationship. Other points were the patient's motivation for therapy, including the obstacles, with observations, conclusions, and agreements. This made the assessment for eligibility a transparent process between the intaker, the patient, and the referring party. Other trainers believed that the intake interview should be predominantly an orientation interview that is as easily accessible as possible, mainly focused on the patient's motivation to follow the training program, thus emphasizing the patient's autonomy.

The topic *of homework* was also discussed. Some thought that homework should be reviewed, not only in the group but also by the trainers, and that it is a missed opportunity not to do so. The advantage of such a review is that it has a tremendously stimulating effect on patients when you give positive feedback on their homework, it gives you an idea of what they do not yet understand, and what concepts need further reinforcement. However, not every trainer shared this opinion. The most common argument against reviewing homework is that it could interfere with the patient's autonomy.

There are other topics on which the working group members disagreed and required further discussion. Freije elaborated on the characteristics of the previously mentioned attitude of trainers toward patients in the Basic VERS training program. This attitude is an active, warm, engaging, enthusiastic attitude. It reflects partly an attitude that the patient is a healthy responsible person who is following a course to manage emotional regulation problems and, at the same time, it reflects some limited "reparenting" as described in schema therapy. It carries the message that, "we start this together, and we complete this together." A trainer supports the patient as he/she discusses the volatile emotions, what triggers him/her, and what would be the best way(s) to manage them. This approach removes the emotion from the interaction between the trainer and patient.

This also makes it easier for the therapist, who often takes the emotional intensity personally, to maintain distance without rejecting the patient. It is an attitude with empathic understanding and patience, which demonstrates understanding for the frustrations and disappointments that patients have had, and that have undermined their self-confidence. These frustrations and disappointments are often reflected in an uncooperative position that patients display, and that can best be interpreted as understandable anxiety and protectiveness against yet another disappointment. In this attitude, trust in the patient is made abundantly apparent. It means an active attitude right from the start to keep people engaged. If patients do not show up to a session, they are called immediately so they can still attend. If they miss the session, there is a discussion of how the lesson went, the homework that was reviewed from the previous session is sent to them, and the content or homework that was difficult is discussed in order to give them the support they need. They always receive positive feedback on what they do well, and they are helped with the aspects they find difficult. Over the course of time their independence increases and they can gradually deal with more empathetic confrontations. Members of the group often do that with each other. Group members want to progress together.

It is beneficial to have this attitude demonstrated to the trainers when they themselves are being trained, and also to the main individual therapists. Presenting VERS as a *pathway/program* may help encourage a sense of togetherness, continuity, perspective, safety, and cohesiveness. VERS integrates well with a variety of other therapies, while serving as a stabilization pathway. Along with the warm connectedness, the *framework* of the actual lesson is always the context which illuminates the things that occur in the present.

Over time, *coordinating the main individual therapy with the VERS training program* has turned out to be very important, and apparently continues to be a focal point. This can occur in a variety of ways, but no guidelines have been established yet. For example, the treatment plan could include agreements regarding how the main individual treatment corresponds with VERS, such that the individual therapy plan might explore the topics offered in the training program more thoroughly. Meeting with the referring parties before the training program begins seems beneficial, but is also difficult to implement.

The main therapist receives a copy of the reinforcement group folder or the VERS binder to learn the pertinent contents of VERS. This can occur by following a training program if needed. There are potentially several ways to coordinate the main individual therapy with the VERS training program, but being practical, realistic, and having an awareness of its importance are the fundamental concepts for achieving that.

*Involving relevant people from the patient's social environment in the treatment* is an area that needs improvement. It is still not routine to view people from the patient's social environment as an important aspect of the treatment program from the very start. They can provide useful information regarding the patient's diagnosis and play a significant role in the treatment, to help them respond compassionately with more understanding, and to feel competent in dealing with their family member's problems. Emotional episodes usually occur when dysfunctional schemas are triggered and the patient is often entangled in a pattern in an unhelpful way. It is of major importance to acquire insight and guidance together to break out of these patterns. The form and frequency contact with the social environment should also have a place in the treatment plan.

Furthermore, it might be productive to emphasize the recognition of people's positive qualities immediately at the start of the therapy and to promote *societal participation*. The principles of Acceptance and Commitment therapy can be an asset with the behavioral goals, gaining awareness of what someone finds valuable, and working towards that in the different domains. This can also be specified in the learning goals, or even in the treatment plan. Over time it can be refined together with the social environment.

Involving *lay experts* is something that can be developed. They have already followed a VERS program and/or other therapies, and have once again been able to structure their lives in a meaningful way. They are able to provide perspective and hope, and encourage people to persist. They also share practical solutions to problems and can share their experiences at various times during the treatment.

Lastly, it is essential that VERS also becomes incorporated into eHealth. It would be very desirable for VERS to have apps for people to use on the spot to make assessments and recordings. This should be taken on with the utmost vigor. We received an app from a reinforcement team member.

## RESEARCH ON VERS

Freije et al. (2002) conducted a pilot study of VERS with a group of 85 Dutch patients from eight clinics. Patients experienced a significant reduction in symptoms on the SCL-90 and the instability factor of the VERS-scale. In comparison with an outpatient norm group, the general level of mental distress decreased on the SCL-90 from above average (244) to below average (207). The anxiety subscale, obsessive-compulsive subscale, total score, and depression subscale decreased the most. Fifty-six patients completed VERS and the dropout rate was 34% (29).

The patients from one clinic within the group had a lower dropout rate (20%) than the others (40%). The training sessions had fewer participants (approximately seven) than usual. An extensive intake was carried out. The patients demonstrated a higher level of involvement. The homework was reviewed and positive supplemental comments were given. An active policy to prevent dropouts was implemented. If a patient reported a desire to withdraw, then the trainer and the patient discussed whether this desire was the result of a dysfunctional schema. Together they would investigate whether withdrawal would help with reaching the patient's goal, and if healthier schemas could be introduced. These findings agree with Hooley and Hoffmann (1999), who found that patients with BPD respond positively to a high degree of involvement, such as reviewing homework and actively preventing dropout.

Freije et al. (2002) recommended conducting a control study in which VERS supplemented the treatment as usual (TAU), and that it should include a greater variety of outcome variables. According to Perkins (2001), a decrease of symptoms does not always mean an increase in quality of life. Measurements of self-esteem, functioning in society, and future perspective would need to take place to assess quality of life.

Dietz (2001) conducted research on the BEST scale, which comprises three subscales: A. Thoughts and feelings; B. Negative behavior; and C. Positive behavior. A factor analysis resulted in the factor "Cognitive, emotional, and behavioral instability," which was shortened to the "Instability factor," which had sufficient internal reliability and validity. The second possible factor that came out comprised two items with an internal consistency of 0.69. This factor signifies the extent to which people would bring the knowledge acquired from the VERS training program into actual practice. She also mentioned that symptoms such as social support, care consumption, emotional lability, self-harm, and other relevant BPD symptoms should be included in future investigations.

In 2003 van Wel led a qualitative preliminary study on VERS I. This became the basis for the revision by Heesterman et al. (2004). Van Wel conducted an RCT in 2004 using 79 patients with BPD randomly assigned to participate in VERS plus TAU or to TAU alone. The other groups included structured individual support, either with or without pharmacotherapy, or TAU, which mainly included social psychiatric supportive care and pharmacotherapy. Assessments were done before and after the intervention and at a one-year follow-up.

VERS plus TAU led to a greater reduction of symptoms than TAU alone. This was also true after one year. Seventy percent of the patients who received VERS plus TAU showed symptomatic improvement, versus 47% of those who received TAU alone. VERS was also associated with greater improvement of the quality of life compared to TAU alone, especially at the follow-up, but there were no differences in terms of the number of suicide attempts or health care utilization. These results support the findings of Blum et al. (2008), who assigned 124 patients with BPD to receive STEPPS plus TAU, or TAU alone. Patients assigned to STEPPS improved more quickly with regard to affect as well as cognition and in the area of impulse control. There were no differences with regard to self-harm behaviors or hospital admissions.

A group of 84 patients who had symptoms of BPD but did not meet the required number of criteria participated in the study by van Wel et al (2009); however, their data were not included in the analysis. Bos et al. (2011) reported the results of the total group (patients with BPD and patients with BPD symptoms). This study showed that general psychopathology and borderline psychopathology improved more in the VERS plus TAU group than in the TAU alone group. The short-term and long-term quality of life also improved for the VERS group. VERS was equally efficacious in participants, regardless of whether they had BPD or just some of the symptoms.

VERS plus TAU was more effective in participants whose initial severity was greater, a finding that mirrored those of Blum et al. (2008). This was found for STEPPS plus TAU as well as for TAU alone, which is probably explained as regression to the mean. This could not explain the greater improvement in all patients in the study conducted by Bos. Bos et al. (2011) mentioned emotional instability, or a dysfunction of the emotion regulation system, as possibly the most distinctive quality for the group with clinical and subclinical BPD. The severity of this quality is a more important criterion for referring a patient to participate in a VERS program than is the diagnosis of BPD.

The guidelines cite the study conducted by Blum et al. (2002). There is evidence for the efficacy of VERS as a supplemental training program in the treatment of BPD.

## THE CURRENT STATE AND FUTURE STATE OF VERS IN THE NETHERLANDS

VERS has a firm place in the treatment armamentarium of BPD in the Netherlands. VERS I is the main training program. We are currently in the most significant transition since the introduction of VERS in the Netherlands. Dimence and Lentis are transferring the VERS I training program rights over to the Trimbos Institute in order to secure further development of the VERS program. We trust that the Trimbos Institute will put VERS, an intellectual property that has been tended to with many hands, on its path into the world with heart and soul. Members of the former working group will remain in the background as consultants for some time (van den Berg, Freije, and Miedema).

The second edition of STEPPS (Blum et al., 2012) was translated in 2014 and will be published by the Trimbos Institute, which will also arrange the training sessions for group leaders. The training program for the patients' social environments has already been published by the Trimbos Institute, and ERT has been issued by a publisher.

The Basic VERS can be ordered directly from Freije. VERS and Parenting and VERS II can be ordered from Lentis. The safeguard of these versions are being discussed.

The hope is that the Trimbos Institute will undertake incorporating VERS into eHealth, develop apps for VERS, and generate research.

Attention should also be given to addressing VERS as a pathway, involving the social support system when the program starts, having lay experts contribute in the sessions, and involving the individual therapist and the patients' social environments more closely. The attitude and competencies for trainers still need refinement. The assessment of eligibility, dealing with homework, and the integration of individual therapy with VERS need further improvement. These issues also provide good topics for further research.

The Netherlands has rigorously developed versions of VERS that are compatible with different target groups of patients who have BPD/EID, and there are still more possibilities for other areas, such as addiction treatment, forensic care, patients with intellectual disabilities, and the basic community mental health services. To summarize, it is a program that continues to inspire further developments.

## REFERENCES

Berg, J. van den (2009). *BOOG, Borderline persoonlijkheidsproblematiek Opvoedings– Ondersteuning Groep*. Deventer and Groningen, Netherlands: Dimence and Lentis. [NB: Will soon be renamed: *VERS en Opvoeding*.]

Black, D. W., Blum, N., Pfohl, B., & St. John, D. (2004). The STEPPS group treatment program for outpatients with borderline personality disorder. *Journal of Contemporary Psychotherapy, 34*, 193–210.

Blum, N., St. John, D., Pfohl, B., Stuart, S., McCormick, B., Allen, J., et al. (2008). Systems training for emotional predictability and problem solving (STEPPS) for outpatients with borderline personality disorder: A randomized controlled trial and 1-year follow-up. *American Journal of Psychiatry, 165*, 468–478.

Blum, N., Bartels, N. E., St. John, D., & Pfohl, B. (2002). Systems training for emotional predictability and problem solving (STEPPS): Group treatment program for borderline personality disorder. Available on CD-ROM from Level One Publishing, Coralville, IA. www.steppsforbpd.com.

Blum, N., Bartels M. A., St. John, D., & Pfohl, B. (2012). *Systems Training for Emotional Predictability and Problem Solving. A group program for the borderline personality disorder*. 2nd ed. Manual available on CD-ROM from Blum's Books.

Blum, N., & St. John, D. (2008). *The STAIRWAYS Treatment Manual CD-ROM* from Blum's Books.

Bos, E. H., Wel, E. B. van, Appelo, M. T., & Verbraak, M. J. (2011). Effectiveness of systems training for emotional predictability and problem solving (STEPPS) for borderline personality problems in a 'real-world' sample: Moderation by diagnosis or severity? *Psychotherapy & Psychosomatics, 80*, 173–181.

Dietz, B. (2001). *Vaardigheidstraining Emotionele Regulatiestoornis (VERS): pilotstudie*. Groningen: Rijks Universiteit Groningen, Clinical Psychology Department, Doctoral dissertation.

Dorrepaal, E., Thomaes, K., & Draijer, N. (2008). *Vroeger en Verder. Stabilisatiecursus na misbruik of mishandeling. Handleiding.* Amsterdam, Netherlands: Harcourt.

Freije, G. K., Dietz, B., & Appelo, M. T. (2002). Behandeling van de borderline persoonlijkheidsstoornis met de VERS: de vaardigheidstraining emotionele regulatie stoornis. *Tijdschrift voor Directieve Therapie, 22*(4), 367–378.

Freije, G. K. (2008). *Basis-VERS.* Self-published. horustafreije@planet.nl

Freije, G. K. (2012). Vaardigheidstraining emotieregulatiestoornis (VERS). In T. Ingenhoven (Ed.), *Handboek Borderline Persoonlijkheidsstoornis 6*(3), 228–237. Utrecht, Netherlands: Uitgeverij de Tijdstroom.

Heesterman, W., Wel, B. van, & Kockmann, I. (2004). VERS. *Vaardigheidstraining Emotie Regulatie Stoornis.* Deventer and Groningen, Netherlands: Dimence and Lentis.

Hooley, J. M., & Hoffman, P. D. (1999). Expressed emotion and clinical outcomes in borderline personality disorder. *American Journal of Psychiatry, 156,* 1557–1662.

Horsselenberg, E., supervisor: Appelo, M. T. (2006). *Werkzame bestanddelen van de VERS.* Groningen, Netherlands, Rijks Universiteit Groningen, Clinical and Developmental Psychology Department, Master's thesis.

Horsselenberg, E. (2006). *Werkzame bestanddelen van de VERS.* Rijksuniversiteit Groningen, Netherlands, Psychology Department, Master's thesis.

Linehan, M. M. (1993). *Cognitive-behavioral treatment of borderline personality disorder.* New York, NY: Guilford Press.

Livesley, W. J. (2007). An integrated approach to the treatment of personality disorder. *Journal of Mental Health, 16,* 131–148.

Perkins, R. (2001). What constitutes success? *British Journal of Psychiatry, 179,* 9–10.

Siegert, E., & Krook, K. (2006). *Omgaan met borderline, psycho-educatieve cursus voor directbetrokkenen.* Utrecht, Netherlands: Trimbos Institute.

Wel, E. B. van, Bos, E. H., Appelo, M. T., Berendsen, E. M., Willgeroth, F. C., & Verbraak, M. J. (2009). Vaardigheidstraining emotieregulatiestoornis (VERS) in de behandeling van de borderlinepersoonlijkheidsstoornis. Een gerandomiseerd onderzoek. *Tijdschrift voor Psychiatrie, 51,* 291–301.

Van Gemert, T. M. van, & Wiersema, H. M. (2007). *Emotieregulatietraining (ERT): Een programma voor adolescenten met emotieregulatiproblemen, Trainershandleiding.* Amsterdam, Netherlands: Uitgeverij Boom.

Van Wel, B., Kockmann, I., Blum, N., Pfohl, B., Heesterman, W., & Black, D. W. (2006). STEPPS group treatment for borderline personality disorder in The Netherlands. *Annals of Clinical Psychiatry, 18,* 63–67.

# 4

# STEPPS in the United Kingdom

RENEE HARVEY ■

STEPPS came to the United Kingdom in 2006 with Nancee Blum's presentation at an international conference in London. Early in 2007 she returned as two National Health Service (NHS) Trusts (in Kent and Sussex) collaborated to organize initial training in the model. The roll-out of training and the implementation of groups have spread rapidly, not only across the two initial counties, but also across the rest of England and Scotland. This chapter will describe some UK-specific issues and adaptations, and also discuss our experience of some more general principles that could apply in any setting. We have developed new versions of the program, one for adolescents and another for use in Primary Care, with further options in the pipeline.

## WHY DID WE CHOOSE STEPPS?

A major change took place in England in January 2003 with the publication of a Department of Health document entitled "Personality Disorder: No Longer a Diagnosis of Exclusion" (National Institute of Mental Health, 2003). The message to NHS Trusts was clear: a new impetus was required to develop services for this population. Some trusts were able to acquire financial backing for the purpose, but in the absence of new funds, services such as Sussex Partnership NHS Foundation Trust needed to find ways to develop services and provide interventions without new money. For Sussex, STEPPS provided a potential solution: an effective, accessible, and economical program, designed to work effectively over a widespread geographical area, with a systems component to provide reinforcement from both professionals and nonprofessionals for the skills being taught in the treatment program. Since its implementation in our community mental health services, STEPPS is not only providing very positive outcomes, it is also popular with service users and clinicians, and the newer adaptations promise increased reach across different service user groups.

## IMPLEMENTATION AND DISSEMINATION IN THE UNITED KINGDOM

The first group, run in Horsham, Sussex, in 2007, led to a more structured uncontrolled pilot study of six groups in 2008 (Harvey, Black, & Blum, 2010). Following this, groups began to be rolled out across Sussex and within two years were running in every community mental health team in the county. In a similar vein, groups spread across Kent and also began in other counties such as Surrey. Another strong group developed in Scotland, followed by a publication (Gracie & Scott-Lodge, 2013). As training courses were made available across the United Kingdom, STEPPS has spread far and wide in a relatively short period (Figure 4.1).

With the shrinking economy and financial pressures, especially on the NHS, services have generally cut back on all therapeutic interventions, and STEPPS has not been an exception. In general, teams are tending to join forces and share facilities and facilitators, but have nonetheless continued to run groups regularly. In many parts of the United Kingdom, it would seem that interest is actually growing in STEPPS because of its cost effectiveness coupled with good clinical outcomes.

### UK Training

Training in the United Kingdom takes place over two days (as elsewhere). It essentially follows the same process, except for the inclusion of UK-relevant content and background information. Training in the United Kingdom has also specifically allowed time for service user (STEPPS "graduates") participation in the training (where available), as well as time for team discussions around local implementation issues. Teams also have time to work on practical exercises using the Emotional Intensity Continuum (EIC) with real-life examples or content from their own work. In certain instances where there has been a relative deficit in basic knowledge and skills in cognitive behavior therapy (CBT), schema therapy (ST), group skills, or even borderline personality disorder, supplementary training has been done. The CBT and ST skills training is a brief supplementary training specifically to enable participants to lead STEPPS groups. (A basic level of training in CBT is one of the requirements for admission to training.) There has also been specific training around the screening and assessment for groups.

1. First STEPPS group: Sussex 2007.

Subsequent areas trained/groups running 2007–2014: Nos. 2 –15

2. Kent
3. Surrey
4. London
5. Essex
6. Milton Keynes
7. Scottish Borders
8. Edinburgh
9. Highland
10. Dumfries & Galloway
11. Manchester
12. Dudley & Walsall
13. Oxfordshire
14. Berkshire
15. Somerset

**Figure 4.1** STEPPS Training: 2007–2014

## Modifications to the Program

Several aspects have been modified to better suit the UK market and to extend its use to different populations. The essential core of the program, its ethos, and manner of delivery have remained the same.

## Changes to the Manual

After the first few groups, three categories of change were made: (1) the spelling, grammar, and vocabulary were anglicized; for example yard work was changed to gardening; (2) some content was made more relevant to a UK population, for example the use of "cheerleading" statements as a way to motivate behavioral changes became "encouraging" statements; (3) our group participants found the writing style of the first edition very complex, with long sentences and overly formalized grammar; for example, cognition instead of thinking. Our modification of the EIC changed headings such as "physical sensations" to what seemed more accessible, namely, "What was my body doing?" and action urges to "What did I want to do?" Service user groups accessing STEPPS in our services seemed to respond more favorably to this direct and simplified approach. In many settings we found individuals who had histories of unfortunate experiences with schooling, who had reading difficulties, or who simply had been unable to acquire skills, perhaps because of emotional and social circumstances during their early years. For these individuals, a simpler format seemed more helpful.

## Other Versions of STEPPS

Initially STEPPS was implemented within secondary mental health services. As the various teams started the program during the first few years, these services were undergoing fundamental changes in how they served people across the whole spectrum of need. Implementation of the national program, Improving Access to Psychological Therapies (IAPT), a program for primary mental health care, meant that increasingly individuals with depression and anxiety disorders were being diverted away from secondary mental health services, a diversion that, in turn, was raising the threshold of complexity of need for the people that IAPT took on. As this has evolved, it became clear that, on the one hand, many people accessing IAPT were struggling with more complex problems than specifically defined DSM-IV Axis I anxiety and/or depression, and that many could arguably be suffering from unidentified or subthreshold personality disorder. On the other hand, clinicians in secondary care were dealing with individuals with increasingly complex presentations, many of whom needed even more specialized and intensive treatment.

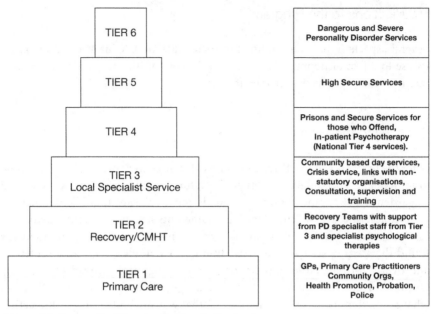

| TIER 6 | Dangerous and Severe Personality Disorder Services |
| TIER 5 | High Secure Services |
| TIER 4 | Prisons and Secure Services for those who Offend, In-patient Psychotherapy (National Tier 4 services). |
| TIER 3 Local Specialist Service | Community based day services, Crisis service, links with non-statutory organisations, Consultation, supervision and training |
| TIER 2 Recovery/CMHT | Recovery Teams with support from PD specialist staff from Tier 3 and specialist psychological therapies |
| TIER 1 Primary Care | GPs, Primary Care Practitioners Community Orgs, Health Promotion, Probation, Police |

**Figure 4.2**  Personality Disorder Services in England

The development of personality disorder services in England was following a classification created by a Department of Health team, whereby provision fell into six categories, shown in Figure 4.2.

Developments in Sussex as specifically related to STEPPS progressed as shown in Figure 4.3, giving rise to our development of other versions of STEPPS specifically for the different populations.

Figure 4.3 shows how STEPPS began at Tier 2 level in Sussex, with the provision of groups in community mental health teams. In Phase 2, Sussex Partnership opened a specialist service, Bluebell House in Burgess Hill in April 2011, for people with more complex needs; for example, struggling with very high levels and frequency of self-harming behavior, high risk for suicide attempts, frequent hospitalizations, and multiple agency and team involvement. This was followed in 2013 by the opening of a second service, Lighthouse in Brighton & Hove. STEPPS and STAIRWAYS are the core skills development programs for both these services; this has led to a variation in the way the model is presented, with both programs embedded within a range of other interventions within a therapeutic setting.

Phase 3 saw the development of STEPPS on two further fronts, in Primary Care, and in Children and Adolescent Mental Health Services (CAMHS). For both of these projects, new versions of the manual have been created.

In Phase 4, Forensic Services have identified the need for a STEPPS program that is simultaneously more intensive, yet with a simpler format. This is now in development.

Each of the versions will now be discussed in turn, with details of the program, implementation issues, outcomes, feedback, and research. They will be discussed in the order in which they were implemented or developed.

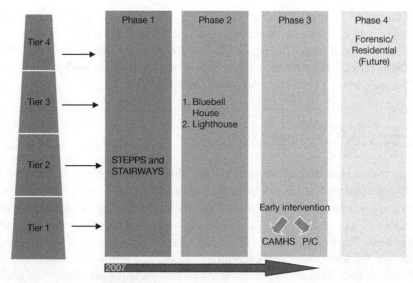

**Figure 4.3** Service Development Map in Sussex

## STEPPS IN VARIOUS SERVICES

### STEPPS in Community Mental Health Services (Tier 2)

Training in the United Kingdom recommends that in community services, referrals to STEPPS groups are made by care coordinators, who are expected to be involved and to help by acting as a "clinician reinforcer" for at least the duration of the program. A screening assessment is made by a team psychologist, who may or may not also be a group facilitator. Recommended screening instruments include the Zanarini Rating Scale for Borderline Personality Disorder (Zan-BPD; Zanarini, 2003), and the Millon Clinical Multiaxial Inventory-III (MCMI-III; Millon et al., 1997). These are chosen to help establish whether BPD is present and to determine what other personality features and DSM-IV Axis 1 problems are present. In most cases the group is not offered to individuals presenting with significant features of antisocial personality disorder or narcissistic personality disorder. Individuals with neurological problems or learning difficulties are not included, although there is interest in developing groups for the latter. Assessors are also advised to not offer places to individuals whose lives are in such chaos that they are unlikely to be able to sustain the pressure of a 20-week course, or where other life demands would make this impossible, such as a planned holiday or medical procedure that would interfere with attendance. A clinical evaluation of motivation and capacity to participate is also made. Some examples will illustrate the kinds of issues that have been encountered. One person told the assessor that she would attend the group, but she absolutely refused to do any kind of homework. Another said she felt she was coerced into the referral and had agreed so she could prove that STEPPS would not work. A third engaged in the group to secure access to her children via the court. In all three cases, the recommendation was that a place not be offered. In all instances, wherever possible, it is recommended that further work is done with individuals to help develop greater readiness for groups rather than absolute refusal, and referral at a later date is considered. Case study 1 describes a case example of a participant who completed STEPPS.

## CASE STUDY 1: JANE, AGED 32

Jane came to mental health services at age 22 following the break-up of a relationship. She informed us, however, that she had been self-harming by cutting herself in various places since the age of 12. A suicide attempt had gone unnoticed when she was 15 and had slept off the effects of swallowing pills. This had also been after being let down by her boyfriend. A pattern of unsuccessful relationships interspersed with other short encounters had led to a termination at 16, and the adoption of her baby at 17. She disclosed on first presentation a history of sexual abuse by a relative which had precipitated the start of the self-harm, and escalating drug and alcohol use. She had been erratic in her engagement with services in the ten years leading up to referral to STEPPS, fluctuating between intense bouts of strong attachment relationships with clinicians who were rejected as soon as she had found another boyfriend.

Jane was somewhat skeptical on the first day of STEPPS. She reacted with surprise and amazement on hearing the symptoms of BPD and realizing that they did describe her, but also others sitting around the table. "I thought 1 was the only alien on the planet," she later remarked, and said how much she had been comforted by the fact that she was not alone, that the struggles she had gone through had a name and were understood, and most of all, that something could be done to help.

Jane attended nineteen out of twenty sessions, always diligently completing the homework tasks. She continued to develop the depth of her understanding of herself, and self-acceptance rather than the harsh self-judgment of the past. Jane was a good example of someone who engaged fully with the program, even creating her own version of the Emotional Intensity Continuum and various other self-help strategies (for example, laminated affirmations stuck all over her house). She went on to establish a stable relationship and had another child. She managed to enroll for literacy and numeracy classes to begin to rebuild her education, and also managed to pass her driving test. Following STEPPS, she engaged with STAIRWAYS, which has helped to consolidate and further develop her learning

NOTE: All case studies are composites created from the histories of real people, structured to demonstrate the differences between "typical" clients from each Tier. All feedback in quotes is taken from direct statements made by STEPPS participants or people (clinicians, family or carers) associated with groups.

The systems component of STEPPS means that as many people in the wider system should be recruited to help reinforce the skills. Family members, friends, therapists and others are all potential reinforcers, and the group participants are encouraged to involve them as much as possible. The initiative lies with the group participant. In the United Kingdom, individuals in community services frequently do not want families involved, or they have families that may either not be helpful or are even a source of difficulties. Group facilitators often work with individuals who are very socially isolated. In an ideal situation, all group participants have a clinician in the team who is skilled and willing to meet with them weekly for a reinforcement session. These clinicians meet regularly for supervision and reflective practice, and, if no family member or friend is available to attend the reinforcer evening session (see course description in Chapter 1), they will attend it to support the group participant. In reality, this has proved hard to achieve. With decreasing numbers of available clinicians in the economic downturn as well as increased caseloads, compromises have been made. In some instances, clinicians have taken on reinforcement in small groups; in other situations they have met less frequently with STEPPS participants. In one service, the group participants were given a room to meet on their own and help reinforce each other's learning. Unfortunately there are many cases where arranged reinforcement is lacking. The difference has been noticeable to patients in those groups and, anecdotally, when participants become aware of inequalities, it has been hard for them to accept. In Sussex the development of online reinforcement is in progress.

One of the early challenges faced by services occurs when STEPPS groups become established initially and it takes time to start offering STAIRWAYS. In the absence of a STAIRWAYS group, it has been reported anecdotally that some individuals retain their skills and go on to do well, while others struggle. One possible explanation relates to what kind of ongoing support is available to the individual when he/she finishes STEPPS. Teams vary widely in their basic attitude and willingness to continue supporting individuals, and one of the ongoing challenges is encouraging and supporting teams to recognize that NICE guidelines (NICE, 2009) recommend long-term input, lasting years, not months or weeks. The ongoing support required here may not necessarily be intensive therapy of one kind or another, but even low-key support may be enough for an individual to feel "held" and to progress with consolidating their skills. As will be reported below, where STAIRWAYS is available, the STEPPS group participants' symptom scores on the Borderline Evaluation of Severity over Time (BEST; Pfohl, et al., 2009) more often show significant improvement.

STAIRWAYS has worked best where it is facilitated by a team of at least four facilitators, who take turns to present in pairs. Each individual facilitator runs two topics back to back, and is joined for the second topic by a different facilitator (a kind of leap-frogging pattern to maintain continuity from one group to the next with only one facilitator changing at any one time, i.e., A + B, then B + C, then C + D, then D + A, etc.). Group members receive a leaflet at the start, introducing the facilitators and specifying dates, times, and presenters for each topic, thereby creating predictability for the participant.

## Tier 2: Research and Outcomes

Harvey, Blum, and Black (2010) present data from the first six pilot groups in Sussex. Referrals were received from community teams in six regions, with 76 individuals initially screened and assessed. Of these, 62 were offered places in groups, the rest were excluded as described previously. Of the 62 who were offered places, three failed to arrive for the start of the groups: one was hospitalized in crisis, another was too ill to attend for physical reasons, and no information was available for the third. A total of 41 out of 59 clients who accepted places in the groups consented to participate in the research. Results for three people were not included, as they had attended a previous STEPPS group. This made a total of 38 individuals included in the study. Groups were set up in six regions, two within functioning day hospital settings, three using rooms in inactive day hospitals, and one in a non-mental health clinic setting. The facilitators included professionals from psychology, nursing, occupational therapy, and social work. Each of the STEPPS groups was also attended by one or two observers, who provided additional assistance with group tasks, monitored adherence to the model, or were there to gain training. Procedures for running the group are described elsewhere in this volume. Participants were expected to have care plans including risk assessments and risk management plans in place and to have been assigned a treatment team member to provide 1:1 skills reinforcement sessions on a weekly basis in addition to any other form of therapy or therapeutic input being received. This was discussed with teams and referrers before the start of the course.

Subjects were assessed at (1) a screening interview; (2) prior to start of the program; (3) during treatment; and (4) at the end of treatment. Pre- and post-treatment measures included the ZAN-BPD; Clinical Outcomes in Routine Evaluation-OM (CORE-OM; Connell & Barkham, 2007), a 34-item self-rating questionnaire measuring psychological distress, covering well-being, symptoms, functioning and risk (part A), and a clinician-rated outcome measure (part B); Beck Depression Inventory-II (BDI; Beck et al., 1996), a 21-item inventory to measure symptoms of depression; and the Positive and Negative Affect Scale—Expanded Version (PANAS-X; Watson & Clark, 1994), a 60-item scale measuring 11 specific affects, providing for mood measurement at two levels. During the STEPPS program, the BEST (Pfohl, et al., 2009) forms were collected for analysis. Results are summarized in Table 4.1 and show significant change in all measures.

Results of BEST questionnaires filled in each week are shown in Figure 4.4. The total score means (SD) dropped from 44.8 (9.9) to 35.3 (14.9). There was a significant drop from Week 1 to Week 20 [Week 1, 44.8 (9.9); Week 20, 35.3 (14.9), $p < 0.001$]. However, because the questionnaire includes items that can only be answered meaningfully once the program has begun (because they are related to doing coursework), and participants are not able to rate this by Week 1,

Table 4.1. PRE- AND POST-INTERVENTION COMPARISONS

| Measure | Subscales: | N | Mean Pre-group | Mean Post-group | Sig. (2-Tailed) |
|---|---|---|---|---|---|
| Beck Depression Inv | | 27 | 40.0 (9.7) | 25.6 (16.1) | 4.5*** |
| CORE: Total | | 24 | 2.4 (0.6) | 1.7 (0.7) | 4.2*** |
| | Well-Being | 24 | 3.0 (0.8) | 2.3 (0.9) | 3.0** |
| | Problem/ Symptoms | 24 | 2.8 (0.7) | 2.0 (0.8) | 4.5 *** |
| | Functioning | 24 | 2.4 (0.5) | 1.7 (0.7) | 4.0** |
| | Risk | 24 | 1.3 (1.0) | 0.8 (0.7) | 3.1** |
| PANAS-X | Negative Affect | 28 | 35.2 (8.1) | 27.0 (9.0) | 4.0*** |
| | Positive Affect | 27 | 18.7 (6.2) | 23.6 (9.6) | −2.3* |
| ZAN-BPD: Total | | 28 | 21.8 (5.3) | 10.7 (8.0) | 7.4*** |
| | Affect | 28 | 8.2 (2.3) | 3.8 (2.9) | 6.9*** |
| | Cognition | 28 | 5.8 (1.8) | 2.8 (2.0) | 7.1*** |
| | Impulsivity | 28 | 3.4 (2.5) | 2.1 (2.2) | 3.0** |
| | Relationships | 28 | 4.4 (1.9) | 2.1 (2.0) | 5.6*** |
| (ZAN-BPD Q 7) | | 24 | 1.3 (1.0) | 0.8 (0.7) | −1.8** |
| BEST (Wk 1 & Post Intervention) | | 27 | 44.8 (9.9) | 35. 3 (14.9) | 4.0*** |
| BEST (Wk 2 & Post Intervention) | | 27 | 42.7 (11.4) | 35.2 (14.9) | 3.3** |

there is a potential source of bias. Calculations were redone, comparing Week 2 with Week 20, and the result was still significant [Week 2, 42.3 (11.4); Week 20, 35.3 (14.9), $p$ <.001].

Table 4.1 shows the comparison between scores on four measures before and after STEPPS and the overall change in BEST scores. It also includes a separate

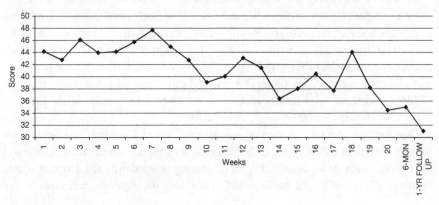

**Figure 4.4** BEST Scores Week 1 to 12 Month Follow-up

line to show the change on the ZAN-BPD question #7, which relates to incidents of self-harm and suicide attempts. All scores showed significant levels of change. It should be noted that the PANAS-X has two subscales, where significant improvement is reflected by a decrease in negative affect and an increase in positive affect. The CORE has four subscales, all of which are scaled to show an improvement as a drop in scores. Included in the table is a comparison of BEST scores between Week 1 of the course and the post-course assessment.

Six months after the reported study, follow-ups were carried out, and one year after the end of the group, measures were repeated. The results are shown in Table 4.2, and Figure 4.1 also reflects these two further measures, with highly significant change.

At the time of the last measures, the researchers re-applied two further instruments that were done at the time of initial referral:

1. Symptom Checklist—Revised (SCL-90-R; Derogatis, 1983). This is a 90-item checklist measuring a variety of Axis I symptoms experienced by users of mental health services. It also provides a Global Severity Index, which has provided a useful index of change in both the US and Dutch studies (Black et al., 2009).

2. Millon Clinical Multiaxial Inventory-III (MCMI-III). This is a 175-item measure of DSM-IV related personality disorders and clinical syndromes. It also provides a measure of Axis I disorders and enables an assessment of relationships between Axis I and Axis II. This was included because of its value in providing a wealth of information regarding personality functioning and to assist in the screening process. Repeating the inventory was aimed at potentially providing information regarding personality level changes that might have occurred.

Table 4.3 shows changes in the SCL-90-R. On the MCMI-III the profiles changed in various ways but, significantly, on the scale measuring BPD there were marked changes between the two measures. This is shown in Table 4.4.

A major weakness of the results, both published and unpublished, is the low number of participants. Drop-out rates were also high (35%). It was gratifying to note, however, that these results confirmed results in other studies. The intention was to follow this up with a full RCT, but it was felt that there was so much change created by STEPPS within teams, increased familiarity with the program, and changed expectations of service users (both those who had been through STEPPS and those who had been told about it) that any study would face too many confounding variables to make it feasible.

One further small study carried out in the United Kingdom has been done to date. Gracie and Scott-Lodge (2013) compared outcome measures before and after preliminary groups run in Highland and reported significant drops in scores on the BEST, the BDI, and the Zan-BPD. Following their groups, measures on the

Table 4.2. Scores on Table 4.1 measures after 6-months and 1-year follow-up

| Measure | N | Mean Pre-group | Mean Post-group | Mean 6-Month Follow-Up Group | Mean 1-Year Follow-Up Group |
|---|---|---|---|---|---|
| Beck Depression Inv | 28 | 40.0 (9.7) | 25.6 (16.1)*** | 34 (12.6)** | 29.3 (13.3)** |
| CORE: Total | 27 | 2.4 (0.6) | 1.7 (0.7)*** | 2.0 (.7)** | 2.6 (2.1) |
| Well-Being | 27 | 3.0 (0.8) | 2.3 (0.9)** | 2.5 (.9)* | 2.5 (1.1)* |
| Problem/Symptoms | 27 | 2.8 (0.7) | 2.0 (0.8)*** | 2.6(.9)* | 2.3 (1.1)* |
| Functioning | 27 | 2.4 (0.5) | 1.7 (0.7)** | 2.2 (.7)* | 2.2 (1.6) |
| Risk | 27 | 1.3 (1.0) | 0.8 (0.7)** | 1.1 (.9) | 1.6 (1.8) |
| PANAS-X | | | | | |
| Negative Affect | 31 | 35.2 (8.1) | 27.0 (9.0)*** | 29 (8.1)** | 26.7 (9.6)** |
| Positive Affect | 31 | 18.7 (6.2) | 23.6 (9.6)* | 25 (7.8) | 22.6 (8.7) |
| Zan-BPD: Total | 31 | 21.8 (5.3) | 10.7 (8.0)*** | 13 (6.8)*** | 9 (6.0)*** |
| Affect | 31 | 8.2 (2.3) | 3.8 (2.9)*** | 2 (1.9)*** | 3.8 (2.6)*** |
| Cognition | 31 | 5.8 (1.8) | 2.8 (2.0)*** | 3.3 (2.4)*** | 2.1 (2.1)*** |
| Impulsivity | 31 | 3.4 (2.5) | 2.1 (2.2)** | 2.4 (2.1)** | 1.6 (1.4)** |
| Relationships | 31 | 4.4 (1.9) | 2.1 (2.0)*** | 6 (4.7) | 1.5 (1.9)*** |
| (ZAN-BPD Q 7) | 21 | 1.3 (1.0) | 0.8 (0.7)** | 0.7** | 1.2 |
| BEST (Wk 2 & Post Intervention) | 24 | 42.3 (11.4) | 33.3 (12.2)** | 35.4 (12.0)** | 31.5 (11.3)*** |

*Table 4.3.* SCORES ON SCL-90-R PRE-INTERVENTION AND 18 MONTHS LATER

| Scale | N | Mean, Initial Assessment | Mean, 12 Months Post-intervention | Significance |
|---|---|---|---|---|
| Somatization | 21 | 57.27 | 52.59 | 0.079 |
| Obsessive-compulsive | 21 | 59.32 | 51.64 | 0.001** |
| Interpersonal sensitivity | 21 | 61.09 | 53.86 | 0.006** |
| Depression | 21 | 62.23 | 50.5 | .000*** |
| Anxiety | 21 | 58.45 | 49.95 | 0.003** |
| Hostility | 21 | 55.18 | 47.64 | 0.006** |
| Phobic anxiety | 21 | 59.64 | 54.95 | 0.03* |
| Paranoid ideation | 21 | 54.55 | 50.27 | 0.02* |
| Psychoticism | 21 | 57 | 50.95 | 0.01** |
| Global severity index | 21 | 60.72 | 52.09 | 0.003** |
| Positive symptom total | 21 | 60.32 | 52.68 | 0.032* |
| Positive symptom distress | 21 | 58.23 | 50.73 | 0.023* |

***: $p < 0.001$
**: $p < 0.01$
*: $p < 0.05$

CORE (Connell & Barkham, 2007) were below clinical cut-off levels. They report that there was a similarly high drop-out rate (35%).

## Tier 2 Program Feedback

Two further sources of information were considered crucial for how STEPPS was to be carried forward in Sussex, namely feedback from clinicians working with the participants and from the participants themselves. The CORE, which formed part of the assessment of participants, allows for measurement of clinician rated outcomes. Table 4.5 shows these results.

*Clinician Feedback*: In all 10 categories, a higher percentage of participants were rated as improved by clinicians. The highest of these was for gains in personal insight and understanding, where 94% of participants were rated as improved. Participants were generally rated as more able to express and explore feelings (87%), and able to use coping strategies or techniques (81%). Clinicians also thought that only 55% of participants showed improvement in their personal relationships. Day-to-day functioning and subjective well-being were rated as improved in 71%, and 61% of participants were rated as showing improvement in symptoms. In the

*Table 4.4.* MCMI-III SCALE C (BORDERLINE) $N = 22$

| Times/Scores | Number of Participants Scoring Below BR 85 | Number of Participants Scoring at BF85 and Above |
|---|---|---|
| Assessment | 11 | 11 |
| 12 Months follow-up | 21 | 1 |

*Table 4.5.* CORE END OF THERAPY FORM

| Benefits of Therapy | | Yes | % | No | % | Not Addressed | % |
|---|---|---|---|---|---|---|---|
| Personal insight/understanding | 31 | 29 | 94 | 1 | 3 | 1 | 3 |
| Expression of feelings/problems | 31 | 27 | 87 | 4 | 13 | 0 | 0 |
| Exploration of feelings/problems | 31 | 27 | 87 | 4 | 13 | 0 | 0 |
| Coping strategies/techniques | 31 | 25 | 81 | 6 | 19 | 0 | 0 |
| Access to practical help | 31 | 16 | 52 | 13 | 42 | 2 | 6 |
| Control/planning/decision making | 31 | 20 | 65 | 11 | 34 | 0 | 0 |
| Subjective well-being | 31 | 22 | 71 | 8 | 26 | 1 | 3 |
| Symptoms | 31 | 19 | 61 | 11 | 35 | 1 | 3 |
| Day to day functioning | 31 | 22 | 71 | 9 | 29 | 0 | 0 |
| Personal relationships | 31 | 17 | 55 | 14 | 45 | 0 | 0 |
| **Medication** | | Yes | % | No | % | N/A | % |
| Change in medication | 31 | 6 | 19 | 25 | 81 | 0 | 0 |

opinions of clinicians, only 52% of participants showed improvements in access to practical help. The form does not clarify whether this refers to a lack of ability to access help or whether help is generally not accessible, either within the individual's private world or from services. The section on change of medication was generally not completed in sufficient detail, although 81% of participants had not changed their medication according to clinician ratings in this study.

*Participant feedback*: Participants generally reacted enthusiastically to the opportunity to provide feedback on their experience. The Group Evaluation Questionnaire in Lesson 19 of the STEPPS manual consists of both open and closed questions. A summary of scoring for closed questions is given in Table 4.6. Responses were initially coded by a research assistant and cross validated by two external volunteers not connected with the research. Open questions included opportunities for participants to comment on what they would like included in future courses and general feedback (e.g., "Overall, what was helpful/not helpful for you in this group?"). Participants were generally happy with the length of the course and the breaks. Negative comments were either that the course was too long or too short. The majority felt their understanding of BPD was better (73%) and that they were better able to cope with their difficulties (90%). They also believed that others thought they were better able to cope (77%). They also found the materials useful (77%). There was greater ambivalence around a specific tool, the reinforcement team skill cards (27% positive, 40% negative). This may relate to the way these were introduced into the teams. Similarly, there was a wider spread of responses regarding how well their individual therapists agreed with the materials. All of this feedback was used to structure how training was carried out, and also helped inform the creation of the first edition of the UK version of the STEPPS manual. Some of the many comments received are given in Box 4.1.

*Table 4.6.* SUMMARY OF PARTICIPANT RESPONSES

| Responses N = 30 | Positive | % | Negative | % | Mixed | % | Uncertain | % |
|---|---|---|---|---|---|---|---|---|
| Length of time right? | 18 | 60 | 9 | 30 | 1 | 3.33 | 2 | 6.67 |
| Understanding of BPD improved? | 22 | 73.3 | 0 | 0 | 3 | 10 | 5 | 16.7 |
| Materials useful? | 23 | 76.7 | 3 | 10 | 4 | 13.3 | 0 | 0 |
| Handle difficulties better? | 27 | 90 | 0 | 0 | 2 | 6.67 | 1 | 3.33 |
| Did 1:1 therapist agree with materials? | 14 | 46.7 | 4 | 13.3 | 1 | 3.33 | 11 | 36.7 |
| Reinforcement team cards helpful? | 8 | 26.7 | 12 | 40 | 5 | 16.7 | 5 | 16.7 |
| Others think you cope better? | 23 | 76.7 | 2 | 6.67 | 2 | 6.67 | 3 | 10 |
| **TOTAL (N = 210)** | **135** | **64.3** | **30** | **14.3** | **18** | **8.57** | **27** | **12.9** |

NOTES:

*Mixed*: a response which contained both positive and negative elements, such as "Some of it was helpful, some not."

*Uncertain*: This score was given when it was unclear what the person meant, or when the comment was not clearly positive or negative, such as "Difficult to say," or a blank answer.

Box 4.1.

**SOME COMMENTS FROM STEPPS PARTICIPANTS**

**How is your understanding of BPD/EID different?**
- I now know I am not alone, there are other people like me and I am not mad.
- Completely different. I now see it as a problem with emotion management, reasonable thinking and life skills.
- Frightening but very informative, put a lot of things into better perspective, also helped my husband and I to be able to communicate.

## How is your life different?

- Being able to understand my emotions, feelings, actions. Using skills, and being more assertive.
- I have hope!!!! I feel less anxious, more positive, less depressed and more in control. I feel I am in a position where I can learn and improve.
- I feel in control and have a great understanding of BPD and realize it's not my fault.

## Do other people see a difference?

- From comments that have been made by various people I can say they think I am coping much better. People have come up to me and said they have noticed a huge difference in me, some have said I seem more grown up and mature. My mum has said I am now likeable and more of a joy to be around, whereas she hated spending much time around me before as we would argue too much. She says there is no comparison to before, I am totally different person. I think before I speak more, I am problem solving, my whole attitude has changed, I am more patient, rational and have less arguments.
- They think I'm changed person. . . Come out of my shell and giving more input towards end. I found my mouth. I'm special now.

---

## STEPPS IN COMPLEX NEEDS/SPECIALIST SERVICES (TIER 3)

Both services in Sussex (Bluebell House and Lighthouse) have opened too recently for sufficient numbers to be reported on. In both cases, STEPPS and STAIRWAYS have been embedded into a therapeutic model with (1) establishing the necessary safety and risk management context; (2) providing time for trust and secure relationships to be built up; and (3) following this, participants need help with developing a wide range of general skills including the ones covered by STEPPS. After this, some may continue onto doing a course of formal psychological therapy. The STEPPS groups we have run in these services have suggested the following:

- The program needs a great deal more opportunity to practice skills under the help and direction of the facilitators. Two additional practice sessions per week are provided.
- Participants frequently need more individual help where reading skills are poor or concentration is impaired for various reasons, including medication.
- Participants may need many more opportunities to try the groups before succeeding, frequently leaving the group and needing to start again.
- Group dynamics have to be managed much more carefully.
- Group facilitators need to be much more tolerant of absences and other disruptions that may arise.

- Groups are currently planning to run with shorter lesson times, with lessons stretched over more sessions, and the course taking longer for participants to complete.

In spite of these challenges, a steady stream of individuals successfully completing groups is now building. Anecdotally, positive feedback is being gathered similar to that just reported, and changes are being observed by others.

These observations are borne out by a small qualitative study by Pipon-Young and Cole (2012), who reported on four women in a medium-security women's unit (one of whom subsequently left the group before completion). Their reflections on the group were presented from both group leaders' and participants' points of view. STEPPS was found to be a useful adjunct to the women's program, with a high level of acceptability among the women. The authors propose that within their setting group dynamics did seem to play a significant role in the running of the group, and that given the well-documented interpersonal difficulties in this group, they felt that some guidance was needed on this in the STEPPS manual. The issue of working in intensive treatment settings with individuals with very complex needs suggests further development of a way to address issues of group dynamics.

For individuals in Tier 3 services, STEPPS and STAIRWAYS form a core part of a program aimed at helping transform the trajectories of their lives. The consistent support over an extended time, with individualized care packages, is

---

## CASE STUDY 2: MAGGIE

Maggie was almost mute when first seen. Locked in a world of terror, flashbacks, hearing voices and various substances (prescribed and other), she found it extremely difficult to open up to begin working in the more intensive setting of the Tier 3 specialist service. She had had an extremely troubled and traumatic history in childhood and right through to her forties, and had little hope that she would ever change. Having been supported by services since her late teens, there did not seem to be many clinicians who worked with her, who thought that significant change was possible. She had been involved in many different services, and repeated hospitalizations.

Change proved to be a long, slow progress. It was clear in this instance that all of the other components of the intensive service were needed to provide the right setting for STEPPS to be helpful. It took three rounds before STAIRWAYS was begun. Very gradually, and with many setbacks, Maggie began the slow process of the very dramatic change that was to be seen. At the time of writing, she had begun to turn to helping others. She had completed a peer recovery training course and was beginning to volunteer in another service, with a view to applying for paid work as a peer support worker.

---

directed to making it possible for a slow transition from being at the receiving end of services to beginning to gain confidence and independence. Providing opportunities to learn peer support skills has also supported participants ("members" of the service) to begin volunteering and even to find paid employment. Case study 2 describes a typical participant.

## STEPPS IN PRIMARY CARE: STEPPS EI

Significant changes to the manual have been adopted for the pilot studies in Primary Care services. To date these have taken place in two separate counties: Sussex and Essex. Preliminary indications were that the manual and number of lessons required shortening. The initial pilots were done with a manual that had been modified to condense some of the sections but, more significantly, to direct the contents at individuals who could be described as pre-diagnostic. Most of these individuals were identified as needing some help with emotional intensity issues, but not being of sufficient complexity to warrant referral into secondary care services.

As these individuals might not relate to the diagnostic elements and more clinical references in the standard STEPPS manual, an important change for the first phase was to modify this language. All references to BPD, diagnosis, illness, and so forth, were removed, and the course description became a program for *Emotional Intensity Difficulties*. The manual for this version, STEPPS EI, was shortened initially to 16 and subsequently to 13 weeks (Blum et al., 2014).

## RESULTS FROM THE FIRST COHORT OF GROUPS

In both Essex and Sussex, selection for inclusion was problematic. Across Essex the groups came from significantly different demographic groups. In one area the group participants struggled with the education level of the manual. In Sussex, the first group included individuals whose needs were at a greater level of complexity than would be expected in Primary Care. This pointed to the need to refine the selection procedure and devise a clear protocol for this.

It also proved difficult to collect formal data from the first groups in a consistent way across the two areas, but outcomes from these groups nevertheless suggest

- Scores on the symptom measures came down. In Sussex they fell just short of significance although there was a trend, and Essex did not formally calculate theirs but observed that scores dropped.
- Subjective reports included improved coping skills, using emergency services less, positive change in attitude, and some clients reported feeling more work-ready (return to employment).
- Participants reported enjoying the group ("passionate about the group") and would recommend the program to others.

The final 13 week version is divided into three modules, a one-week introductory session, and two modules of 6 weeks each. It is designed to provide greater flexibility, as group participants have the option of doing Module 1, Modules 1 plus 2, or all three. Preliminary feedback is "overwhelmingly positive." A research study is now in progress to evaluate STEPPS EI formally.

## STEPPS IN CHILDREN AND YOUNG PEOPLES' SERVICES: STEPPS YP

Three pilot groups were carried out in Brighton in 2012–2015, with a group of 16–17 year-olds. This included the innovation of running a parallel group with the participants' parents/carers. Several measures were taken before and after the groups. There was also a focus group held with each of the two participant groups (young people and their families/carers).

*The Parents'/Carers' Group*: For the first meeting, the young people and their parents and carers met in one large group. After an introduction covering general housekeeping rules, the outline of the course, and guidelines covering issues such as confidentiality and information sharing, the two groups were split. The groups ran in parallel, covering the same content. The difference was that while the young people were directly learning skills, parents/carers were informed that they were not doing the course for themselves but were gaining the information for supporting their family member. They were encouraged to make themselves available to their family member for support, but to allow themselves to be guided by the young person regarding the nature and frequency of support. It was thus made clear to the young people that they should feel in control of how they were receiving support. Results of the STEPPS YP evaluation suggest

- Quantitative measures were not able to provide meaningful information for the first group as there had been a high drop-out rate, and it was difficult to analyze the data obtained. However, anecdotally there was an improvement in symptoms.
- Feedback from the young people suggested they found the group very valuable, and that it was effective in helping them gain coping strategies.
- Feedback from parents suggested that they observed significant changes in the young people and valued the group very highly. Their own group was a source of great support to them, and they reported that it made a difference to them personally and in their relationships with their young person. Box 4.2 summarizes comments from both groups.
- During the second group, two of the young people were able to find work, and attributed their ability to do this and to meet the challenges to the skills they gained from the group.

Box 4.2.

## Feedback from STEPPS-YP Young People, and Their Parents/Carers

**From the young people:**
- It has helped me to look differently at my emotions and know that it's okay to feel that way.
- It has helped a lot. I am more aware when I am vulnerable to harm.
- I have had to face up to my difficulties and have been taught how to better communicate myself to others.
- I can communicate better and no longer self-harm.

**From their parents/carers:**
- The only people who understand what I'm going through are *here*, on a Tuesday night.
- Trying to understand what I may have done, and working with guilt feelings.
- I have backed off, and she is taking responsibility—for the first time.
- My husband and I both feel we have changed and have noticed this change of behavior in one another.
- I can see changes in front of my eyes, I'm not sure I can believe it yet!
- This has been a godsend.
- I feel we have a future—a future as mum and daughter—as friends—and as her reinforcer which is how we laughingly refer to me! However... It's early days – will the change last? There is a lot of secrecy—I don't really know yet.
- Thank you for giving us our children back.

---

- During the third group, dramatic improvements were noted in the number of emergency room visits, hospital bed-days, and crisis incidents (including police involvement). Beginning from a high baseline, these outcome parameters had all reduced to zero.

As with STEPPS EI, there is a need to refine the selection procedure for STEPPS YP. In the pilot groups parents and carers played a significant role in encouraging the young people to maintain attendance. There had been a high drop-out rate to start with (50–60%); this improved significantly by the third group (2%). There were also significant systemic issues in securing and maintaining clinician involvement in the referral teams. Some of these issues relate to the shrinking of teams and high demands on clinicians together with growing numbers of referrals. STEPPS facilitators will continue to develop ways to support teams and expand the skills reinforcement opportunities for group participants.

## CONCLUDING REMARKS

STEPPS and STAIRWAYS appear to be flourishing in the United Kingdom, especially given the constraints imposed by the economic situation and changes in services. By being very economical and relatively easy to train, they offer a useful addition to the menu of choices for individuals with BPD. The future promises further versions that will be made available to an even wider service user group.

## REFERENCES

Beck, A. T., Steer, R. A., & Brown, G. K. (1996). *Manual for the Beck Depression Inventory-II*. San Antonio, TX: Psychological Corporation.

Black, D. W., Blum, N., Pfohl, B., St John, D., McCormick, B., & Allen, J. (2009). Predictors of response to Systems Training for Emotional Predictability and Problem Solving (STEPPS) for borderline personality disorder: an exploratory study. *Acta Psychiatr Scand, 120*, 53–61.

Blum, N. S., Bartels, N. E., St. John, D., Pfohl, B. (with Harvey, R., Henley-Cragg, P., Burgess, J., Parrott, M., Sussex Partnership Trust NHS). (2014). Managing Emotional Intensity: A Resource for Younger People. Iowa City, IA: LevelOne Publishing.

Connell, J., & Barkham, M. (2007). *Core-10 User Manual*, Version 1.1. Rugby, England: Core System Trust & Core Information Management Systems Ltd.

Derogatis, L. R. (1983). *SCL-90-R Administration, Scoring, and Procedures Manual II*. Towson, MD: Clinical Psychometric Research.

Gracie, J., & Scott-Lodge, L. (2013). First STEPPS: Outcomes from Systems Training for Emotional Predictability and Problems Solving (STEPPS) groups for patients with borderline personality disorder in NHS Highland. *DCP Scotland Review, 8*, 10–15.

Harvey, R., Black, D. W., & Blum, N. (2010). Systems Training for Emotional Predictability and Problem Solving (STEPPS) in the United Kingdom: A Preliminary Report. *Journal of Contemporary Psychotherapy, 40*, 225–232.

Millon, T., Davis, R., & Millon, C. (1997). *MCMI-III: Millon clinical Multiaxial Inventory-III, Manual*, 2nd ed. Minneapolis, MN: National Computer Systems.

National Institute for Mental Health in England. (2003). *Personality disorder: No longer a diagnosis of exclusion*.http://www.nimhe.org.uk

NICE. (2009). *Borderline personality disorder: Treatment and management*. NICE Clinical guideline 78. Available at www.nice.org.uk/CG78 [NICE guideline].

Pfohl, B., Blum, N., McCormick, B., St. John, D., Allen, J., & Black, D.W. (2009). Reliability and validity of the Borderline Evaluation of Severity over Time: A new scale to measure severity and change in borderline personality disorder. *Journal of Personality Disorders, 23*, 281–293.

Pipon-Young, L., & Cole, S. (2012). A preliminary evaluation of a Systems Training for Emotional Predictability and Problem Solving (STEPPS) group in a women's forensic medium secure unit. *Clinical Psychology Forum, 239*, 35–39.

Watson, D., & Clark, A. L. (1994). *The PANAS-X: Manual for the positive and negative affect schedule; expanded form*. Iowa City, IA: University of Iowa.

Zanarini, M. C. (2003). Zanarini rating scale for borderline personality disorder (ZAN-BPD): A continuous measure of DSM-IV borderline psychopathology. *Journal of Personality Disorders, 17*, 233–242.

# 5

# STEPPS in Correctional Settings

NANCEE S. BLUM AND DONALD W. BLACK ■

"Emotional instability and impulsivity contribute substantially to the challenges affected people face. . . . They are also at disproportionate risk of becoming entangled in the criminal justice system."

—ROBERT TRESTMAN, PhD, MD

This chapter provides an overview of Systems Training for Emotional Predictability and Problem Solving (STEPPS) in correctional systems in Iowa and elsewhere. The program was introduced to the Iowa Department of Corrections (IDOC) and data have shown it to be effective in reducing symptoms specific to borderline personality disorder (BPD). In addition, the program has been shown to boost mood and negative affect, reduce disciplinary infractions, and reduce self-harm behaviors in offenders. The authors describe the problems and pitfalls of implementing the program in prisons and other correctional settings.

## PREVALENCE OF BPD IN PRISON

We have worked closely with the IDOC since 2005 to integrate STEPPS into the routine care of offenders with BPD in our work as consultants to the department. It had become clear from the literature and our own work that BPD is common in offender populations; other than routine psychiatric care provided by prison psychiatrists, consisting mainly of medication management, there was little specific treatment for BPD. We sought to close that gap by implementing STEPPS and monitoring outcome. The process was slow and began in fits and starts, but it has now become established.

*Table 5.1.* FREQUENCY OF BORDERLINE PERSONALITY DISORDER IN PRISON SETTINGS

| Study | Place | No. of Subjects | Diagnostic Instrument | Percentage with BPD |
|---|---|---|---|---|
| Jordan et al., 1996 | North Carolina | 805 women | CIDI | 28 |
| Singleton et al., 1997 | United Kingdom | 2371 men 771 women | SCID-II | 19 (19, men; 20, women) |
| Riesco et al., 1998 | Spain | 56 men | IPDE | 41 |
| Blackburn & Coid, 1999 | United Kingdom | 164 men | SCID-II | 57 |
| Zlotnick, 1999 | Rhode Island | 85 women | SCID-II | 49 |
| Davison et al., 2001 | United Kingdom | 62 men* | PDQ-4, SCID-II | 44 (PDQ-4) 45 (SCID-II) |
| Dunsieth et al., 2004 | Ohio | 113 men** | SCID-II | 28 |
| Black et al., 2007 | Iowa | 198 men 22 women | SIDP-IV | 30 (27, men; 55, women) |

CIDI = Composite International Diagnostic Interview; SCID-II = Structured Clinical Interview for DSM-IV Axis II Personality Disorders; IPDE = International Personality Disorder Examination; PDQ-4 = Personality Disorder Questionnaire; SIDP-IV = Structured Interview for DSM-IV Personality.
* Convicted of violent and sexual offenses.
** Convicted of sexual offenses.

Our personal observation in working with offenders is that many of the men and women had unrecognized BPD. The literature confirmed our suspicions, as several researchers had shown that the disorder is common in this setting (see Table 5.1). There are several published studies that are directly relevant and help put our findings into perspective. In a sample of 164 violent male offenders in England, Blackburn and Coid (1999) reported that 57% met criteria for BPD. Jordan et al. (1996) assessed 805 women entering prison in North Carolina and reported that 28% had BPD, while Zlotnick (1999) reported that 49% of 85 women offenders incarcerated in Rhode Island met criteria for BPD. Lastly, in a large survey of incarcerated persons in the United Kingdom, Singleton et al. (1997) determined that 19% of 2,371 men and 20% of 771 women had BPD. While none of the studies are directly comparable because of differences in study populations and assessment methods, each points to the frequency with which BPD is seen in prisons in both the United States and the United Kingdom, rates that are particularly high among the subset of violent male offenders. These figures can be directly compared with those reported from the Epidemiologic Catchment Area sample (Swartz et al., 1990), in which the prevalence of BPD in the general population has been estimated at 1.8%.

These studies led us to design and conduct our own prevalence survey, which we embedded in a larger study on the prevalence of mental illnesses in the Iowa prison system led by colleague and forensic psychiatrist Tracy Gunter, now at Indiana University (Gunter et al., 2008). The study began in 2004 and took over a year to complete. A random selection of newly committed offenders was interviewed at the Iowa Medical and Classification Center (IMCC), Oakdale, Iowa, outside of Iowa City where the University of Iowa is located. To ensure that our research team was safe, we did not include violent offenders, those requiring special programming (e.g., close supervision, segregation, seclusion), or those requiring maximum security. Women were purposely oversampled so that their percentage in the study was approximately twice that in the Iowa prison population. The IMCC serves as a reception facility for the IDOC, wherein all new offenders are admitted for intake and reception activities, including a health screen, basic orientation to Iowa's correctional system, risk assessment, and institutional assignment. The process lasts from four to six weeks, after which offenders are assigned to one of nine correctional facilities throughout Iowa to serve their sentence. As in all such studies, we required subjects to give written, informed consent. The data were confidential and protected by a Federal Certificate of Confidentiality. To assess mental disorders and addictions, the Mini International Neuropsychiatric Interview—Plus (MINI-Plus) was then administered by trained interviewers (Sheehan et al., 1998). After starting data collection, we decided to add an assessment for BPD. We used the BPD assessment module taken directly from the Structured Interview for DSM-IV Personality (Pfohl et al., 1997), which has been shown to be reliable and valid. The questions directly map to the nine DSM-IV criteria for BPD. The module is included in the Appendix.

The screen was administered to 220 offenders (22 women, 198 men). Over 90% of the sample had at least one self-reported BPD symptom, the most frequent being impulsivity, followed by displays of inappropriate anger, unstable mood, suicidal thoughts/behaviors, and transient paranoid ideation (Figure 5.1).

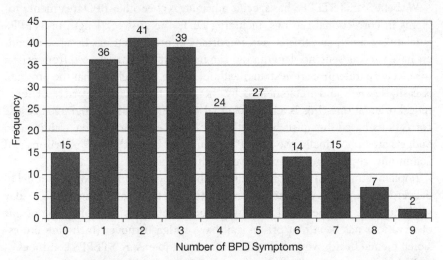

**Figure 5.1** Frequency Distribution of Number of BPD Symptoms in Men and Women Offenders

SOURCE: Reprinted with permission from Black, D.W., Gunter, T., Allen, J., Blum, N., Arndt, S., Wenman, G., & Sieleni, B. (2007). Borderline personality disorder in male and female offenders newly committed to prison. *Comprehensive Psychiatry*, 48, 400–405.

We found that 27% of the men and 55% of the women met criteria for BPD according to our screener (Black et al., 2007). We concluded that because so many men met criteria for BPD that, at least in prison settings, the disorder should be considered as part of a routine psychiatric differential diagnosis, particularly when the presenting complaints involve emotional instability, anger dyscontrol, impulsivity, or repeated episodes of self-harm.

We also found that offenders with BPD were more likely to have a history of mental health treatment, report greater interference in functioning due to their psychiatric disorder, and report having a lower quality of life than the other offenders. We concluded that offenders with BPD experience substantial psychological distress, which impairs their ability to function in important life domains.

## IMPLEMENTATION OF STEPPS IN PRISON

Despite the prevalence of BPD in corrections, and its clear association with behavioral and management problems in prisons, few treatment programs had been implemented in Iowa or elsewhere. Dialectical behavior therapy (DBT), perhaps the most widely discussed treatment program, has been modified for use in prisons (Nee and Farman, 2005), but no manuals had been published or disseminated. Because of this unmet need, we worked closely with the IDOC to integrate STEPPS into the routine care of offenders. We made it clear to corrections staff that the program supplements but does not replace other treatments or services an offender may be receiving such as medication or individual psychotherapy.

We believe that STEPPS has specific advantages over other BPD treatment programs in correctional settings, including DBT. The 20-week length of STEPPS is relatively short, and this is very important in prison settings because offenders have varying sentence lengths and can be transferred or released from prison (or receive parole/probation status) without notice. We believe that the program is easily learned and implemented by therapists from a wide variety of theoretical orientations. This is a significant advantage over other programs because corrections-based therapists have little time for extensive additional training and budgets are tight. Finally, the STEPPS manual can be used "as-is" in prisons and community corrections and extensive modifications are unnecessary.

Implementing STEPPS required that we begin by training prison personnel to deliver the program. We asked interested therapists to participate in a 1–2 day workshop; this has been followed by periodic "refresher" sessions. One of our observations has been that prison staff have a high turnover (including professional mental health workers), which means that to ensure STEPPS continues as a viable program, periodically we have to organize full-bore training sessions for newly hired therapists (and others who may have attended past sessions).

Our training workshops begin with a thorough discussion of BPD, including its epidemiology, course, possible causes, diagnosis and assessment, and clinical management. We introduce staff members to a screening module taken from the Structured Interview for DSM-IV Personality (SIDP-IV; Pfohl et al., 1997) to help identify offenders with BPD who may be suitable for STEPPS. After training, co-author Nancee Blum has made herself available by phone or teleconferencing for postsession supervision.

We have worked mainly in medium to low security areas within the IDOC and have not needed special security measures. As delivered in the prison setting, STEPPS sessions have the same look and feel as its counterpart delivered in the community. Prison therapists follow detailed lesson plans with the key elements including psychoeducation about BPD, emotion management skills training, and behavior management skills training. We have emphasized throughout this book that the *systems* component is unique to the program and helps distinguish it from other group treatment programs that have been developed for persons with BPD. This element involves a one-time 2-hour evening session for system members. The facility may choose to record this session for staff on other shifts. Because inmates are confined to prison, we have broadened the definition of "system member" to include corrections officers and other prison staff members, in addition to family members and friends on the offender's approved visitor list. These individuals are educated about BPD and how best to respond consistently to the offender in order to reinforce newly learned skills.

Offenders receive a folder for the handouts given at the beginning of each session. Handouts contain materials pertaining to the skill being taught in that lesson, as well as homework assignments to be completed between sessions. Sessions are typically conducted in a classroom setting whenever possible, with participants seated at a table and facing a marker board or chalkboard. The typical clinical format is one 2-hour session weekly; some facilities have modified this to 60–90 minute sessions twice weekly and one or two optional 60-minute homework sessions, which may be helpful for offenders who have learning difficulties. Offenders who are able to grasp the materials easily are encouraged to attend the homework sessions to help those who may have more difficulty.

As with STEPPS in other settings, sessions are highly structured with specific therapist guidelines for each session, materials needed, and the homework assignment. Each skill builds upon the previously taught skills. A constant theme is that "most of the work is done between sessions." That is, while specific skills are taught during group sessions, offenders are expected to practice them during the week between sessions. Beginning with the third lesson, each session begins with a specific relaxation activity, such as progressive muscle relaxation.

Group participants start each session by filling out the Borderline Evaluation of Severity over Time, or BEST, a self-report questionnaire to rate their symptoms of BPD, and record the result on a graph to measure their progress. (The BEST is included in the Appendix). Use of specific skills is identified from the previous week and homework is reviewed; for example, regarding how an offender applied the skill or skills learned at the previous session. A new skill is then introduced.

## FIRST CORRECTIONS STEPPS STUDY

In collaboration with the IDOC, we were asked to assess the efficacy STEPPS in the prison system for the purpose of program evaluation. For that reason, the study was not considered research and there was no need to obtain informed consent from offenders who had participated in STEPPS. The data were collected by prison personnel; deidentified data were later turned over to us for analysis and dissemination.

In our first study, we reviewed the experience of 12 women incarcerated at the Mt. Pleasant Correctional Facility in Mt. Pleasant, Iowa, a medium security facility (Black et al., 2008). We concluded that STEPPS produced measureable improvements in mood and behavior, was well accepted by therapists and offenders, and could easily be integrated into the correctional setting and benefit offenders.

The women had been identified clinically as borderline, but their BPD was confirmed using the BPD screening module described earlier in the chapter. To assess improvement, we used the BEST to assess thoughts, feelings, and behaviors associated with BPD (Pfohl et al., 2009). The BEST was developed by our group as a companion to the STEPPS program and is described in Chapter 2. The Positive and Negative Affectivity Scale (PANAS; Watson and Clark, 1994) was used to assess positive and negative dispositions. The Beck Depression Inventory (BDI; Beck, 1978) was used to assess mood severity. This simple battery is easy to collect from offenders and provides quality data for evaluation. We also asked that the prison collect data on suicide attempts, self-harm, and prison infractions.

The assessments were collected at baseline and Weeks 4, 8, 12, 16, and 20 of the program. We administered the Client Satisfaction Questionnaire-8 (Atkkinson and Greenfield, 1999) at Week 20 to assess offender satisfaction with the program. Adherence to the manual was rated on a 5-point scale, a score of 5 denoting "excellent" adherence; a score of 4 ("good") or higher was considered acceptable. Adherence to the model was rated as excellent (4.9 out of 5). (The adherence scale is included in the Appendix.)

The offenders ranged in age from 19 to 49 years with a mean of 34.8 years. Ten were Caucasian and two were African-American. Nine women (75%) completed high school and four attended college. Five women (42%) were married, five had never married, and two were divorced. Ten women (83%) were employed at the time of their incarceration. Four women (33%) had a co-occurring diagnosis of antisocial personality disorder. Seven women (58%) had a lifetime substance use disorder and seven (58%) had at least one prior arrest on an alcohol- or drug-related charge. Eleven women (92%) had a past psychiatric hospitalization with a median of three. Nine women (75%) had received individual psychotherapy, and of these women, five had also engaged in group psychotherapy. None received concurrent individual psychotherapy. The mean number of prior convictions was 10.3 with a median of 8. The mean length of prison sentence was 10.2 years with median of 10 years. All but one woman had served less than one year of her sentence.

Eleven women (92%) were prescribed psychotropic medication; 10 took an antidepressant, seven a sedative/hypnotic, four a mood stabilizer, four an anxiolytic, and two an antipsychotic. The mean number of medications was 2.5. One subject dropped out after the baseline assessment and another dropped out after week 12 because both were discharged from prison. All other subjects completed the program and had attended all 20 sessions.

Improvements in BPD-related symptoms, depression, and negative affectivity were assessed by comparing means at baseline to those in subsequent weeks using a linear mixed-effects model. Significant improvements were seen on the BEST, PANAS negative affectivity scale, and the BDI. Significant effect sizes ranged from 0.41 for the PANAS negative affectivity scale to 0.86 for the BDI. Because there were so few prison infractions, and only one suicide attempt and self-harm incident each, we were unable to assess improvement on these variables. Mean Client Satisfaction Questionnaire-8 (CSQ-8) scores were 27.0, which indicated high levels of satisfaction with the program. Developed as a multidimensional rating of client satisfaction with mental health services (e.g., therapists, program, outcome), scores can range from 8 to 32.

## SECOND CORRECTIONS STEPPS STUDY

With the encouragement of the IDOC, we have added to the sample as the number of STEPPS participants has grown. Prison staff members have continued to collect data on the BEST, PANAS, BDI, and suicidal behaviors, self-harm, and disciplinary infractions. Recently, we evaluated the experience of 77 offenders who had participated in STEPPS, including 14 men and 63 women. They had been enrolled in one of seven groups taking place in prison; 10 offenders had enrolled in a community corrections based group. The latter were individuals who were on probation or had been paroled from prison.

In this analysis, offenders ranged in age from 19 to 50 years with a mean of 31.4 years. Forty offenders (89%) were prescribed psychotropic medication; 36 (80%) took an antidepressant, 10 (22%) a sedative/hypnotic, 20 (44%) a mood stabilizer, 11 (24%) an anxiolytic, 18 (45%) an antipsychotic, 17 (38%) a benzodiazepine, and 15 (33%) a pain medication. Offenders were prescribed a mean of 3.0 psychotropic medications.

Five offenders (7%) dropped out after the baseline assessment, 14 (21%) dropped out after week 4, 7 (10%) dropped out after week 12, and 41 (61%) completed all 20 sessions. In the community corrections sample, 3 subjects (30%) dropped out after the baseline assessment, 6 (60%) dropped out after week 4, and 1 (10%) dropped out after week 12. Thus, 41 offenders (53%) completed the 20-week program. Most drop-outs occurred either due to transfers or discharges, or because the offender was segregated due to disciplinary problems.

Improvements in BPD-related symptoms, mood, and negative affectivity were assessed by comparing means at baseline to those in subsequent weeks using a linear mixed-effects model. Significant improvements were seen on the total BEST score and all three subscales, PANAS negative affectivity scale, and the BDI. Significant effect sizes ranged from 0.69 for PANAS negative affectivity to

1.30 for the BEST total score. Improvement in PANAS positive affectivity was not significant.

There were significant reductions in suicidal behaviors and disciplinary infractions. At baseline, 14% of the sample had at least one suicidal behavior in the past 4 weeks; 26% had at least one disciplinary infraction. At week 20, 5% of the sample had at least one suicidal behavior in the past last 4 weeks and 17% had at least one disciplinary infraction. Improvement in suicidal behavior was tested with the mixed-effects logistic regression model. The mean slope estimates were negative and significant ($p = .029$ and $p = 0.043$ for suicidal behaviors and disciplinary infractions, respectively). The results are summarized in Table 5.2.

Baseline severity measures were the most robust predictors of improvement and were inversely related to improvement in BPD-related symptoms, mood, and positive and negative affectivity. This finding is consistent with our findings (Black et al., 2009) on response predictors based on the randomized controlled trial of Blum et al. (2008), but also the trial reported by Bos et al. (2011). In other words, offenders with higher symptom levels gained the most from treatment and were more likely than others to have measureable improvements.

*Table 5.2.* Changes in Symptom Severity, Depression, and Positive and Negative Affectivity for 77 Offenders Participating in STEPPS

| Outcome | Baseline Mean | SD | Week 20 Mean[1] | Test of improvement Slope | SE | d | F | df | p-value |
|---|---|---|---|---|---|---|---|---|---|
| BEST | | | | | | | | | |
| Thoughts/ feelings | 21.1 | 7.5 | 12.4 | −0.42 | 0.06 | 1.12 | 57.1 | 1 | <.001 |
| Negative behaviors | 8.4 | 3.7 | 5.2 | −0.16 | 0.02 | 0.87 | 61.3 | 1 | <.001 |
| Positive behaviors | 10.2 | 3.0 | 7.4 | 0.14 | 0.03 | 0.94 | 27.2 | 1 | <.001 |
| Total | 34.3 | 11.1 | 19.5 | −0.72 | 0.08 | 1.30 | 78.1 | 1 | <.001 |
| BDI total | 25.5 | 13.5 | 10.6 | −0.73 | 0.08 | 1.08 | 85.7 | 1 | <.001 |
| PANAS | | | | | | | | | |
| Positive affectivity | 28.2 | 8.5 | 30.2 | 0.11 | 0.07 | 0.26 | 2.7 | 1 | .103 |
| Negative affectivity | 27.6 | 9.1 | 20.5 | −0.31 | 0.06 | 0.69 | 23.8 | 1 | <.001 |

[1] Because not all subjects were assessed at week 20, the mean is derived from the linear mixed-effects model mean intercept and slope estimates.
BEST = Borderline Estimate of Severity Over Time; BDI = Beck Depression Inventory; PANAS = Positive and Negative Affect Schedule.

source: Reprinted with permission from Black, D. W., Blum, N., McCormick, B., & Allen, J. (2013). STEPPS group treatment program for borderline offenders. *Journal of Nervous and Mental Disease, 201,* 124–129. © 2013 Lippincott Williams & Wilkins, Inc.

Box 5.1.

**COMMENTS FROM OFFENDERS WHO HAVE ATTENDED STEPPS**

"I have positive tools to help with my emotional intensity disorder."

"People have noticed a big change in me."

"I don't blow up as big."

"I understand my disorder better."

"I can handle problems better than I ever did before."

"I only came because it was a condition of my probation but I am so glad I did!"

---

Offenders gave the program high marks. Satisfaction was measured with the CSQ-8 in 37 of 41 offenders who completed the program. The mean score in offenders was 28.5 with 27% achieving the scale maximum of 32. Again, using the CSQ-8 to rate overall satisfaction, the offenders' mean score was 28.5. This compares favorably to the mean score of 28.2 reported by Blum et al. (2008) for STEPPS participants; this is much higher than the score of 22.6 reported in those assigned to treatment as usual. Comments from some of the offenders appear in Box 5.1.

Data collection is ongoing and there are now 115 subjects who have participated in STEPPS, including 22 men and 93 women.

*Antisocial Subanalysis.* Antisocial personality disorder in offenders was predictive of greater improvement in BDP-related symptoms assessed with the BEST ($P = 0.032$) and positive affectivity assessed using the PANAS ($P = 0.007$). This finding is consistent with our randomized controlled trial in the community (Blum et al., 2008). While the finding is counterintuitive, perhaps it should be seen as a call not to automatically exclude those with ASPD from STEPPS.

## CURRENT STATE OF STEPPS IN CORRECTIONS

While we have focused on our experience in Iowa, other prison systems have integrated STEPPS into their treatment programs for offenders with BPD. These include prisons in Minnesota, Wisconsin, Texas, South Dakota, Colorado, California, and Indiana.

## FUTURE OF STEPPS IN CORRECTIONS

Our work has shown that BPD is common and problematic in correctional systems, but also that STEPPS can be successfully integrated into the care of men and women offenders in correctional settings. We have shown that STEPPS can lead to clinically significant improvement, producing robust improvements in borderline specific symptoms, mood, and negative affectivity. The decrease in negative affectivity suggests that offenders feel less hopeless and have fewer negative self-impressions. Importantly, STEPPS leads to a decrease in disciplinary incidents and self-harm behaviors, which is crucial in prisons, where these behaviors can be especially challenging. Offenders also experienced an *increase* in positive behaviors such as following through with therapy plans. These changes reflect the emphasis of STEPPS to teach people skills to help self-regulate their intense emotions and maladaptive behaviors. The systems component of STEPPS can easily be modified for the correctional setting to include corrections offices and other personnel with whom the offender regularly interacts.

## REFERENCES

Attkisson, C. C., & Greenfield, T. K. (1999). The UCSF Client Satisfaction Questionnaire (CSQ) scales: The Client Satisfaction Questionnaire-8. In by M. E. Maruish (Eds.), *Psychological testing: Treatment planning and outcome assessment,* 2nd ed. Hillsdale, NJ: Erlbaum.

Beck, A. T. (1978). *Depression inventory.* Philadelphia, PA: Philadelphia Center for Cognitive Therapy.

Black, D. W., Blum, N., Eichinger, L., McCormick, B., Allen, J., & Sieleni, B. (2008). Systems Training for Emotional Predictability and Problem Solving (STEPPS) in women offenders with borderline personality disorder in prison: A pilot study. *CNS Spectrums, 13,* 881–886.

Black, D. W., Blum, N., Pfohl, B., St. John, D., McCormick, B., & Allen, J. (2009). Predictors of response to Systems Training to Emotional Predictability and Problem Solving (STEPPS) for borderline personality disorder: an exploratory study. *Acta Psychiatrica Scandinavica, 120,* 53–61.

Black, D. W., Gunter, T., Allen, J., Blum, N., Arndt, S., Wenman, G., & Sieleni, B. (2007). Borderline personality disorder in male and female offenders newly committed to prison. *Comprehensive Psychiatry, 48,* 400–405.

Black, D. W., Blum, N., McCormick, B., & Allen, J. (2013). STEPPS group treatment program for borderline offenders. *Journal of Nervous and Mental Disease, 201,* 124–129.

Blackburn, R., & Coid, J. W. (1999). Empirical clusters of DSM-III personality disorder in violent offenders. *Journal of Personality Disorders, 13,* 18–34.

Blum, N., St. John, D., Pfohl, B., Stuart, S., McCormick, B., Allen, J. . . . Black, D. W. (2008). Systems Training for Emotional Predictability and Problem Solving (STEPPS) for outpatients with borderline personality disorder: A randomized controlled trial and 1-year follow-up. *American Journal of Psychiatry, 165,* 468–478.

Bos, E. H., Wel, E. B. van, Appelo, M. T., & Verbraak, M. J. (2011). Effectiveness of systems training for emotional predictability and problem solving (STEPPS) for borderline personality problems in a 'real-world' sample: Moderation by diagnosis or severity? *Psychotherapy & Psychosomatics, 80,* 173–181.

Davison, S., Leese, M., & Taylor, P. J. (2001). Examination of the screening properties of the Personality Diagnostic Questionnaire 4+ (PDQ-4+) in a prison population. *Journal of Personality Disorders, 15,* 180–194.

Dunsieth, N. W., Nelson, E. B., Brusman-Lovins, L. A., Holcomb, J. L., Beckman, D., Welge, J. A., Roby ... McElroy, S. L. (2004). Psychiatric and legal features of 113 men convicted of sexual crimes. *Journal of Clinical Psychiatry, 65,* 293–300.

Gunter, T., Wenman, G., Sieleni, B., Allen, J, Arndt, S., & Black, D. W. (2008). Frequency of mental health and addictive disorders among 320 men and women entering the Iowa prison system. *Journal of the American Academy of Psychiatry and the Law, 36,* 27–34.

Jordan, B. K., Schlenger, W. E., Fairbank, J. A., & Caddell, J. M. (1996). Prevalence of psychiatric disorders among incarcerated women. II. Convicted felons entering prison. *Archives of General Psychiatry, 53,* 513–519.

Nee, C., & Farman, S. (2005). Female prisoners with borderline personality disorder: Some promising treatment developments. *Criminal and Behavioral Mental Health, 15,* 2–16.

Pfohl, B., Blum, N., McCormick, B., St. John, D., Allen, J., & Black, D. W. (2009). Reliability and validity of the Borderline Evaluation of Severity over Time: A new scale to measure severity and change in borderline personality disorder. *Journal of Personality Disorders, 23,* 281–293.

Pfohl, B., Blum, N., & Zimmerman, M. (1997). *Structured Interview for DSM-IV Personality Disorders (SIDP-IV).* Washington, DC: American Psychiatric Press.

Riesco, Y., Perez Urdaniz, A., Rubio, V., Izquierdo, J. A., Sánchez Iglesias, S., Santo, J. M., et al. (1998). The evaluation of personality disorders among inmates by IPDE and MMPI. *Actas Luso Espaniola De Neurologia, Psiquiatria, Y Ciencias, 26,* 151–154.

Sheehan, D., Lecrubier, Y., Sheehan, K. H., Amorim, O., Janavs, J., Weiller, E., et al. (1998). The Mini International Neuropsychiatric Interview (MINI). *Journal of Clinical Psychiatry, 59*(suppl 20), 22–33.

Singleton, N., Meltzer, H., & Gatward, R. (1997). *Psychiatric morbidity among prisoners: Summary report.* United Kingdom: Government Statistical Service, Department of Health.

Swartz, M. S., Blazer, D., George, L., & Winfield, I. (1990). Estimating the prevalence of borderline personality disorder in the community. *Journal of Personality Disorders, 4,* 257–272.

Watson, D., & Clark, L. A. (1994). *The PANAS-manual for the positive and negative affect schedule: expanded form.* Iowa City, IA: The University of Iowa.

Zlotnick, C. (1999). Antisocial personality disorder, affect dysregulation, and childhood abuse among incarcerated women. *Journal of Personality Disorders, 13,* 90–95.

# 6

# STEPPS in a Residential Therapeutic Community in Italy

ALDO LOMBARDO ■

This chapter describes the implementation of STEPPS in a residential therapeutic community in Rome. It outlines how Italian Therapeutic Communities serve patients with a variety of diagnoses who often require specialized help to manage their overly intense emotions. The author describes the evolutionary adaptation of the therapeutic community to the demands of a changing psychiatric patient population, and how the gradual integration of STEPPS and sociotherapy has provided residents and staff with a common language. This has led to greater cohesion; general improvement in perceived quality of life; enhanced mutual support; and an increase in trust, empathy, and personal awareness among patients. The author highlights the challenges associated with this implementation and illustrates the adjustments made to the weekly therapeutic program. The STEPPS Manual was translated into Italian, and training was provided to staff members of selected communities. The chapter also addresses ways to use STEPPS on a daily basis as homework for residents and as support training for social rehabilitation workers with no background in cognitive-behavioral therapy.

In 2010, I was looking for a suitable program for residents of the Raymond Gledhill Therapeutic Community. The patients needed a program that would give them a set of new skills and strategies to deal with their overly intense emotions. Our patient's diagnoses had gradually changed from schizophrenia to bipolar disorders, drug abuse, and personality disorders—primarily borderline personality disorder (BPD). When I learned of STEPPS, I was struck by its potential because it was a well-structured, time-limited program that appeared suited to our setting. Earlier attempts to introduce general skills training undertaken by a cognitive therapist and later by a dialectic behavior therapy (DBT) trainer did not meet the needs of our patients. Even though the Raymond Gledhill Therapeutic

Community is a resilient organization capable of taking up the challenges posed by patients with complex needs, I felt that a suitable psychoeducational scheme to improve the efficacy of our sociotherapeutic approach was needed.

The implementation in Italy of the 1998 Basaglia psychiatric reform law marked the closing chapter of the previous psychiatric hospital system (Burti, 2001). Despite resistance on the part of many psychiatrists who foresaw dangers and warned of the pitfalls of this law, many Italian psychiatric hospitals were closed. Wards for acute psychiatric patients could not have more than 15 beds; the units were tasked with discharging patients as quickly as possible, preferably within 1–2 weeks in an effort to ward off the risk of institutionalization should the patient stay for greater lengths of time. However, no training was provided to personnel or to family members who were saddled with the responsibility of taking charge of these psychiatric patients as if they were mental health professionals. It is interesting to note, in passing, that the psychiatrist and policy maker Franco Basaglia, after whom the law was named, had himself been influenced by Maxwell Jones and his notion of the problems of a single member of a therapeutic community (TC) becoming the problem of the TC itself. He believed that just as society was responsible for the mental suffering of its members, it followed that society, as a community, ought to provide the answers to the very psychiatric problems to which it had contributed.

Soon after the Basaglia law of May 1978, many patients found themselves with nowhere to go other than to private clinics or hastily put up shelters provided by genuinely motivated people of a charitable and concerned disposition, as much as by shrewd businessmen. As a result, the Regional Health Authorities were on the lookout for forms of accreditation that could deal with new alternative services such as unstaffed apartments, supervised hostels, group homes, day centers, and cooperatives managed by patients (Tansella, 1986). There was a growth in psychiatric residences after 1997. By the year 2000, according to a national survey of residential facilities by De Girolamo et al. (2005), there were 1,374 residential centers throughout Italy.

Drawing inspiration from professionals who favored psychological and psychodynamic approaches of a pre-medication era, TCs became alternatives to the traditional medical model, which had found itself unable to deal with the complex needs of psychiatric patients whose condition did not warrant hospitalization but required close and continued supervision (i.e., patients with BPD).

## THE RAYMOND GLEDHILL THERAPEUTIC COMMUNITY

Together with two other colleagues, in 1991 we established the Raymond Gledhill TC in Rome. Initially our efforts centered around group work as we tried to help patients break away from their "sick" role. We did this by enabling them to find ways to empower them with more responsibilities and chores within the TC and by actively working together to make consensus-driven choices that created a safe environment. Over time, demand for treatment diverted more and more from chronic psychotic illnesses to mood and personality disorders, often associated with the effects of drug abuse, and this influenced our approach and our need to acquire new and different skills.

Because I had previous training there, I looked to the United Kingdom as an excellent source from which to draw information and practical know-how. I had learned of an approach called *Sociotherapy* (Whiteley, 1986), which had been introduced by Maxwell Jones in the 1960s at the Henderson Hospital for psychopaths and severely disturbed borderline personality disorders and which had proved to be very effective (Dolan, Warren, Menzies, et al. 1996). Historically, Henderson Hospital is considered the mother of psychiatric TC approaches. The concept of the TC and its attenuated form—the therapeutic milieu—caught on after World War II and dominated the field of inpatient psychiatry throughout the 1960s in that country (Main, 1989). More recently, the development of "mini" therapeutic communities in the United Kingdom put the country at the cutting edge of the BPD recovery movement.

In 1997, I attended a 3-day residential workshop called Living Learning Experience (LLE) in Kent, where I experienced the role of patient in a sociotherapeutic environment. It was here that I became better acquainted with the traditional TC residential approach for severe BPD based almost exclusively on group work (i.e., no one-to-one therapeutic relationship between therapists and patients).

## RATIONALE FOR INTEGRATING TREATMENTS WITH EMOTIONAL REGULATION TRAINING FOR BPD

What are the needs of these patients as a psychiatric category? Much can be learned from listening to what former patients have to say.

- "The truth is that before you change you do not know who you really are; what you really want."
- "As I always felt lonely and unsure of myself, I joined in and adapted to people like me. Drinks and drugs at the beginning were just an excuse to be with other people; later on they became my main preoccupation as 'addict' and the sense of feeling insecure and unsafe remained."
- "A borderline is terrified you might die if you feel too much pain, so you must act quickly."
- "Let's face it, doctor; we don't need medicines, we need limits . . . limits, yes, but with love!"

These statements provide a good indication of the major BPD problem areas and the inability of the patient to deal with the kind of emotional intensity that underlies impulsivity, fear of dying, unsuccessful social skills, and vacillating personal life pursuits. Emotional intensity leading to excessive forms of acting-out is very difficult to tackle, as it interferes with the therapeutic patient/therapist relationship; it makes mentalization impossible and leads to treatment drop-out. In other words, the needs of BPD patients suggest that for a treatment to be effective, the therapy should synergistically address the three main features of BPD: (1) cluster interpersonal relationships; (2) cluster affects/impulsivity; and (3) cluster self-image/identity.

We addressed these three clusters in typical residential TC style, with sociotherapy and psychotherapy. Psychotherapy is important primarily as a listening process with understanding coming from the therapists' interpretation. It facilitates trust and repairs attachment, both of which are necessary for a more stable emotional life and interpersonal relationships.

Sociotherapy, on the other hand, involves a more active process of role distribution, because it induces self-image and behavioral changes by allowing new and more satisfactory ways of coping with interpersonal interactions: "Sociotherapy is the re-learning of social roles and interpersonal behaviour through the experiencing of social interactions in a corrective environment" (Whiteley, 1986).

Our TC might benefit greatly by transforming its former milieu therapy into sociotherapy; however, I could see that the combination of social and psychotherapeutic approaches to the TC milieu did not adequately meet the "cluster affects/impulsivity" target of the new category of referrals; that is, people with complex needs and the tendency to self-medicate deep personal distress with alcohol and street drugs, justifying integrated forms of treatment (dual-diagnosis; Sciacca, 1991). The lack of effectiveness from the medical model's response to these new complex service demands put more pressure on our TC to harness its resilience and expertise to successfully engage with the new challenges posed by dual-diagnosis and severe personality disorders. New approaches were needed and I actively sought out practical tools for sociotherapy to work in synergy with other specialized, specific emotional-control training.

## COGNITIVE SCIENCES AND PSYCHODYNAMIC SYNERGY

My interest in BPD and the consequences of disorganized attachment and childhood traumas on the brain grew in parallel with new evidence of neuronal plasticity and the effects of new learning and repetition on the brain's capacity to modify circuits and synapses (Rakic, 2002). The growth of cognitive-behavioral therapies was shedding light on the effect of trauma on areas of the brain dealing with memory and frontal-cortex inhibiting-functions responsible for dissociation. In the majority of our BPD referrals one could identify previously unrecognized forms of posttraumatic stress disorder (PTSD) or significant childhood trauma in their past. This correlation with BPD is now sufficiently documented (Gunderson et al., 2013; Sack et al., 2013). Classen et al. (2006) proposed two types of personality disorders linked to PTSD depending on whether patterns of attachment were organized or not. This distinction is useful for the purpose of elaborating BPD therapeutic needs. Treatment plans should address attachment issues as well as undertaking better strategies to cope with impulsive/defensive reactions linked to trauma.

## LOOKING FOR THE "MISSING ELEMENT"

By the end of 2009, a significant number of our PD patients appeared to require special forms of trauma treatment; for example, eye movement desensitization therapy. When sociotherapy was developed in the 1960s, little was known about the brain's capacity to modify circuits responsible for emotional control through specific learning patterns and repetition. A form of social skills training was introduced by Stuart Whiteley, at the Henderson Hospital, who maintained that, "Normal development incorporates both individually felt emotional experiences—attachment and loss, coping with frustrations, expressing anger and enduring anxiety and despair—and more socially orientated and behavior, taking on responsibilities and assuming roles. Treatment should therefore take into account both psychotherapy and sociotherapy processes" (Whiteley, 1986).

Given our setting, and the patients' varying backgrounds, traditional TC sociotherapy and "learning from experience" could not be applied by the book. We came to realize how important it was for traumatized persons to have time to feel safe and confident enough to address painful and vivid memories. I still recall the feeling of helplessness I experienced as one resident struggled with her history of child abuse. During the group therapy sessions, it was plain to see her helplessness as the recall of her trauma kept coming up, especially now that her own daughter was the same age as she had been when her abuse began; she often needed extra time and support from other members at the end of a group session. Her suffering and anger not only seemed to paralyze her, but clearly affected other group members. Encouraging the patient on the path to self-awareness was necessary, but not sufficient to alter long-standing automatic negative patterns and dysfunctional reactions. Although well-intentioned, our approach was taking far too long to achieve tangible results in these patients even when they actually stayed long enough to complete the three phases of the program. The drop-out rate surpassed conservative expectations.

Another issue concerned older patients with a history of childhood abandonment. Not only were they unable to prevent themselves from acting out (e.g., storming out of the community in a dramatic huff), but when they later regained their composure, the realization of the effects of their uncontrolled bouts on the others in the group only served to increase their psychological pain.

I concluded that emotionally caused behaviors such as outbursts of anger or the inability to deal with frustration, could be better managed using specific cognitive strategies. I was of the opinion that traditional sociotherapy could be improved by teaching patients new ways to respond to the triggers of their dysfunctional automatic emotional reactions. In short, we had to find the missing element to improve their "cortical functions" and to seek this element through a cognitive-behavioral approach.

Teaching new coping strategies to people with emotional dysregulation and making sure they practice these strategies is essential for the road to recovery. Research supports the view that BPD is associated with a failure of fronto-limbic inhibitory function (Silbersweig et al., 2007). Traumatic experiences can also impair cortical inhibiting functions of control of lower parts of the brain governing emotions, mainly the amygdala (Quirk, et al., 2003). Therefore, traumatized patients and emotionally neglected people need strengthening of the cortical inhibiting functions of limbic regions such as the insula, amygdala, or anterior cingulate cortex, by learning new skills. It was reassuring to learn that I was not the only psychiatrist convinced that psychodynamic approaches and cognitive therapies should be integrated (Lewis, 2006). Travi et al. (2010) produced an interesting study that describes this kind of experiment in the psychiatric ward of Arezzo General Hospital where, together with his co-workers, he employed a group psycho-educational approach defined as "cognitive-behavior group therapy." The method was systematically applied from March 2004 to December 2009. Travi used five indicators of effectiveness: (1) participation in psycho-educational sessions by patients; (2) frequency of re-admission to hospital; (3) ward atmosphere; (4) frequency of aggressive and violent behavior; and (5) users' and family members' satisfaction with services in the ward. His study produced excellent results and stimulated my desire to learn more about his program. Eventually, I visited The Retreat in York, England which happens to be the first and oldest TC, set up by William Tuke in 1796. The Retreat is where psychiatrist Chris Holman, who directs the BPD unit, integrated the dialectical behavior therapy approach with a modified form of sociotherapy to adapt it to local hospital requirements of more effective treatment for severe BPD cases (Acorn Project, 2007).

## STEPPING INTO STEPPS

By chance, I came across a BPD-related blog where I read about the STEPPS program. The work by Blum et al. (2008) showed that patients receiving STEPPS along with their regular care experienced a wide range of improvements in their levels in depression, negative affect, disturbed cognitions, impulsivity, and overall interpersonal functioning. If I looked to STEPPS as a positive addition to our program, it was also because it would not interfere with our traditional sociotherapy format and would allow us to address the "cluster affects/impulsivity" of our patients with personality disorders without recourse to too many changes. I had spent years in search of suitable forms of cognitive tools and appropriate social skills training to integrate with sociotherapy in order to manage BPD patients. I felt that STEPPS was what I had been seeking.

## DIALECTICAL BEHAVIOR THERAPY VERSUS STEPPS

Before I learned of STEPPS, I had intended to replicate the model used at The Retreat in York and reproduce the Acorn Project at our own TC. At that time, the official DBT Training Course was too expensive, so I invited a psychologist who was expert in DBT to provide me and other staff members with some training.

With my background in psychoanalysis, I have to confess that I struggled with part of the training. Recalling my visit to The Retreat, I remembered my encounter with a patient who was about to be discharged—an intelligent woman of Anglo-Italian descent, with a secondary school diploma. As a BPD patient exposed to DBT treatment for nearly a year, she was more qualified than I in DBT. While she shared her DBT manual with me with enthusiasm, the extensive homework exercises, diagrams, and acronyms made me wonder how suitable DBT was for the patients in our TC. In view of the amount of homework and the many sessions to attend, I felt that those who wanted to pursue the entire 12-month DBT treatment must have unusually high levels of motivation. Nonetheless, I decided to let members of my staff continue their training lessons.

After completing the fourth and last module of the DBT course for my staff, our psychologist trainer moved to Tuscany, which meant there was no way we could now undergo the necessary supervision. My trained staff tried to apply the emotional regulation and interpersonal efficacy modules but, as I had suspected, soon realized they were too complex and lengthy for our residents. Whether because of the inability of our patients to deal with the amount of work, the DBT protocol mandated individual and group sessions that did not fit well with our sociotherapy format, or perhaps our staff's overly high expectations vis a vis the severely disturbed residents, we decided to set DBT aside. We felt that we needed to look further, and it seemed that STEPPS might fit our needs.

Compared with our earlier experience with social skills training, psychoeducational approaches, and DBT, STEPPS appeared promising for three reasons. First, it was based on an integrated systems-based framework that called for active support by fellow residents. Homework supervision could be carried out by fellow residents or by staff members other than psychologists, because the homework itself was both simple and of short duration. Importantly, family members would be able to learn ways to deal with their loved one's emotional intensity. Patients were expected to spend some time at home before finally being discharged, which would allow the family to practice their newly acquired skills and put them to the test. Second, the STEPPS program itself was relatively simple to learn and put into practice. This had the added bonus of making the training course shorter (only 20 weeks) and less expensive, thus giving patients the chance to have more training sessions if required, even in cases of premature discharge. Third, perhaps most important, STEPPS had been shown to improve mood and other affective symptoms, where DBT had been less effective (Rizvi, 2011).

In November 2009, I contacted Nancee Blum for information on training. She, along with Norm Bartels, Don St. John, and Bruce Pfohl, had developed the STEPPS manual. I was then put in contact with Renee Harvey, a consultant psychologist and STEPPS trainer from the United Kingdom, who agreed to help us implement STEPPS. I attended her "One-Day Introductory STEPPS Meeting" in Horsham, England a few months later, where she gave a presentation with slides, figures, and research findings. She also invited two enthusiastic former users to answer questions about their experience with the program and its advantages over the many other approaches they had tried during their many years of BPD treatment.

## THE APPLICATION OF THE ITALIAN VERSION OF STEPPS MANUAL IN A RESIDENTIAL TC

With help from other co-workers, I undertook the translation of the STEPPS manual into Italian. Acting on Nancee Blum's advice, we chose the UK adaptation of the text (2009), because it was more recent. We stayed as faithful as possible to the text, as well as to its layout. The translation was painstaking work, and the release of a second edition of the American version of the STEPPS Manual (Blum et al., 2012) meant that we had to repeat the process. As soon as the first draft was ready, we invited Renee Harvey to present an intensive training workshop in May 2011.

We launched our first 20-week course in September of the same year. Barbara Sartini, our rehabilitation technician (a profession akin to the British occupational therapist) followed the manual instructions together with Daniel Isopo, another TC worker. We wished to test the impact of STEPPS on our patients by scrupulously following the manual. We selected only patients with BPD for our first course, and because we had only a few patients with this diagnosis, we asked our nearest branch to allow three of their BPD patients to join the STEPPS course and act as though they were outpatients. A total of eight participants met regularly for the 2-hour sessions for 20 weeks. The meetings took place in an area set aside for this purpose in the main TC building, where a separate entrance reproduced exactly what one would expect for an outpatient program. As STEPPS was specifically designed for outpatient service users, we wanted to explore the effect of our training on the residents (four from the main TC building and three from nearby) by letting them behave as though they were outpatients.

## ADAPTATION AND INITIAL RESISTANCE

A pivotal component of the STEPPS program is for users to identify a reinforcement team, that is, a support network of people on hand in times of crisis and who will serve as the person's homework coach. These people can be friends, family members, professional staff of the treatment systems, or other providers. In our case, the residents decided to rely on one another as well as the TC workers to make up the reinforcement team. The three members from the other TC branch were assigned support by a worker who had attended Harvey's STEPPS course. The result was encouraging, and feedback from participants at the end of the 20-week course was quite positive. It was touching to see how certain participants ascribed great importance to receiving a certificate of completion ("Diploma"). It was the first time for many that they felt as though they had accomplished something worthwhile.

Emboldened by the success of this first course, we organized another, aimed this time for our entire resident body, including those not diagnosed with BPD. The results showed that STEPPS could be employed successfully, even in people who did not meet full BPD criteria. Not all TC workers were convinced, however,

despite these initial encouraging results. Their skepticism was leveled at the dubi-
ous recourse of enforcing cognitive behavioral practices with patients who, so far
as their training in psychodynamics pointed out, would have benefitted primarily from mentalization and secure attachment. Another issue was the perceived
contradiction that staff members were being asked to study STEPPS in a working environment that normally relied upon mutual agreement. Some staff members were highly critical of my proposal, which they saw as being at odds with
the traditional approach based on consensus and empowerment and, as a result,
their resistance increased. One worker in particular felt the TC was betraying the
rationale of its psychological framework, especially the principle (one of the four
basic TC principles) of culture of inquiry (Campling, 2001) upon which sociotherapy relies, and walked out. Other workers were more flexible and less resistant
to STEPPS. In witnessing the patients' positive responses, they were able to see
that the program was compatible with the psychodynamic TC system of recovery,
based on detecting the unconscious destructive forces at work.

It gradually became apparent that the STEPPS program was capable of integrating methodological constructs such as mindfulness, schema recognition (with its
connected automatic negative thoughts), and verbalization of emotions—all of
which contribute synergistically to the improvement of self-awareness and effective self-control. At the time, because we had no clear evidence that this new tool
could indeed be gainfully adapted to our approach, I decided that the best course
of action was to verify how welcome STEPPS had been at our TC. At the end of
the second cycle, I requested that the participants complete a questionnaire and
give their impression of how STEPPS was impacting our sociotherapy program.

## ACCEPTANCE BY PATIENTS

The following questionnaire was distributed to all residents (see Figure 6.1).

1. Should we continue to keep STEPPS in our TC program? Yes. . . . No. . . .

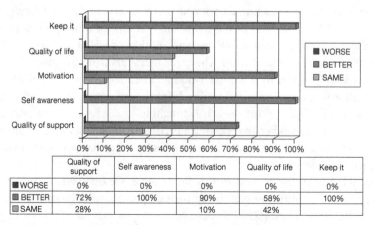

| | Quality of support | Self awareness | Motivation | Quality of life | Keep it |
|---|---|---|---|---|---|
| ■ WORSE | 0% | 0% | 0% | 0% | 0% |
| ■ BETTER | 72% | 100% | 90% | 58% | 100% |
| ■ SAME | 28% | | 10% | 42% | |

**Figure 6.1** Responses to Survey of TC Residents about the Usefulness of STEPPS

Now that you have done the STEPPS training, how would you rate the following indicators? Answer: the same, worse, or better:

2. Quality of life in the TC
3. Motivation
4. Self-awareness
5. Quality of support provided to you by the TC
6. Which part of STEPPS did you find most useful?
7. What would you change in order to allow a better use of STEPPS in the community?
8. Do staff members use the same STEPPS language?

As can be seen from Fig. 6.2, the answer to "Which part of STEPPS was most useful?" was "Challenging filters & ANTs" (automatic negative thoughts); this was followed by "Stop and manage." The former derives from schema therapy, the latter from the field of mindfulness. Both highlight how Blum's idea of integrating various tried-and-tested systems of care in a progressive, structured fashion is successful and mutually reinforcing.

The answer to "What would you change in order to allow a better use of STEPPS in the Community?" was "nothing" or "I don't know," indicating that none of the 20 topics felt redundant, unwelcome, or unneeded. "Do staff members consistently use STEPPS-related language in their dealings with you?" The answer to this was inconsistent, as people often left the "Yes" or "No" space blank. This was hardly surprising in view of the initial lukewarm interest shown by some TC workers toward the new approach. In spite of this, catchwords such as "pots" (the diagram referred to when learning how to evaluate and self-assess the Emotional Intensity Continuum during or soon after an episode), filters, and ANT (automatic negative thoughts) began to come up more and more often in staff and community meetings.

Useful Tools Preference

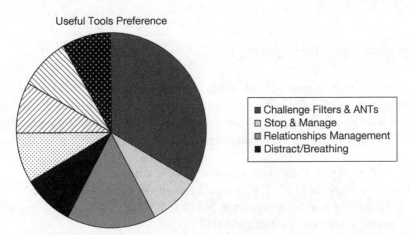

**Figure 6.2** Pie Chart Showing Distribution of Responses to "Which Part of STEPPS Was Most Useful?"

In response to the question, "Have you noticed any changes in our TC after the STEPPS course and if so, what?" the answers could be clustered as follows:

1. More meaningful activities and "group cohesion" (a more tightly knit group)
2. Increased motivation levels among residents
3. Increased mutual support
4. Growth in trust, empathy, and understanding of self (self-awareness)
5. Improved understanding of shared vocabulary for better communication with staff

All this showed that STEPPS had a positive impact on the TC. By the third course, even a physician (and TC worker by vocation) wanted to go through the experience herself. At the end of the 20-week module she said, "I believe everyone here should do the course, regardless of the diagnostic label; this helps everybody to live better." Her contribution validated the confirmation by former patients that STEPPS was beneficial to all concerned. Two months later, another former patient said to me, "You know, a year ago I was seriously thinking of leaving the community and the only thing that kept me here at the time was STEPPS! I could not allow myself to miss out on it."

By now, the relevance of STEPPS for our residents was unquestionable. The need to carry out this training more often meant that we had revise our timetable of weekly activities. We introduced new therapeutic sessions, bearing in mind the STEPPS modules. These weekly sessions were counting and breathing relaxation, mindfulness exercises, body work to improve bodily emotional appraisal, schema therapy to deepen our understanding and management of negative filters (for example, by talking to the schema in an "empty chair"), as well as creativity inspired sessions to enrich our collection of positive, "safe-place" images to turn to mentally in times of need. Figure 6.3 outlines our working week adaptation to the STEPPS module.

## ACCEPTANCE BY TC STAFF

Patients as participants seemed satisfied. What about staff? What were their thoughts about STEPPS? What impressions did they glean from the patients' attitudes after its introduction? A questionnaire with the following questions was distributed to all TC workers soon after the third STEPPS cycle.

1. In light of your daily observation of patients' attitudes following the introduction of STEPPS, how would you rate its usefulness for them? Please give your score on a scale from 1 to 7, where 1 = Totally useless, a waste of time and 7 = Indispensable tool.
2. How useful do you think STEPPS-Sociotherapy integration is for TCs? Please give your score on a scale from 1 to 7 as in #1.

| Time | Monday | Tuesday | Wednesday | Thursday | Friday | Saturday | Sunday |
|---|---|---|---|---|---|---|---|
| Ore 8.00 | Breakfast | Breakfast | Breakfast | Breakfast | Breakfast | Breakfast | |
| 9.00–10.00 | CM CHECK-IN | CM CHECK-IN  Case Review | CM CHECK-IN | CM CHECK-IN | CM CHECK-IN | CM CHECK-IN | CM CHECK-IN |
| 10.30–11.35 | Social Skills Training (DISTANCING)  OR – | Studying Emotions (COMMUNICATE) | Crafts Marmelade | | Social Skills Training (CHALLENGE A.N.T.)  OR | | |
| 10.30–11.35 | Group Psychotherapy | | Artistic expressions (DISTRACT) | Sport | Group Psychotherapy | | |
| | | Medications | | | | | |
| | | Large CT Meeting | PREPARATION GROUP | | | | |
| 13.15 | Lunch | STAFF | Lunch | Lunch | Lunch | Lunch | |
| | Free Time | Free Time | Free Time | Free Time | Free Time | Free Time | |
| 16.–17.15 | Artistic expressions (DISTRACT) | Programs Group & Community improvement | STEPPS COURSE | Schema Therapy Group (FILTERS CHALLENGING) | Problem Solving – Task Group (MANAGE) | MEANINGFUL FILM | |
| 18–18.30 | CM CHECK-OUT | CM CHECK-OUT | CM CHECK-OUT | CM CHECK-OUT | CM CHECK-OUT | | |
| 18.30–18.45 | Diary Homework | Diary Homework | Diary Homework | Diary Homework | Diary Homework | | |
| | Free Time | Free Time | Free Time | Free Time | Free Time | Free Time | Free Time |
| 20:00 | Dinner | Dinner | Dinner | Dinner | Dinner | Dinner | Dinner |
| 23:00 | Closure | Closure | Closure | Closure | Closure | Closure | Closure |

Figure 6.3  Weekly Schedule for STEPPS Activities Adapted for the TC

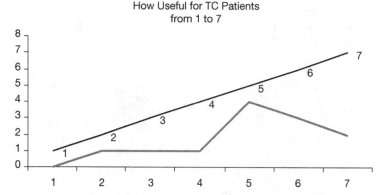

**Figure 6.4** Responses regarding the usefulness of STEPPS to TC Residents

3. Following the introduction of STEPPS in our TC, would you say that the overall quality of life for the residents has (a) stayed the same; (b) changed a little bit; (c) improved somewhat; or (d) significantly changed for the better?
4. Would you be willing to undergo the full STEPPS cycle as a participant? Yes; No.

The answers to the four questions are shown in Figs. 6.4, 6.5, 6.6, and 6.7,. We also asked participants to describe how they experienced the adjustments to the program that were necessary as a result of STEPPS and how they reacted to the training; we also encouraged them to provide suggestions on what steps should be taken to improve the integration of STEPPS into our TC.

All mentioned experiencing some difficulties at the beginning in having to adapt to STEPPS-derived concepts and language that, of course, were new to them. Virtually all expressed satisfaction and appreciation of our trainers while stressing the importance of practicing more pot forms and challenging filters.

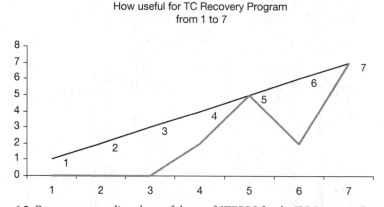

**Figure 6.5** Responses regarding the usefulness of STEPPS for the TC Recovery Program

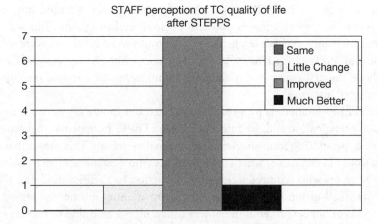

**Figure 6.6** Responses by TC Staff Regarding Quality of Life in TC Residents Who Had Participated in STEPPS

After the third course, it is worth noting that the majority of staff members placed the implementation of STEPPS as a recovery tool for psychiatric rehabilitation at "nearly indispensable" (score 6), and one person even considered it "indispensable" (score 7). It is worth mentioning that the two night-shift workers, who see less of the patients, also gave the same answers. This further confirmed the general perception that the introduction of STEPPS to our TC program was helpful and was delivering scalable results.

## FURTHER ADJUSTMENTS

After the fourth course, our confidence increased to the point where we felt there was room for additional adjustments. For example, ongoing psychoeducational weekly group sessions called Gruppo Programmi were implemented, consisting of personalized programs for individual priority needs. Because the second part

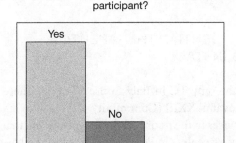

**Figure 6.7** Responses by TC Staff Regarding Whether They Would Participate in STEPPS

of STEPPS (lessons 13 to 20) deals with behavioral issues, we used this section to improve the organization of patients' personalized programs. This was done by incorporating its schedules, grids, and diagrams. As a result, we were able not only to shorten the inpatient cycle for future users, but also to concentrate more heavily on the first part of the manual that emphasizes the effective management of emotional intensity.

Our STEPPS facilitators proposed that because our inpatients were accustomed to group participation and the daily 30-minute STEPPS homework, they would be capable of benefitting from shorter cycles in smaller groups. This meant that more cycles would be available, whether for patients who needed refresher sessions or for newcomers who required a timely introduction to STEPPS modules. During the daily small-group homework session, one patient at a time was tasked with sharing his or her review with the others concerning which skill or tool was most valuable from among the following: (a) "pot form"; (b) stepping back and breathing; (c) filters and challenging automatic negative thoughts; (d) communicating emotions with words; (e) weekly applied skills review. It is worth noting that those more experienced patients who had grasped the usefulness of such skills realized that they worked wonders for their self-awareness and were more than willing to review them daily in small groups with other residents. These are people who are now being labelled in the United Kingdom as "experts by experience."

A former TC member who regarded the "pot form" as very useful for her self-control joined our weekend training course to share how STEPPS continued to be of help to her. She stressed that the repetition of numerous pot forms was a very effective way to get to know oneself more intimately. Through this tool she came to realize that she need not define herself merely as a mentally ill person, the way she used to think of herself when she was released from the psychiatric ward, but that she was a person. Now that she was a person, she had complex problems to tackle and skills to learn and practice and she had been able to acquire this knowledge via the work she had covered at the TC, including the functional social role playing. Her endorsement is testament to the powerful synergy that can occur between sociotherapy (with its functional role distribution in the TC) and the cognitive approach in the quest to track down people's personal and more private reactions when they are cast in roles different from the "sick role" they had been labelled with and become accustomed to.

## STEPPS IN RESIDENTIAL THERAPEUTIC COMMUNITIES IN ITALY

Presently, ours is the only TC in Italy to use STEPPS. There is a charity called Comunità Papa Giovanni XXIII (Community of Pope John XXIII), offering social and psychiatric services to the poor and the downtrodden, that provides psychiatric residential recovery centers in Rimini and Vicenza and has received sociotherapy training in the last five years, and more recently STEPPS training, from our organization. In the past, the few Italian TC directors who, like myself, thought it necessary to add the cognitive approach to the treatment of dysfunctional behaviors in residential settings had decided to opt for DBT ["Crest" Milano; "Casa di Lodesana"—Fidenza (Pr); "Villa dei Pini" Firenze]. Interest in cognitive behavioral approaches for BPD, other than DBT, is limited because of few published research studies in other areas. Randomized controlled trials (RCTs) are difficult to conduct. Nonetheless, apart from DBT, no other cognitive approaches for BPD had been developed, tested, and shown to be effective until Blum et al. (2008) demonstrated the efficacy of STEPPS for people with BPD. The popularity of DBT is such that even as late as 2009, the NICE Clinical Guideline (NICE, 2009), offered the following recommendation: "In the case of women with a borderline personality disorder for whom reducing recurrent self-harm is a priority, consider a comprehensive dialectical behavior therapy (DBT) programme" (p. 21).

The only TC we have trained so far in the STEPPS and Integrated Sociotherapy (SIS) approach is part of the Community of Pope John XXIII. As a member of the International Associations of the Faithful, it is an association of the Faithful of Pontifical Right and active in 26 countries. It has a staff of 138 and 2,174 members. Worldwide, the Association has opened 520 centers, 298 of which are family homes, and runs several projects to assist vulnerable people with various needs.

For years we had been running LLE-style residential training workshops for staff of this organization. In October 2013, we were asked to train 10 staff members to use STEPPS. In November, three facilitators trained by us ran their first 20-week course with a small group of patients (two TC residents and four outpatients). It was completed in April 2014. The facilitators reported to us that none of the participants in the group had pure BPD. One dropped out after a few sessions while another had to leave due to a job offer that she did not want to turn down. The next two inpatients used other TC residents for their reinforcement team. One outpatient chose her sister and her neighbor. The last member of the group, who was rather withdrawn and suspicious and chose never to reveal his surname, was described as being the most meticulous and efficient member. What was important for us was the enthusiasm proclaimed by the participants at the end of the course and likewise that of the facilitators, who told us how excited they were at the idea of launching another STEPPS course very soon. "We have recruited twelve participants already and many more are queuing up! . . . we are so very excited, nobody could stop us now." "We are waiting for STAIRWAYS in a year's time."

All this is very promising for the promotion of STEPPS in Italy. Its credibility can only increase with each success and a large role in its promotion will be played by the direct testimony of former TC residents, whether BPD or not, who have successfully completed the program and can attest to its efficacy. I felt a great deal of responsibility for translating the manual so that it was easy to understand and put into practice, as well as pioneering its use in Italy. I want to be certain that Italian facilitators will feel confident about using it from the very start.

The positive feedback from both patients and trainees encourages us to move quickly onto the next stage, which is to disseminate STEPPS among Italian professionals, showing them how it is possible to integrate this powerful rehabilitation

tool with the traditional TC approach. Given the positive outcome of our exploration of its potential, we now feel entitled to coin a definition for this approach, and
that is "STEPPS Integrated Sociotherapy" (SIS). We made a formal presentation of
STEPPS and SIS to a number of psychiatrists and members of the Italian Society
for Psychosocial Rehabilitation (SIRP) at the National Congress held in Salerno
in September 2014.

## THE STEPPS MANUAL AND TRAINING

Great care went into the translation of the manual, and although some paraphras-
ing was necessary, we did our best to closely replicate the original format. We
decided to print only the facilitator's part of the manual; the remaining four parts
were reproduced in PDF format on a CD that was included with the manual.
It is worth mentioning that Italian consumers/facilitators with no cognitive-
behavioral training or understanding had some difficulty with the "pot form,"
the diagram referred to when learning how to evaluate and self-assess the EIC
during or soon after an episode. We all know how pivotal this diagram is for the
STEPPS approach, and how much it is appreciated by the patients themselves.
Our STEPPS trainers therefore went to some lengths in presenting a more user-
friendly explanation of the diagram in keeping with the Italian language and cultural background; for example using colored cartoons of expressed emotions and
dramatic representations of role-playing.

We followed the advice of our Dutch colleagues, who have more than 10 years
of STEPPS training experience, about the best way to allot the manual the importance it deserves and how to undertake the most efficient teaching method. The
training consisted of an intensive 2-day workshop and participants are awarded a
certificate upon completion. The number of participants ranged from 6 to 10 and
never exceeded 12. The frequency of these workshops initially was twice a year.
Diplomas are handed out to facilitators only when they have successfully undertaken two STEPPS 20-week courses with their patients. We also realized very
early on in our experience how important the addition of role playing proved to
be for the trainee, as well as their rehearsal of how to deliver the first few STEPPS
lessons to participants. Role playing was considered fun and received the top rating in these workshops.

## RESEARCH ISSUES

While the effectiveness of STEPPS has undoubtedly been confirmed (van Wel
et al., 2006; Blum et al., 2008; Bos et al., 2010; Bos et al., 2011), research is still
required regarding its integration with sociotherapy in residential centers.
Traditional training of TC workers is likely to be influenced by facts and concepts derived from our experience of integrating STEPPS in residential settings.
We are at the stage where performance levels of this integration have yet to be

demonstrably outlined, and we can only hope that research will develop in this direction. The only research study to date is that carried out by Boccalon et al. (2012) on an inpatient unit in Milan (see Chapter 7). The study showed that this integration has great promise for BPD, particularly in severe cases exacerbated by co-morbidities, as STEPPS can be effective in reducing the number of both self-destructive behavior episodes and hospitalization rates.

All psychiatric TCs in Italy treat patients with psychosis and personality disorders. Our experience has shown that STEPPS is a versatile tool, suitable for both patient and staff needs, and that it has a significant impact on the recovery process in residential settings. The implementation of STEPPS goes beyond assisting individuals to deal with depressive moods, suspiciousness, or other psychological distress more effectively; it also sets up a common language that facilitates communication overall and throughout the TC. As a result, it serves to foster the concept I defined as *cohesion* in my book *"La comunità psicoterapeutica. Cultura, strumenti, tecnica"* (Lombardo, 2007, pp. 197–201). In this book, *cohesion* is flanked by *empathy* and *norms* (my so-called NEC Formula), and all three tenets interact to secure a balanced *therapeutic atmosphere* in residential settings.

Another important aspect of a common language is that it gives patients a far greater chance of being "heard" even when they are in the throes of an intense bout, threaten to leave, engage in harming themselves or act aggressively or otherwise frighten people. The gentle reminder that they can challenge their filter activation for dealing with the associated distorted thoughts helps maintain contact with the person even at the height of a meltdown. Patients are encouraged to carry the STEPPS skills memory cards with them at all times, and to turn to them when they fall prey to an episode of intense emotional activation. We have had resounding proof of how SIS can effectively operate in reducing levels of aggression, improving the ability to tolerate individual episodes, and raising the quality of mutual support. All these factors are of indubitable benefit on rates of clinical effectiveness, which then translates into reduced costs, reduced medication needs, shortened length of stay and, and last but definitely not least, lasting improved quality of life after discharge. All of these factors warrant further research.

It is our view that, in the future, the curriculum for health professionals such as occupational therapists, psychiatric rehabilitation technicians, psychologists, psychotherapists, and psychiatrists requires a course on STEPPS as a fundamental recovery tool. For the moment, we can only hope that more TCs will integrate STEPPS into their clinical work in the near future so that a greater number of people can benefit from its powerful effects and learn to value it, just as we valued it from the very beginning.

## REFERENCES

Acorn   Project.   (2007).   http://www.theretreatyork.org.uk/services/specialist-adult-services/the-acorn-programme.html

Blum, N., Bartels M. A., St. John, D., & Pfohl, B. (2012). *Systems Training for Emotional Predictability and Problem Solving. A group program for the borderline personality disorder.* 2nd ed. Manual available on CD-ROM from Blum's Books.

Blum, N., Pfohl, B., St. John, D., Stuart, S., McCormick, B., Allen, J., Arndt, S., & Black, D. W. (2008). Systems Training for Emotional Predictability and Problem Solving (STEPPS) for outpatients with borderline personality disorder: A randomized controlled trial and 1-year follow-up. *American Journal of Psychiatry, 165*, 468–478.

Boccalon, S., Alesiani, R., Giarolli, L., Franchini, L., Colombo, C., Blum, N., & Fossati, A. (2012). Systems Training for Emotional Predictability and Problem Solving (STEPPS): Theoretical model, clinical application, and preliminary efficacy data in a sample of inpatients with personality disorders in comorbidity with mood disorders. *Journal of Psychopathology, 18*, 335–343.

Bos, E. H., van Wel, E. B., Appelo, M. T., & Verbraak, M. J. P. M. (2011). Effectiveness of Systems Training for Emotional Predictability and Problem Solving (STEPPS) for borderline personality disorder in a "real-world" sample: Moderation by diagnosis or severity? *Psychotherapy and Psychosomatics, 80*, 173–181.

Bos, E. H., van Wel, E. Bas, Appelo, M. T., & Verbraak, M. J. P. M. (2010). A Randomized controlled trial of a Dutch version of Systems Training for Emotional Predictability and Problem Solving for borderline personality disorder. *Journal of Nervous & Mental Disease, 198*(4), 299–304.

Burti, L. (2001). Italian psychiatric reform 20 plus years after. *Acta Psychiatrica Scandinavica, Supplementum 410*, 41–46.

Campling, P. (2001). Therapeutic community. *Advances in Psychiatric Treatment, 7*, 365–372.

Classen, C. C., Pain, C., Field, N. P., & Woods, P. (2006). Posttraumatic Personality Disorder: A Reformulation of Complex Posttraumatic Stress Disorder and Borderline Personality Disorder. *Psychiatric Clinics of North America, 29*(1), 87–112.

De Girolamo, G., Picardi, A., Santone., G., Falloon, I., Morosini., P., Fioritti., A., Micciolo., R., PROGRES Group. (2005). The severely mentally ill in residential facilities: a national survey in Italy". Psychological Medicine, *35*, 421–431.

Dolan, B., Warren, D., Menzies, D., & Norton, K. (1996). Cost-offset following specialist treatment of severe personality disorders. *Psychiatric Bulletin, 20*, 413–417.

Gunderson, J. G., Weinberg, I., & Choi-Kain, L. (2013). *Borderline Personality Disorder. FOCUS*, 11,129–145.

Lewis, L. (2006). Enhancing mentalizing capacity through dialectical behavior therapy skills training and positive psychology. In J. G. Allen & P. Fonagy (Eds.), *Handbook of mentalization-based treatment* (pp. 171–182). Chichester, England: Wiley Ltd.

Lombardo, A. (2007). *La comunità psicoterapeutica. Cultura, strumenti, tecnica.* Milan, Italy: Franco Angeli Editore II Edizione aggiornata, pp.197–201.

Main, T. (1989). *The Ailment and other psychoanalytic essays.* London, England: Free Association Books.

NICE Clinical Guideline 78 (2009). Borderline personality disorder: Treatment and management. National Institute for Health and Clinical Excellence. http://www.nice.org.uk/nicemedia/pdf/CG78NICEGuideline.pdf

Quirk, G. J., Likhtik, E., Pelletier, J. G., & Pare, D. (2003). Stimulation of medial prefrontal cortex decreases the responsiveness of central amygdala output neurons. *Journal of Neuroscience, 23*, 8800–8807.

Rakic, P. (2002). Neurogenesis in adult primate neocortex: An evaluation of the evidence. *Nature Reviews Neuroscience, 3*, 65–71.

Rizvi, S. L. (2011). Treatment failure in dialectical behavior therapy. *Cognitive and Behavioral Practice, 18*, 403–412.

Sack, M., Sachsse, U., Overkamp, B., & Dulz, B. (2013). Trauma-related disorders in patients with borderline personality disorders. Results of a multicenter study. *Nervenarzt, 84*, 608–614.

Sciacca, K. (1991). *An integrated treatment approach for severely mentally ill individuals with substance disorders.* New Directions for Mental Health Services, No. 50, Chapter 6: San Francisco, CA: Jossey-Bass.

Silbersweig, D., Clarkin, J. F., Goldstein, M., Kernberg, O. F., Tuescher, O., Levy, K. N., Brendel, G. . . . Stern, E. (2007). Failure of frontolimbic inhibitory function in the context of negative emotion in borderline personality disorder. *American Journal of Psychiatry, 164*, 1832–1841.

Tansella, M. (1986). Community psychiatry without mental hospitals—the Italian experience: A review. *Journal of the Royal Society of Medicine, 79*, 664–669.

Travi, M., Cappuccini, M., Pinzaglia, L. Serafini, U. & Cesari, G. (2010). Valutazione nell'SPDC di Arezzo di "L'Intervento Cognitivo-Comportamentale di Gruppo in SPDC". *Nuova Rassegna di Studi di Psichiatria*, (1), 1–10.

Van Wel, B., Kockmann, I., Blum, N., Pfohl, B., Black, D.W., & Heesterman, W. (2006). STEPPS group treatment for borderline personality disorder in The Netherlands. *Annals of Clinical Psychiatry, 18*, 63–67.

Whiteley, J. S. (1986). Sociotherapy and psychotherapy in the treatment of personality disorder: discussion paper. *Journal of the Royal Society of Medicine, 79*, 721.

# 7

# Introducing STEPPS on an Inpatient Unit in Italy

ANDREA FOSSATI, ROBERTA ALESIANI,
SILVIA BOCCALON, LAURA GIAROLLI,
SERENA BORRONI, AND ANTONELLA SOMMA ■

## INTRODUCTION

Borderline personality disorder (BPD) is a common mental disorder associated with high rates of suicide, severe functional impairment, high rates of comorbid mental disorders, intensive use of treatment, and high costs to society (Leichsenring et al., 2011). Available evidence suggests that BPD is more stable than mood disorders but less consistent over time than previously thought (e.g., Gunderson et al., 2003; Skodol et al., 2005b; Zanarini et al., 2006; Sanislow et al., 2009). In particular, BPD features tend to decline over time (e.g., Zanarini et al., 2006), but this process does not imply a parallel improvement of BPD subjects in their psychosocial functioning. BPD subjects have more functional impairment and higher use of treatment than do subjects suffering from major depression (Bender et al., 2001; Skodol et al., 2002). Although some BPD subjects may have good psychosocial functioning (26%), most of them (80%) lose this level of functioning over time and do not regain it (Zanarini et al., 2010).

This point has major implications for treating subjects with BPD. On the one hand, the reduction in the number of diagnostic criteria over time does not negate the need for treatment as the borderline patient ages, because psychosocial functioning typically does not improve over time. At the same time, the deterioration in psychosocial functioning also limits the person's financial resources. This outcome limits the ability of many BPD patients to pay for costly therapies. Thus, the availability of treatment programs for BPD that do not place an economic burden on BPD patients and are designed to help BPD patients with problem solving in their daily life is clinically relevant, particularly in the treatment of older and mostly disadvantaged BPD patients.

There are several evidence-based psychotherapies whose efficacy in treating BPD has been shown in randomized clinical trials (Leichsenring et al., 2011). These therapies are beneficial with respect to clinically relevant symptoms (e.g., deliberate self-harm, suicidal behavior, frequency of hospital admissions, depressive symptoms, general symptom distress, drop-out rate, etc.), although they do not lead to remission in most patients. Yet despite their efficacy in treating BPD, these psychotherapies share limitations that may hamper their availability to particular subgroups of patients. One concern is that the treatments are costly and involve significant therapist training, which limits their usefulness (Blum et al., 2002). Moreover, they require extended commitment over time and regular attendance to sessions; these requirements may exceed the available personal and psychosocial resources of most compromised BPD patients.

The relative instability of BPD criteria over time has another implication for clinical management of BPD patients that is frequently overlooked. With fewer symptoms over time, personality disorders become more highly correlated with each other and less distinct as individual disorders (Sanislow et al., 2009). In older patients, clinicians may prefer to focus on personality dimensions such as emotion dysregulation (Zanarini et al., 2007) and impulsivity (Links et al., 1999; McGlashan et al., 2005). These are core features of BPD and cut across several other personality disorders, rather than relying on diagnostic categories that may prove inadequate to capture BPD psychopathology. As a consequence, time-limited, inexpensive treatments that are targeted at emotion and behavior regulation may represent the treatment of choice for older BPD patients.

While impulsivity and emotion dysregulation represent two core features of BPD, recurrent suicidal threats or gestures are the symptom that probably makes the greatest demands on mental health resources (Paris, 2004). The risk of severe suicidal attempts—or even completed suicide—is known to increase when BPD co-occurs with major depression, depressive episodes during the course of bipolar I/II disorder, or substance dependence disorder.

BPD is frequently associated with comorbid axis I and axis II disorders (Grant et al., 2008; Lenzenweger et al., 2007; Skodol et al., 2005a); 84.5% of patients with BPD met criteria for having one or more 12-month axis I disorders, and 73.9% met criteria for another lifetime PD diagnosis (Grant et al., 2008; Lenzenweger et al., 2007). In particular, BPD is most frequently associated with mood disorders, anxiety disorders, and disorders associated with substance misuse (Grant et al., 2008; Lenzenweger et al., 2007; Skodol et al., 2005a); with a lifetime prevalence of 39%, posttraumatic stress disorder is common, but not universal in BPD patients (Grant et al., 2008).

We believe the high comorbidity of BPD should not be overlooked in clinical practice. When treating BPD patients with comorbid mental disorders (e.g., mood and anxiety disorders), clinicians should be sensitive to the following issues:

1. "Acute" symptoms frequently mediate the contact between the BPD patient and the clinician. In other words, BPD patients often seek help not for their BPD symptoms, but instead for accompanying major

depression or panic attacks. In fact, the patient may not be aware that he or she has BPD.

2. BPD patients with comorbid mental disorders may find it difficult to separate the impairment in daily life from the major depression from the impairment due to their BPD features.

3. BPD patients with co-occuring mental disorders may expect that the pharmacological treatment which may be effective for the co-occurring axis I disorder—or non-PD mental disorders in *DSM-5* (American Psychiatric Association, 2013) Section II jargon—should also lead to remission of their personal and interpersonal difficulties related to BPD.

4. BPD patients with comorbid non-PD mental disorders (e.g., bipolar disorder, major depression, panic disorder, etc.) need specific treatment of the co-occurring non-PD mental disorder; in this situation, effective management of the BPD should be integrated with the treatment for the co-occurring disorder; thus it is important that effective treatments for BPD do not disrupt the treatment of the non-PD mental disorder, but rather are complementary.

5. BPD patients with comorbid non-PD mental disorders may require hospital admissions because of the course and treatment of their co-occurring mental disorder, but they should avoid unnecessary hospital admissions which may be related to life difficulties associated with the BPD. In this situation, the phase of treatment in the inpatient unit may represent an important occasion not only for treating the non-PD mental disorder (e.g., bipolar disorder, major depression, panic disorder, etc.), but also for initiating treatment for the BPD, which should continue in the outpatient clinic after hospital discharge.

6. When mood disorders and substance use disorders are present, treatment of the BPD should place a special emphasis on emotion regulation and suicide prevention; a systems component can be useful here, that is, the patient and those within his or her system should be included.

The STEPPS program fits well with these goals.

## IMPLEMENTATION IN THE INPATIENT SETTING

Our team is specialized in diagnosing and treating PD patients with co-occurring mental disorder diagnoses and works in close connection with the Mood Disorder Inpatient Unit of the San Raffaele Hospital of Milano, Italy. Over the years, we have admitted many patients referred by physicians working in the Mood Disorder Inpatient Unit for psychotherapy treatment who shared the following common features:

1. They were inpatients in their 40s, 50s, or older, mostly women.
2. They were receiving appropriate pharmacological treatment for their mood disorder.

3. They met BPD criteria or manifested prominent BPD features that represented a major clinical problem, such as emotion dysregulation, impulsive behavior, unstable relationships, and anger outbursts.
4. They had poor insight regarding their BPD symptoms; patients considered their BPD features as a moral failing, or considered them as manifestations of their mood disorder.
5. They suffered from either major depression or bipolar disorder.
6. They made several suicide attempts before index admission unrelated to the course of their mood disorder.
7. They had been admitted previously to psychiatric inpatient units because of problematic behaviors (e.g., destroying things, suicidal gestures, physical fights, etc.) that appeared unrelated to their mood disorder.
8. BPD rather than mood disorder was the major cause of impairment in their global functioning.
9. They had a lengthy history of unsuccessful psychotherapy treatment.

These patients were pessimistic about benefitting from psychotherapy, while expressing disappointment with the pharmacological treatment because "medications only made depression less present in my life, but it did not solve any of my real problems." Many alternated between considering themselves as bad people who were not worth anything and feeling rageful and frustrated because of the raw treatment they had received in their lives. For many, despair was a shared feeling and suicide was "always a viable option; it is my emergency exit ... my triumph." Many faced divorce and/or had dysfunctional relationships with their relatives; loneliness was a common existential condition for the majority of them. Most had tried various psychotherapies over the years in an attempt to seek relief from their emotional pain, but none of these attempts was successful. This led many to consider themselves as damaged objects "that cannot be repaired; maybe, I should be simply dismissed." Many had not worked in years and faced severe economic difficulties.

Our goal was to help these patients not only to reduce their BPD symptoms, but also to improve their day to day functioning. We wanted them to know that it was not too late to consider the possibility of building a worthwhile life. We did not wish to expose these patients to a further therapeutic failure.

When we learned about the STEPPS program (Black et al., 2004; Blum et al., 2002; 2008), we recognized that STEPPS would suit our patients well. The program was economical, was explicitly designed to be added to existing treatment, was time-limited (our patients could see the results in months, rather than in years), had clearly defined goals and strategies, fostered the patients' commitment through "homework assignments" (e.g., cards, emotion diaries), helped the patients to generalize what has been discussed during STEPPS session topics to real-life situations, and was effective in reducing self-destructive behaviors and helping to stabilize emotional instability. But because STEPPS was developed as an outpatient program for treating BPD, we had to modify it in order to start the program during an inpatient stay (about 1 month) and to complete it after hospital discharge.

## MODIFICATIONS/TRANSLATION TO STEPPS

We translated the STEPPS manual into Italian and, with the help of Nancee Blum, we modified the program to fit the needs of our borderline inpatients with co-occurring mood disorder diagnoses. In particular, the STEPPS program was adapted as follows:

1. The psychoeducational intervention was started during the hospital stay after mood disorder symptoms had improved in order to promote patients' insight and to increase motivation.
2. Session frequency was increased from once to twice weekly and each session length was reduced to 45 minutes from 2 hours. The logic behind this modification was to increase the number of days during a week in which patients felt actively engaged in a group and to reduce abandonment fears during the days between sessions.
3. The overall number of sessions was increased from 20 to 30.

Our BPD patients with co-occurring mood disorders were frequently in their 50s, and most had histories of several unsuccessful psychotherapy trials. These experiences led them to be skeptical of entering another treatment program. Moreover, the majority were concerned about the cost of psychotherapy. Although several studies documented the efficacy of the STEPPS program in addition to other treatments for BPD (see Chapter 2), no studies were available on the efficacy of the STEPPS as a stand-alone treatment. Nonetheless, research evidence showed that skills-training was an important element to successful treatment (Shearin & Linehan, 1994). Thus, we chose to implement STEPPS as a stand-alone treatment for our BPD inpatients with co-occurring mood disorders.

We started our first STEPPS inpatient group in March 2009. It should be emphasized that our patients participated in the STEPPS program as the only treatment for BPD symptoms, but received routine psychiatric treatment for their mood disorder. Monitoring the efficacy of the STEPPS in our inpatient group and answering the question, "Does STEPPS work also as a stand-alone treatment for BPD?" were priority issues.

## EXPERIENCE WITH STEPPS

Based on these considerations, it is difficult to disentangle our clinical experience with STEPPS from research. In a sense, the clinical needs of our patients informed our research questions, and research findings guided our clinical applications of STEPPS.

Our first experience with STEPPS was a group of severely impaired BPD inpatients with co-occurring mood disorders. In order to be referred to this "experimental" treatment for BPD, inpatients had to meet the following criteria:

1. A *DSM-IV* diagnosis of either major depression or bipolar disorder according to the clinicians who were following them in treatment
2. Receiving a successful mood stabilizing treatment for at least two years
3. A *DSM-IV* BPD diagnosis that explained most of the difficulties experienced by the patients when they were euthymic, according to the clinicians treating them for their mood disorder
4. A history of self-destructive behaviors unrelated to the mood disorder
5. At least two previously failed psychotherapy trials for BPD
6. IQ greater than 75
7. Informed consent to participate in the STEPPS program for inpatients

From March 2009 to March 2010, 20 inpatients (17 women, 3 men) with a mean (*SD*) age of 46.9 years (*SD* = 8.0) with BPD and a co-occurring mood disorder who met all the inclusion criteria were recruited for the program. The mean number of hospitalizations before entering STEPPS was 3.50 (*SD* = 2.3) and the mean (*SD*) number of suicidal attempts was 2.1, (*SD* = 2.7). The findings of this first experience with STEPPS in the inpatient setting have been published (Boccalon et al., 2012). Six months after completing the program, a number of encouraging findings were observed. Patients who completed the program showed a significant and progressive decrease in the number of self-destructive behaviors (ANOVA $\chi^2$ = 11.47, $p < 0.01$) and hospitalizations (ANOVA $\chi^2$ = 16.85, $p < 0.001$). ANOVA showed a significant decrease of the "distrust" cognitive filter over time ($\chi^2$ = 7.68, $p < 0.05$). In our BPD inpatient group, "distrust" was significantly associated with the number of BPD features ($r = 0.43$, $p < 0.01$) and with the number of suicide attempts before entering STEPPS ($r = 0.71$, $p < 0.01$). We also found that patients experienced a significant decrease in emotion dysregulation (i.e., Emotional Intensity Continuum scores) over time ($\chi^2$ = 58.71, $p < 0.005$).

However, the drop-out rate from STEPPS treatment was high (11 patients, or 55%). There were no differences in number of hospitalizations and self-destructive behaviors between subjects who completed the program and subjects who dropped out. The presence of more histrionic (Mann-Whitney $U$ = 23.5, $p < 0.01$) and passive-aggressive (Mann-Whitney $U$ = 32.5, $p < 0.05$) traits was the only significant difference between the two groups. We considered several possible explanations, ranging from the necessity of therapists to get fully acquainted with STEPPS, to the impact of the modifications that were introduced to the original STEPPS program. On the other hand, we realized that a 55% drop out rate in BPD patients who previously had a 100% drop-out rate actually represented a 45% increase in the success rate!

Starting with these considerations and the encouraging findings on the clinical usefulness of STEPPS for our BPD inpatients, we considered reducing the drop-out rate a priority for our team. We held regular team meetings in order to check for adherence to the STEPPS manual, and sought advice from Nancee Blum and others. Moreover, we thought it important to know the patients' factors influencing the drop-out rate in order to develop motivational interventions tailored specifically to the difficulties for inpatients with BPD which could improve the patient's commitment to STEPPS.

Based on our previous experience, we added a motivational intervention before starting STEPPS during the inpatient phase, particularly for those patients with co-occurring histrionic and passive-aggressive features. Moreover, we chose to focus on fine-tuned instruments for personality assessment to improve our understanding of factors related to dropping out.

Thus, during 2012 we selected a second sample of inpatients with BPD and co-occurring mood disorders who participated in the STEPPS program as the sole treatment for their BPD features (Alesiani et al., 2014). Participants who completed the program were followed for 12 months after successfully completing STEPPS. Consistent with our earlier experience, our sample included 32 subjects recruited from inpatients at the Mood Disorders Center, Department of Clinical Neurosciences, Hospital San Raffaele-Turro, Milan.

Inclusion criteria were: (1) a *DSM-IV* mood disorder (bipolar or unipolar) diagnosis by clinical judgement, in long-term treatment for at least 2 years; (2) a *DSM-IV* diagnosis of BPD or severe PD with prominent borderline traits and a history of suicidal attempts or self-harm acts, and emotional and behavioral dysregulation, even in the euthymic period; (3) failed 2 or more psychotherapy trials; (4) IQ over 75 or an education level beyond primary school; (5) ability to give informed consent. The sample consisted of 6 men (19%) and 26 women (81%); the age range was 26 to 63 years (mean = 44.4 years, SD = 9.3 years). Thirteen percent were college graduates, 62% had a high school qualification, and 25% had a junior high school qualification. Sixteen subjects (50%) had a diagnosis of unipolar disorder, 5 (16%) had bipolar disorder, type I, and 11 (34%) bipolar disorder, type II. Six subjects (19%) had a comorbid axis I disorder: anxiety disorder (3%) or substance abuse (16%). Thirteen subjects (41%) met criteria for narcissistic personality disorder, 10 (31%) BPD, 5 (16%) histrionic personality disorder, 4 (13%) passive–aggressive (negativistic) personality disorder, and 4 (13%) personality disorder not otherwise specified (the sum of the percentages was higher than 100% due to comorbidity of Axis II diagnoses). As was observed in our first STEPPS inpatient sample, all subjects had severe personality dysfunction, as indicated by a history of multiple hospitalizations (*M* = 3.7, *SD* = 2.6) and suicidal attempts before entering the STEPPS program (*M* = 2.3, *SD* = 2.5). For these reasons, they were considered complex and not suited for individual psychotherapy.

In this second study, we refined and extended the assessment battery. In line with our previous study, the axis I diagnoses were assessed by the clinical judgment of expert psychiatrists according to *DSM-IV* criteria. The axis II assessment was carried out during hospitalization after acute symptom remission. In addition to the clinical referral diagnosis of BPD, all subjects were interviewed with the Structured Clinical Interview for DSM-IV Axis II Personality Disorders (SCID-II; First et al., 1994) by trained raters blind to the study hypotheses. In addition, all subjects filled out self-report questionnaires including the Temperament and Character Inventory-Revised (TCI-R; Cloninger, 1999), the Barratt Impulsiveness Scale-11 (BIS-11; Patton, Stanford & Barratt, 1995), the Aggression

Questionnaire (AQ; Buss & Perry, 1992), the Attachment Style Questionnaire (ASQ; Feeney, Noller, Hanrahan, 1994), the Narcissistic Personality Inventory-40 (NPI-40; Raskin & Hall, 1979; Raskin & Terry, 1988), and the Hyper-Sensitive Narcissism Scale (HSNS; Hendin & Cheek, 1997). The self-report questionnaires were filled out four times: at baseline (T0), at end of treatment (T1), at 6-month follow-up (T2), and at 12-month follow-up (T3).

During treatment, patients were also required to complete a daily diary using the Emotional Intensity Continuum (EIC; Blum et al., 2012; Blum et al., 2008; Boccalon et al., 2012). The EIC is a self-report visual analog scale which operationalizes the concept of varying levels of emotional intensity on a 1–5 scale where 1 is feeling calm and relaxed and 5 is feeling out of control. The goal is for the patient to monitor their emotional intensity over time and to become more adept at predicting the course of an emotional episode and to identify and anticipate stressful situations that lead to destructive behaviors. They also learn specific skills to manage these situations. In this study, weekly averages data were evaluated through the single daily scores; then the longitudinal course of these weekly averages was observed.

The Filters Questionnaire (Blum et al., 2012), was administered at the beginning of the program, the end, and at 6 and 12 month follow-up. The Filters Questionnaire is a 60-item Likert-like self-report questionnaire that STEPPS participants use to identify negative and distorted thoughts based on 10 cognitive schemas: emotional deprivation, abandonment, mistrust, defectiveness/social undesirability, failure to achieve, vulnerability to harm and illness, self-sacrifice, subjugation, unrelenting standards and entitlement.

To confirm STEPPS efficacy at 12-months, we selected the following outcome criteria: (a) reduction in the number of hospitalizations related to self-harm acts; (b) reduction in the number of suicidal attempts; (c) reduction of the perceived emotional intensity levels and changes in scores on the Filters Questionnaire; and (d) changes in the scores on the self-report questionnaires.

To identify predictors of drop-out, we analyzed the following variables: (a) demographic features (sex, marital status, school level and job); (b) axis I diagnosis; (c) axis II categorical and dimensional diagnosis; and (d) personality features.

Efficacy data at 12-month follow-up in this sample were highly encouraging and consistent with those observed in our previous study (Boccalon et al., 2012). Inpatients who completed the program showed a significant decrease in the number of hospitalizations (ANOVA $\chi^2 = 18.7$, $p < 0.001$), both at the end of the treatment and at the 12-month follow-up. In particular, the mean ($SD$) number of hospitalizations changed from 4.1 ($SD = 2.7$), to 0.3 ($SD = 0.5$). ANOVA showed a significant decrease in suicidal attempts during and after STEPPS, until the 12-month follow-up ($\chi^2 = 16.071$, $p < 0.01$). The mean ($SD$) number of suicidal attempts changed from 3.2, ($SD = 3.8$), to 0 (i.e., we did not observe any suicide attempts during and after STEPPS). ANOVA showed a significant decrease in EIC scores during STEPPS, $\chi^2 = 74.0$, $p < 0.001$.

The actions we took to reduce the drop-out rate from STEPPS for inpatients based on the results of our previous study (Boccalon et al., 2012) were only partially successful. In this second sample, 17 (53%) subjects completed the treatment. The drop-out rate was 47%. Drop-out analysis showed no significant differences with regard to sex, marital status, school level or job between the inpatients who dropped out and those who completed the program. Likewise the Axis I and Axis II categorical diagnoses did not discriminate between the two groups. Those who dropped out from STEPPS were significantly different from those who completed the program on the following aspects:

1. Histrionic PD traits: inpatients who dropped out had a mean number of histrionic personality disorder traits ($M = 2.8$, $SD = 1.7$) that was significantly higher than the average number of traits observed among completers ($M = 1.6$, $SD = 1.5$), Mann-Whitney $U = 75.5$, $p < 0.05$.
2. TCI-R Self-Transcendence Total score: inpatients who dropped out from STEPPS showed an average Self-Transcendence total score of 80.8 ($SD = 13.2$; i.e., 75th percentile of the distribution of Self-Transcendence scores in the Italian normative sample), whereas the inpatients who completed the program showed an average Self-Transcendence total score of 64.0 ($SD = 14.9$; i.e., 33th percentile of the distribution of Self-Transcendence scores in the Italian normative sample). The difference in the Self-Transcendence total score between the two groups was highly significant (Mann-Whitney $U = 38.5$, $p < 0.005$).

In particular, Self-Forgetful was the Self-Transcendence facet most significantly discriminating the two groups (Mann-Whitney $U = 41.0$, $P = 0.004$). In particular, inpatients who dropped out showed an average score on the Self-Forgetful facet of 34.2 ($SD = 5.8$; i.e., between the 75th and 90th percentile of the distribution of Self-Forgetful facet scores in the Italian normative sample), whereas participants who completed STEPPS showed a mean Self-Forgetful score of 26.1 ($SD = 7.8$; i.e., between the 33th and 50th percentile of the distribution of Self-Forgetful facet scores in the Italian normative sample).

Thus, according to TCI-R scores, the average personality profile of inpatients who were unable to complete the STEPPS program was composed of the following temperament and character scores:

a. Novelty Seeking: $M = 105.4$, $SD = 9.4$ (i.e., 75th percentile of the distribution of Novelty Seeking scores in the Italian normative sample)
b. Harm Avoidance: $M = 114.9$, $SD = 12.6$ (i.e., 90th percentile of the distribution of Harm Avoidance scores in the Italian normative sample)
c. Reward Dependence: $M = 102.6$, $SD = 13.3$ (i.e., between the 50th and 66th percentile of the distribution of Reward Dependence scores in the Italian normative sample)
d. Persistence: $M = 110.6$, $SD = 19.8$ (i.e., 33th percentile of the distribution of Persistence scores in the Italian normative sample)
e. Self-Directedness: $M = 116.2$, $SD = 23.6$ (i.e., 10th percentile of the distribution of Self-Directedness scores in the Italian normative sample)

   f.  Cooperativeness: $M = 121.8$, SD = 19.4 (i.e., between the 10th and 25th
       percentile of the distribution of Cooperativeness scores in the Italian
       normative sample)
   g.  Self-Transcendence: $M = 80.8$, SD = 13.2 (i.e., 75th percentile of the
       distribution of Self-Transcendence scores in the Italian normative
       sample)

In other words, inpatients who dropped out had low scores on Self-Directedness
(SD) and Cooperativeness (C), and high scores in Self-Transcendence (ST), suggesting severe and complex personality difficulties characterized by persistent
problems with pursuing goals (low SD), antagonistic relationships with other
people (low C), and a possible tendency towards dissociation and/or magical
thinking (i.e., high ST).

   Thus, we analyzed the interactions of the three TCI-R character scales, comput-
ing quantitative measures of magical thinking according to Cloninger's theory
(Cloninger, 1999). In particular, when the magical thinking index was computed
(ST × (max SD score–actual SD score)), the drop-out group showed on average
a higher magical thinking score ($M = 6.9$, SD = 2.6) than the completers' group
($M = 5.4$, SD = 1.6; Cohen d = 0.7, 1-tailed $P < 0.05$).

   3. Suicidal attempts before STEPPS: interestingly, the mean number of
      suicidal attempts (before index admission) for the inpatients who did not
      complete STEPPS was 1.3, SD = 1.6, whereas inpatients who completed
      the program showed a mean (SD) of suicide attempts (before index
      admission) of 2.9, SD = 2.9 for completers. We observed a trend toward
      statistical significance for this comparison, Mann-Whitney $U = 67.0$,
      $P = 0.06$, which seemed to indicate that the higher the number of
      suicidal attempts before STEPPS, the less likely the patient is to drop out.

Our second study seemed to confirm the efficacy of STEPPS in reducing the number of suicidal attempts and hospitalizations. Indeed, these changes appeared to
be stable at the 12-month follow-up. The emotion management skills and group
setting seemed to help patients cope with emotional crises, without resorting to
dysfunctional behaviors. The stability at 12-month follow-up suggested that our
patients were able to use these skills even after the end of the treatment; emotional
crises could not be avoided, but could be managed in ways that were not self-
destructive. Indeed, our inpatients were able to use more adaptive strategies and
increase their self-efficacy. In particular, EIC data suggested that our inpatients
who completed the STEPPS treatment continued to experience distressing events,
but their impact on inpatients' lives decreased over time, as reflected by the lower
levels of emotional intensity that were perceived by our inpatients.

   In our sample of severely impaired BPD inpatients with co-occurring mood
disorder diagnoses, the positive effect of the treatment on the cognitive aspects
(filters) did not seem to be stable over time. The ending of the treatment and loss
of support provided by the group setting were likely to make it more difficult for

patients to challenge distorted thoughts. The lack of changes in self-report measures of adaptive and maladaptive personality features was somewhat expected, because the impact of STEPPS was evident primarily in emotion regulation and crisis management.

Our second study increased our understanding of the drop-out issue. To address factors that may predict which patients may not be suitable candidates for STEPPS is a core aspect of good clinical management. Our second study findings confirmed our previous data on the link between histrionic personality disorder and the risk of not completing STEPPS, showing that inpatients who dropped out had significantly more histrionic traits than those who completed the program. This result seems to suggest that STEPPS may be challenging for inpatients with prominent infantile, suggestible, inauthentic and attention-seeking features, even in the presence of a motivational intervention before starting the program. Because of the structured, active, and directive format of the treatment, BPD inpatients with a mood disorder and prominent histrionic features may suffer from sharing the focus of attention. Moreover, they were likely to have more difficulties engaging themselves in an authentic therapeutic process.

The results of the TCI-R profile analysis strongly suggested that we had to take into account not only personality disorder features, but also personality functioning if we aimed to successfully reduce the drop-out rate. The TCI-R profile of the inpatients who were not able to complete the program was significantly characterized by high scores in Self-Transcendence. This seems to suggest that while all the BPD inpatients in our second study had a severe impairment in the self- (i.e., Self-Directedness) and interpersonal (i.e., Cooperativeness) functions of personality, inpatients who dropped out were characterized by a significantly higher degree of immaturity and wishful thinking, when compared to participants who completed the STEPPS program. These inpatients were likely to have marked difficulties with commitment to a reality-oriented approach. By definition, STEPPS is a treatment that could be defined as "reality-oriented"; filling out daily diaries, completing homework assignments and the structured format of the program require a reality-oriented mode of functioning. The results of our second study lead us to hypothesize that the intrinsic characteristics of STEPPS may represent an obstacle to compliance with the treatment for selected BPD inpatients with co-occurring mood disorder; indeed, attention-seeking behavior and emotional lability (i.e., prominent histrionic features), and/or the tendency to take refuge in daydreaming as the favorite way to deal with personal or life difficulties (i.e., magical thinking) characterized our BPD inpatients who were not able to complete the program.

The results gave us another important clinical indication that STEPPS was particularly well-suited for BPD inpatients with co-occuring mood disorders characterized by severe self-destructive behavior. Indeed, inpatients who had more suicidal attempts before STEPPS appeared to be more committed to the treatment and more able to complete the program than less suicidal inpatients. Interestingly, our data appeared to suggest that BPD inpatients who dropped out were less severely impaired than the BPD inpatients who completed the STEPPS treatment, at least in regard to suicidal behavior. In turn, the interaction among magical thinking, attention-seeking behavior, and relative lack of severe self-destructive behavior may reduce the motivation in this subgroup of BPD inpatients with co-occurring mood disorders.

These findings lead us to re-think the motivational intervention for BPD inpatients at risk for drop-out from STEPPS treatment in order to address two major issues:

a)  challenging the patient's hidden expectation that obtaining relief from BPD features would mean they might lose attention and support from significant others, which may underlie patient's attention-seeking behavior; and

b)  fostering the patient's sense of self-efficacy and ability to take responsibility for her/his actions, in order to reduce the patient's need for flights into magical thinking.

Moreover, the association between prominent histrionic features and risk of drop-out from STEPPS lead us to consider placing special attention on the management of emotional crises in these BPD inpatients.

Finally, our second study strongly supported the clinical usefulness of extending the personality assessment of BPD inpatients with a co-occurring mood disorder who are candidates for STEPPS well beyond the DSM-IV (and DSM-5) categorical model of personality disorders. The lack of a link between Axis I/Axis II categorical diagnosis and drop-out, and the presence of a link between specific personality features (histrionic traits and the Self- Transcendence dimension) and drop-out could suggest the desirability of adopting a dimensional approach in the treatment of BPD inpatients with co-occurring mood disorders. Our findings are also in line with the growing recognition (Clark, 2007; Tyrer, 2005; Verheul, 2005) that a "stand-alone" categorical approach may have limited clinical utility, particularly in the case of severely impaired BPD patients.

In terms of clinical management, these findings led us to extend the dimensional measures of dysfunctional personality traits, introducing the Personality Inventory for DSM-5 (PID-5; Krueger et al.,2012), the Difficulties in Emotion Regulation Scale (DERS; Gratz & Roemer, 2004) and the Pathological Narcissism Inventory (PNI; Pincus et al., 2009) in the assessment process of our BPD inpatients with co-occurring mood disorders, as well as computer-administered measures of impulsivity, theory of mind, and ability to correctly identify emotional states.

The results of the second study pushed us to persist in exploring new strategies to improve inpatients' commitment to treatment, considering the 12-month efficacy of STEPPS in reducing suicidal risk, number of hospital admissions, and emotional intensity.

Thus, we introduced two simple modifications to the previous STEPPS inpatient treatment:

1. Inpatients in STEPPS treatment were given the opportunity to call an emergency number when they were experiencing a crisis. Inpatients participating in STEPPS were instructed that if any of our team were available, they could receive immediate help; otherwise (as in the case of extreme emotional distress occurring in the middle of the night), they could call and leave a message on the answering machine in order to be contacted as soon as one of the team members was available. The reason behind this proposal was to help the patient act safely during an emotional crisis, offering immediate help (if possible) or at least substituting potentially self-damaging acts (including impulsive acts as binge drinking, gambling, etc.) with help-seeking behavior positively reinforced by the therapists' realistic availability (in a sense, it was a way to foster secure attachment relationships in our BPD inpatients).
2. Paying special attention to our inpatients' emotional crises by giving the opportunity to manage the emotional turmoil in vivo during STEPPS group sessions. We thought this could represent an adaptive response to the attention-seeking behaviors of our BPD inpatients who were at high risk of dropping out.

These interventions produced another question that should be answered, "Do these modifications work?" This question led us to carry out the third study on STEPPS for BPD inpatients with co-occurring mood disorders. In 2013 we selected a third sample of BPD inpatients with co-occurring mood disorders who were referred for STEPPS treatment during their hospital stay. Our third study actually had three major aims: (a) testing whether our modifications were effective in reducing the drop-out rate from the STEPPS among our inpatients; (b) evaluating which components of emotion dysregulation were particularly effective, at least in a group of BPD inpatients with co-occurring mood disorders; (c) getting further evidence of the efficacy of the STEPPS treatment in reducing the number of suicidal attempts and hospital admissions in BPD inpatients with co-occurring mood disorders.

The third study group was composed of 24 BPD inpatients with co-occurring mood disorder diagnoses; inclusion criteria were identical to those in our previously described studies. Twenty (83.3%) were female and four (16.7%) were male, mean (SD) age was 41.0 years (SD = 8.9). All inpatients received a clinical diagnosis of BPD by the clinicians who were following them in treatment for mood disorders. According to SCID-II interview, 11 inpatients (45.8%) met the criteria for a BPD diagnosis, five inpatients (20.8%) received a diagnosis of narcissistic personality disorder, four (16.7%) received a histrionic personality disorder diagnosis, and six (25.0%) received a diagnosis of mixed personality disorder (percentages exceeded 100% because of multiple diagnoses). Bipolar disorder, type II ($n = 12$, 50.0%) and major depression ($n = 8$, 33.3%) were the most frequently diagnosed mood disorders. The mean (SD) number of hospital admissions before STEPPS treatment was 3.4 (SD = 2.8), and the mean (SD) number of attempted suicides was 2.1, (SD = 2.3).

When compared to inpatients who participated in our second study, the present inpatient sample was characterized by a younger age (41 years vs. 44 years), a higher base rate of bipolar disorder, type II, and a higher rate of SCID-II BPD diagnoses.

Although these differences make it difficult to accurately estimate the impact of sampling differences on the results in our third study, only seven participants (29.2%) dropped out and 17 participants (70.8%) completed the program. Thus, the drop-out rate in our third study was close to the drop-out estimates reported in the literature on evidence-based treatments for BPD (Barnicot et al., 2011), perhaps due to our modifications.

In this study, BPD inpatients with co-occurring mood disorders who completed STEPPS were administered the DERS and the EIC before starting STEPPS during the inpatient phase, when they completed the program, and six months after finishing STEPPS. In this sample, the DERS total score at baseline correlated significantly with the number of BPD criteria met according to the SCID-II interview ($r = 0.41$, $P < 0.05$); a trend toward statistical significance was observed for the correlations between the DERS total score at the baseline and the number of suicidal attempts before STEPPS ($r = 0.38$, $P < 0.06$).

Among our BPD inpatients who completed STEPPS, the baseline DERS total score was on average 121.2 (SD = 18.7), whereas mean DERS total scores of 107.5 (SD = 28.3) and 107.0 (SD = 29.9) were observed at the end of the program and at six-month follow-up, respectively. ANOVA showed that the decrease of the DERS total score was significant ($\chi^2 = 7.82$, exact $P < 0.05$). Wilcoxon test showed that on average the DERS total score at baseline was significantly higher than DERS total scores at the end of STEPPS (Wilcoxon $z = 2.61$, exact two-tailed $p < 0.01$), and at six-month follow-up (Wilcoxon $z = 2.61$, exact two-tailed $p < 0.01$), respectively. No significant differences were observed between DERS total scores at the end of STEPPS and at six-month follow-up (Wilcoxon $z = 0.43$, exact two-tailed $P > 0.60$). A similar pattern of change during and after treatment in our BPD inpatient sample was observed for the DERS Goals (ANOVA $\chi^2 = 6.06$, exact $P < 0.05$), and Impulse scale scores (ANOVA $\chi^2 = 6.45$, exact $P < 0.05$).

Consistent with our previous studies, in the subgroup of BPD inpatients with co-occurring mood disorder who were able to complete the program, the mean (SD) number of attempted suicides changed from 2.1 (SD = 2.3), before entering STEPPS to 0 at the end of the program, to 0.1 (SD = 0.3), at six months follow-up (ANOVA $\chi^2 = 19.4$, exact $P < 0.001$. Similar outcomes held also for the reduction in the average number of hospital admissions (not due to the course of the co-occurring mood disorder) which changed from 3.4 (SD = 3.1), before entering

STEPPS, to 0.2 (SD = 0.4), and 0.3 (SD = 0.47), at the end of STEPPS and at six-month follow-up, respectively (ANOVA $\chi^2$ = 22.2, $P$ < 0.001).

Although the lack of a control group and the differences in relevant sample characteristics prevent us from drawing definitive conclusions, the results of our third study seem to indicate that phone calls for crisis management and in vivo management of emotional crises during STEPPS group sessions may have been effective in reducing the frequency of drop-out when STEPPS was used as the exclusive treatment of BPD inpatients with co-occurring mood disorder diagnosis. This finding encouraged us to keep these modifications, although further data are necessary before accepting their effectiveness.

The significant decrease of the DERS scores observed during STEPPS treatment suggested that STEPPS may be particularly effective in increasing emotion regulation, improving the patient's self-perception of being able to master her/his intense emotions. STEPPS seems to have helped our BPD inpatients with co-occurring mood disorders internalize effective strategies of emotion regulation which they were able to use in their daily lives, even in the absence of a structured therapeutic setting.

In particular, the data suggest that STEPPS improves emotion regulation in BPD inpatients with co-occurring mood disorders in two major ways:

1. Boosting the patient's abilities to develop goal-oriented behaviors during emotional crises which led to downregulation of negative emotions (i.e., reduction of DERS Goals scale scores)
2. Inhibiting the patients' tendency toward "acting without thinking" (i.e., impulsively) when they are in a state of intense, negative emotional arousal (i.e., reduction of DERS Impulse scale scores)

In our opinion, this finding does not indicate that STEPPS works by simply improving emotion regulation; the data appear to suggest *how* STEPPS works in fostering emotion regulation abilities in BPD inpatients with co-occurring mood disorders. Improving adaptive goal-setting capacities and inhibiting impulsive reaction during emotional crises seemed to represent major features in the process of emotion regulation based on the STEPPS program. Interestingly, these two components of emotion regulation may activate a cycle in which fostering adaptive goal-setting leads to reduction of impulsive behavior during negative emotional activation, and the STEPPS ability to promote behavioral control leads to increased ability to identify effective strategies for emotion regulation during states of negative emotional arousal in BPD inpatients with co-occurring mood disorders.

Although we performed only "open label," uncontrolled studies of the efficacy of STEPPS treatment for BPD inpatients with co-occurring mood disorders, we found in three independent samples that STEPPS significantly reduced the number of hospital admissions (not related to mood disorder course) and the frequency of suicide attempts, even when it was used as the only treatment for BPD features in these patients.

## CURRENT STATE OF STEPPS IN INPATIENT SETTINGS

Since 2009, both our patients and the academic community have given us invaluable suggestions to further our work with STEPPS. The program has become the treatment of choice for BPD inpatients with co-occurring mood disorders at San Raffaele Hospital of Milano, Italy. Currently, all inpatients with mood disorders and a clinical diagnosis of BPD are referred to our team during weekly meetings with the psychiatrists working in the Mood Disorder Unit of San Raffaele Hospital. The enthusiasm that STEPPS treatment raised among both our colleagues and our patients led us to propose adding the STAIRWAYS program in order to help our patients consolidate, and even extend the STEPPS results.

Besides the clinical application of STEPPS, we are insisting on two major goals of our team: a) exchanging ideas with other teams using STEPPS in institutional settings in Italy and around the world; and b) disseminating our experience with STEPPS in mood-disordered BPD inpatients to other psychiatrists and clinical psychologists working with borderline inpatients with different co-occurring mental disorder diagnoses. In other word, we are trying to keep a close connection to the big STEPPS family, while trying to export the STEPPS to inpatient settings different from a university clinic highly specialized in treating mood disorders. BPD patients may suffer from a number of co-occurring mental disorders, ranging from post-traumatic stress disorder to substance misuse disorders. The presentation of our experience with STEPPS during the post-graduate course in psychopharmacology for psychiatrists working in the Italian National Health System as well as in private practice represents one of the most important occasions for us to disseminate the STEPPS model to different inpatient settings. It also represents an attempt to create a network of clinicians (and researchers) interested in using the program in Italy—we know that it is challenging work, but we feel it is worth doing.

STEPPS dramatically changed the future for many of our BPD inpatients with co-occurring mood disorders, showing them that they were able to overcome their difficulties and live with their emotions without self-destructive behaviors; indeed, for many of our BPD inpatients, STEPPS was helpful in restoring a sense of hope and self-worth in previously hopeless patients who considered themselves as "problems with no solution." We are convinced that STEPPS can help BPD with many other co-occurring mental disorders; disseminating the program among Italian psychiatrists is the best way to make STEPPS available to their clients with co-occurring posttraumatic stress disorder, anxiety disorders, substance dependence disorders, etc.

Currently, we are working on improving the motivational phase for inpatients at high risk of dropping out (i.e., BPD inpatients with prominent histrionic PD features and/or magical thinking) prior to their participation in the treatment program. In other words, we are not trying to identify the best candidates for STEPPS treatment; rather, we are trying to make the STEPPS a self-enhancing experience for all our BPD inpatients, rather than only for a (more or less wide) subgroup.

## FUTURE OF STEPPS IN INPATIENT SETTING

To summarize our STEPPS agenda for the next few years, we emphasize the following:

1. Although several randomized clinical trials (RCTs) have documented the efficacy of the STEPPS, we believe an RCT should be conducted to consolidate the evidence of efficacy of the STEPPS treatment for BPD inpatients with co-occurring mood disorders.

2. Disseminating STEPPS among Italian psychiatrists to make the program available to a growing number of BPD inpatients and outpatients with co-occurring mood disorders, with other co-occurring mental disorders, or without a co-occurring mental disorder. This would make it possible to start a rich exchange of clinical observations and suggestions, which could lead to multi-center studies designed to evaluate the program's efficacy in the treatment of BPD inpatients (and outpatients as well) with co-occurring mood disorders, or with different diagnostic co-occurrences.

3. A number of different psychotherapies appear effective for BPD patients, including STEPPS (Somma et al., 2014). Thus, the question, "Does STEPPS work?" has received a resounding "yes." This leaves us to ask, "How does STEPPS work?" Starting from this general question, we plan to carry out a process study, designed to evaluate at which point major changes occur, which treatment components are most effective, and which materials (forms, questionnaires, diaries, etc.) are particularly helpful to clients. Issues concerning patient motivation for treatment and how they change during the STEPPS program, therapeutic alliance during the STEPPS program, and dynamics among group participants could also be considered in process studies to evaluate how they impact efficacy and drop-out rate.

## REFERENCES

Alesiani, R., Boccalon, S., Giarolli, L., Blum, N., & Fossati, A. (2014). Systems Training for Emotional Predictability and Problem Solving (STEPPS): Program efficacy and personality features as predictors of drop-out-an Italian study. *Comprehensive Psychiatry, 55*(4), 920–927.

Barnicot, K., Katsakou, C., Marougka, S., & Priebe, S. (2011). Treatment completion in psychotherapy for borderline personality disorder: A systematic review and meta-analysis. *Acta Psychiatrica Scandinavica, 123*(5), 327–338.

Bender, D. S., Dolan, R. T., Skodol, A. E., Sanislow, C. A., Dyck, I. R., McGlashan, T. H., . . . Gunderson, J. G. (2001). Treatment utilization by patients with personality disorders. *American Journal of Psychiatry, 158*(2), 295–302.

Black, D. W., Blum, N., Eichinger, L., McCormick, B., Allen, J., & Sieleni, B. (2008). STEPPS: Systems training for emotional predictability and problem solving in women offenders with borderline personality disorder in prison-a pilot study. *CNS Spectrums*, *13*(10), 881–886.

Black, D. W., Blum, N., Pfohl, B., & John, D. S. (2004). The STEPPS group treatment program for outpatients with borderline personality disorder. *Journal of Contemporary Psychotherapy*, *34*(3), 193–210.

Blum, N. S., Bartels, N. E., St John, D., & Pfohl, B. (2012). *Systems Training for Emotional Predictability and Problem Solving*. STEPPS 2nd ed. Coralville, IA: Level One Publishing (Blums Books); 2012 [www.steppsforbpd.com].

Blum, N., Pfohl, B., John, D. S., Monahan, P., & Black, D. W. (2002). STEPPS: A cognitive-behavioral systems-based group treatment for outpatients with borderline personality disorder—a preliminary report. *Comprehensive Psychiatry*, *43*(4), 301–310.

Blum, N., John, D. S., Pfohl, B., Stuart, S., McCormick, B., Allen, J., . . . Black, D. (2008). Systems Training for Emotional Predictability and Problem Solving (STEPPS) for outpatients with borderline personality disorder: A randomized controlled trial and 1-year follow-up. *American Journal of Psychiatry*, *165*(4), 468–478.

Boccalon, S., Alesiani, R., Giarolli, L., Franchini, L., Colombo, C., Blum, N., & Fossati, A. (2012). Systems Training for Emotional Predictability and Problem Solving (STEPPS): Modello di intervento, adattamento clinico e dati preliminari di efficacia in un campione di pazienti ricoverati con diagnosi di disturbo dell'umore e disturbo di personalità. *Journal of Psychopathology*, *18*, 335–343.

Buss, A. H., & Perry, M. (1992). The aggression questionnaire. *Journal of Personality and Social Psychology 63*, 452–459.

Clark, L. A. (2007). Assessment and diagnosis of personality disorder: Perennial issues and an emerging reconceptualization. *Annual Review of Psychology*, *58*, 227–257.

Cloninger, C. R. (1999). *The Temperament and Character Inventory–Revised*. St. Louis, MO: Center for Psychobiology of Personality, Washington University.

Feeney, J. A., Noller, P., & Hanrahan, M. (1994). Assessing adult attachment. In M. B. Sperling, W. H. Berman (Eds.), *Attachment in adults: Clinical and developmental perspective* (pp. 128–152). New York: The Guilford Press.

First, M. B., Spitzer, R. L., Gibbon, M., Williams, J. B. W., & Benjamin, L. (1994). Structured clinical interview for DSM-IV Axis II personality disorders (SCID-II), version 2.0. New York, NY: Biometrics Research Department, New York State Psychiatric Institute.

Grant, B. F., Chou, S. P., Goldstein, R. B., Huang, B., Stinson, F. S., Saha, T. D., . . . Ruan, W. J. (2008). Prevalence, correlates, disability, and comorbidity of DSM-IV borderline personality disorder: Results from the Wave 2 National Epidemiologic Survey on Alcohol and Related Conditions. *Journal of Clinical Psychiatry*, *69*(4), 533–545.

Gratz, K. L., & Roemer, L. (2004). Multidimensional assessment of emotion regulation and dysregulation: Development, factor structure, and initial validation of the difficulties in emotion regulation scale. *Journal of Psychopathology and Behavioral Assessment*, *26*(1), 41–54.

Gunderson, J. G., Bender, D. S., Sanislow, C. A., Yen, S., Rettew, J. B., Dolan-Sewell, R., . . . Skodol, A. E. (2003). Plausibility and possible determinants of sudden 'remissions' in borderline patients. *Psychiatry*, *66*(2), 111–119.

Hendin, H. M., & Cheek, J. M. (1997). Assessing hypersensitive narcissism: A reexamination of Murray's Narcissism Scale. *Journal of Research in Personality*, *31*(4), 588–599.

Leichsenring, F., Leibing, E., Kruse, J., New, A. S., & Leweke, F. (2011). Borderline personality disorder. *Lancet*, *377*, 74–84.

Lenzenweger, M. F., Lane, M. C., Loranger, A. W., & Kessler, R. C. (2007). DSM-IV personality disorders in the National Comorbidity Survey Replication. *Biological Psychiatry, 62*(6), 553–564.

Links, P. S., Heslegrave, R., & Reekum, R. V. (1999). Impulsivity: Core aspect of borderline personality disorder. *Journal of Personality Disorders, 13*(1), 1–9.

Krueger, R. F., Derringer, J., Markon, K. E., Watson, D., & Skodol, A. E. (2012). Initial construction of a maladaptive personality trait model and inventory for DSM-5. *Psychological Medicine, 42*, 1879–1890.

McGlashan, T. H., Grilo, C. M., Sanislow, C. A., Ralevski, E., Morey, L. C., Gunderson, J. G., . . . Pagano, M. (2005). Two-year prevalence and stability of individual DSM-IV criteria for schizotypal, borderline, avoidant, and obsessive-compulsive personality disorders: Toward a hybrid model of axis II disorders. *American Journal of Psychiatry, 162*(5), 883–889.

Paris, J. (2004). Half in love with easeful death: The meaning of chronic suicidality in borderline personality disorder. *Harvard Review of Psychiatry, 12*, 42–48.

Patton, J. H., Stanford, M. S., & Barratt, E. S., (1995). Factor structure of the Barratt Impulsiveness Scale. *Journal of Clinical Psychology, 51*, 768–774.

Pincus, A. L., Ansell, E. B., Pimentel, C. A., Cain, N. M., Wright, A. G., & Levy, K. N. (2009). Initial construction and validation of the pathological narcissism inventory. *Psychological Assessment, 21*(3), 365.

Raskin, R. N., & Hall, C. S. (1979). A narcissistic personality inventory. *Psychological reports, 45*(2), 590–590.

Raskin, R., & Terry, H. (1988). A principal-components analysis of the Narcissistic Personality Inventory and further evidence of its construct validity. *Journal of Personality and Social Psychology, 54*(5), 890.

Sanislow, C. A., Little, T. D., Ansell, E. B., Grilo, C. M., Daversa, M., Markowitz, J. C., . . . McGlashan, T. H. (2009). Ten-year stability and latent structure of the DSM–IV schizotypal, borderline, avoidant, and obsessive-compulsive personality disorders. *Journal of Abnormal Psychology, 118*(3), 507.

Shearin, E. N., & Linehan, M. M. (1994). Dialectical behavior therapy for borderline personality disorder: theoretical and empirical foundations. *Acta Psychiatrica Scandinavica, 89* (379), 61–68.

Skodol, A. E., Gunderson, J. G., Shea, M. T., McGlashan, T. H., Morey, L. C., Sanislow, C. A., . . . Stout, R. L. (2005a). The collaborative longitudinal personality disorders study (CLPS): Overview and implications. *Journal of Personality Disorders, 19*(5), 487–504.

Skodol, A. E., Pagano, M. E., Bender, D. S., Shea, M. T., Gunderson, J. G., Yen, S., . . . & McGlashan, T. H. (2005b). Stability of functional impairment in patients with schizotypal, borderline, avoidant, or obsessive compulsive personality disorder over two years. *Psychological Medicine, 35*(3), 443–451.

Somma, A., Blum, N., Black, D., Alesiani, R., Boccalon, S., Giarolli, L., Borroni, S. . . . Fossati, A. (2014). Evidenze empiriche di efficacia del System Training for Emotional Predictability and Problem Solving (STEPPS) nel Trattamento del Disturbo Borderline di Personalità: Una Meta-Analisi degli Studi Pubblicati. *Psicoterapia Cognitiva e Comportamentale, 20*, 197–198.

Tyrer, P. (2005). The problem of severity in the classification of personality disorder. *Journal of Personality Disorders, 19*(3), 309–314.

Verheul, R. (2005). Clinical utility of dimensional models for personality pathology. *Journal of Personality Disorders, 19*, 283–302.

Zanarini, M. C., Frankenburg, F. R., Reich, D. B., & Fitzmaurice, G. (2010). The 10-year course of psychosocial functioning among patients with borderline personality disorder and axis II comparison subjects. *Acta Psychiatrica Scandinavica, 122*(2), 103–109.

Zanarini, M., Frankenburg, F., Hennen, J., Reich, D., & Silk, K. (2006). Prediction of the 10-year course of borderline personality disorder. *American Journal of Psychiatry, 163*(5), 827–832.

Zanarini, M., Frankenburg, F., Reich, D., Silk, K., Hudson, J., & McSweeney, L. (2007). The subsyndromal phenomenology of borderline personality disorder: A 10-year follow-up study. *American Journal of Psychiatry, 164*(6), 929–935.

# 8

# Treatment of Borderline Personality Disorder in Adolescents

MARIEKE SCHUPPERT, PAUL EMMELKAMP,
AND MAAIKE NAUTA ■

Personality traits like extraversion, neuroticism, and conscientiousness can be recognized at an early age, but tend to increase steadily over the years (Roberts et al., 2006). More extreme traits can be associated with an increased risk for personality pathology. However, both clinicians and researchers have been reluctant to diagnose personality disorders (PD) before age 18. One of the consequences of this reluctance is that relatively little research has been done on (symptoms of) PDs in adolescence, and more specifically, on borderline personality disorder (BPD). In recent decades, the development of BPD has increasingly become a focus of interest. Several studies have found ample evidence for a reliable and valid diagnosis in adolescence (e.g., Crawford et al., 2008; Paris, 2003; Miller, Muehlenkamp, & Jacoboson, 2008; Schuppert et al., 2012a). In epidemiological studies, BPD in adolescence was found to be a predictor for psychosocial dysfunction later in life. In a 20-year follow-up study (Children in the Community Study, CIC), Winograd et al., (2008) found that borderline symptoms at a mean age of 13.7 years predicted lower social functioning and life satisfaction, and a higher consumption of health care services. Youth with borderline symptoms fulfilled more BPD criteria, more axis I disorders (especially mood disorders and addiction), and showed more general impairment at 20 years' follow-up.

The prevalence of BPD in adolescence is roughly estimated at 1–3% (Bernstein et al., 1993; Lewinsohn et al., 1997). This figure goes up to 10–14% when milder cases are included (Bernstein et al., 1993), or when self-reports are used (Chabrol et al., 2004). Despite the growing body of evidence for a reliable diagnosis of BPD in adolescence, the high prevalence, and the associated serious adverse consequences, only a few age-specific therapeutic interventions have been developed and evaluated for the treatment of BPD symptoms in youth (Chanen & Kaess, 2012).

Unfortunately, the consequences for long-term functioning in untreated adolescents with borderline personality pathology are serious.

## Etiology of BPD

Personality disorders are generally considered to have their origin in multiple causes. Two main factors can be distinguished: biological factors, including genetic predispositions, and psychosocial factors (for a recent review, see Chanen & Kaess, 2012).

## Biological Factors

Personality traits are heritable to a certain degree, and so are personality disorders (Emmelkamp and Kamphuis, 2007). Twin studies in adult BPD patients have shown inconsistent results: heritability estimates up to 69% have been found (Torgersen et al., 2000), but more recent studies report a range from 35 to 45% (Distel et al., 2011; Kendler et al., 2008; Torgersen et al., 2008). Bornovalova et al., (2009) conducted a longitudinal study with adolescent twins over a period of 10 years, with time intervals of 3–4 years. They concluded that genetic factors play a greater role in both stability and change of borderline traits, compared to environmental factors. Gunderson et al., (2011) conducted a family study with 132 BPD probands, 134 controls without BPD, and 102 probands with a lifetime diagnosis of major depressive disorder (MDD). They concluded that BPD (and its four main characteristics: affective, interpersonal, behavioral, and cognitive symptoms) aggregates in families. In a large multivariate twin modeling study, Kendler et al., (2008) concluded that genetic risk factors for personality disorders do not reflect the typology in DSM-IV. One genetic factor reflected vulnerability and/or negative emotionality for personality disorders in general. Two more specific genetic factors indicated high impulsivity/low agreeableness, and introversion. However, no specific genes have yet been identified in relation to BPD.

More recently, research focused on the interaction between genes and environment. Specific environmental life events have been identified that moderate the genetic and environmental interaction on BPD features (Distel et al., 2011). Among these factors are being a victim of sexual and/or violent assault, job loss, or divorce. Individuals who were exposed to one of these life events showed higher environmental variance for BPD features, leading to a lower heritability of BPD features. Also, a correlation between genes and environment was found for some life events. This indicates that the genes influencing BPD features also increase the risk to be exposed to certain life events (Distel et al., 2011). However, the risk factors that have been identified do not suggest a specific psychopathological pathway to BPD. Comparable findings have been described in research on MDD and posttraumatic stress disorder, identifying the same kind of environmental risk factors in combination with genetic factors (Sartor et al., 2012).

Other biological factors have been found in the neurotransmitter system and in brain structures that are related to behavioral and affective symptoms of the disorder. For example, opioids are involved in feelings of pleasure or soothing, but also in stress responses and sadness. Oxytocin is associated with attachment, the ability to trust others, and to read social interactions, whereas vasopressin has been implicated in aggression regulation, especially in intimate relationships (for an overview see Stanley and Siever, 2010). Disturbances in these three systems have been found in BPD patients, but replication of the investigations and additional research is needed to obtain a better understanding of the neurobiological basis of BPD. For example, little is known about the "post or propter" of these findings (whether disturbances in neuropeptides are preceding borderline personality disorder or whether they are a consequence of the disorder, a consequence of life events, or a combination of factors), since there is little longitudinal research on this subject in children and adolescents. A few structural neuroimaging studies have been published in adolescent BPD, but no functional neuroimaging studies (Chanen and Kaess, 2012). Reduced orbitofrontal cortex volumes and decreased anterior cingulate cortex volume were found. Findings in adult BPD neuroimaging studies (like structural changes in the corpus callosum, and reduction of hippocampal or amygdala volumes) could not be demonstrated in adolescents. To conclude, recent findings of neurobiological studies are interesting and promising and shed a new light on the development of (borderline) personality disorders. However, the findings are contradictory and inconclusive, and further research is needed to unravel this complex field.

## Psychosocial Factors

A history of early childhood trauma, neglect, sexual abuse and/or maltreatment is strongly related to the development of BPD symptoms (Johnson et al., 1999; Paris, 2003; Silk et al., 1995; Zanarini et al., 1997). Most of these studies have used retrospective information, which probably will have produced a recall bias (Hufford and Shiffman, 2003). Another complicating factor is the fact that many of the possible risk factors are highly correlated, and difficult to disentangle (Bradley et al., 2005). BPD symptoms were increased in adolescents with a history of sexual assault, even in individuals with less genetic vulnerability. Prospective studies on environmental risk factors are scarce. Again, these risk factors are not very specific for the development of BPD, but have also been found in other psychiatric disorders e.g., depression and anxiety disorders (Hovens et al., 2012).

Growing up in a dysfunctional family and parental rearing styles have also been found to be related to the development of BPD traits (Paris, 2003). The main theories about the relationship between family factors and the development of BPD are psychodynamically oriented. It has been suggested that BPD has its cause in mothers that did not allow their child to separate, i.e., were overprotective (Materson and Rinsley, 1975). In the last decades, there has been an increasing interest in the interaction between parenting, genetically influenced temperamental factors, childhood adversities, and parental psychopathology (Paris, 2003; Paris, 2008). Insecure and disorganized attachment may underlie one of the core symptoms of BPD: difficulties in interpersonal relationships. Though the scientific support is still small, all theories suggest a causal relationship between separation and/or attachment problems and the development of BPD. It is conceivable that these problems in early childhood are an even bigger challenge for parents with psychopathological problems themselves.

Only a few studies have investigated actual parenting behavior in relation to BPD features in adolescents, all in community rather than clinical samples. Only one study reported on parental overprotection: the Children in the Community (CIC) study ($n$ = 776) reported that maternal overinvolvement had no direct impact on a persistence or an emergence of BPD 2.5 years later. However, the combination of maternal overinvolvement with maternal inconsistency was a predictor of BPD (Bezirganian, et al., 1993). In another paper based on data from the CIC study, low parental affection and aversive parenting were both associated with an elevated risk for BPD in the offspring (Johnson, et al., 2006). Maternal hostility was also associated with BPD features in adults in a community sample of mothers ($n$ = 162) with low income (Carlson, et al., 2009).

Parental rearing may be explained partly by parental psychopathology. Indeed, a recent overview focusing on parenting behavior of mothers with BPD concludes that several factors play a part in the poor psychosocial functioning in their children (Stepp, et al., 2011). Among these factors are insensitive communication (critical, intrusive, and frightening), role confusion (i.e., addressing the child as a friend or parent), and increased risk of abuse. In line with these findings, stronger associations between negative parenting styles and personality disorder symptoms were found in students that grew up with a parent with PD than in students that grew up with a parent without PD (Cheng et al., 2011), but this was not investigated specifically for borderline PD.

Schuppert et al. (2012b) investigated the role of parental rearing as well as parental psychopathology in relation to BPD features in youth. The study compared current maternal parenting behavior in a clinical sample of referred adolescents (14–19 years) with BPD features ($n$ = 101) to a healthy control group ($n$ = 44). Data from the adolescents, as well as from their biological mothers, were collected. Actual parental rearing styles (overprotection, rejection, emotional warmth as assessed with the EMBU), and psychopathology in mothers (general psychopathology assessed with the SCL-90 and personality traits assessed with the PDQ-4) were entered in a hierarchical logistical regression model to examine which factors account for differences between adolescents with BPD features and healthy controls. Based on previous research on the development of BPD, they hypothesized that adolescents with BPD features and their mothers would report less emotional warmth, more rejection, and more overprotection, as compared to healthy controls. In view of the transgenerational transmission of BPD (Stepp et al., 2011), they expected mothers of BPD adolescents to report more cluster B symptoms and more general psychopathology compared to mothers in the healthy control group.

The main results of the study are as follows: (1) Adolescents with current elevated levels of BPD features report higher levels of parental rejection, overprotection, and lower emotional warmth. (2) Mothers of adolescents with BPD features report more general psychopathology and cluster C personality symptoms, but no more cluster A and cluster B symptoms. (3) Three variables were the strongest predictors of BPD features in adolescents, namely the parental rearing styles of less emotional warmth and more overprotection, and more general psychopathology in mothers.

Contrary to expectations, no elevated levels of maternal cluster B personality traits were found in mothers of adolescents with BPD features. However, higher levels of maternal cluster C traits were found in this group; mothers with increased levels of cluster C (anxious, fearful) personality traits may raise their children with more overprotection, and thus increase the risk of BPD in their offspring. Even more, in combination with general psychopathology (e.g., anxious/depressive symptoms), those mothers may be unstable and unpredictable, and thus arouse instability in children who are already vulnerable for the development of BPD features.

Higher levels of emotional warmth were found in the control sample than in the clinical sample. Both parent and adolescent personality factors have been found to be relevant for explaining emotional warmth as parenting behavior (Haan et al., 2012). It has been suggested that emotionally stable parents are less anxious, and are therefore better able to handle problematic behavior in their adolescent children (Haan et al., 2012). Further exploration of moderators in the pathway to BPD is necessary, in order to develop interventions that aim at specific components of the disorder.

## BORDERLINE PATHOLOGY OR NORMAL DEVELOPMENTAL PHASE

Adolescence is a developmental stage of changes in different fields: somatic, cognitive (for instance conceptual thinking), and social (maturity of identity, sexuality, and autonomy). Youth is generally considered to be impulsive, stubborn, and reckless. Such a period of "Sturm und Drang" has long been regarded as an essential phase for the development of the self. However, research has shown that for the vast majority of adolescents, this developmental phase should not be characterized as a time of heavy turmoil, and that most adolescents manage to make the transition to adulthood without serious problems. On the other hand, in spite of the fact that adolescence is not a time of extreme turmoil, it is a period of increased risk taking behavior (Crone et al., 2008; Steinberg & Morris, 2001). The prevalence of suicide attempts is rather high (Lewinsohn et al., 1996). Impulsivity, affect dysregulation, and identity disturbance are normal developmental phenomena, at least to some level, and are mostly transient. Indeed, there is a decrease in risk taking behavior in the course of adolescence, and an increase in more rational decision making (Crone et al., 2008).

Especially in milder forms, it is often difficult to distinguish BPD from normal development, which complicates the diagnostic process. Duration and severity of the borderline symptoms, the disruption of family life, and the adverse consequences (e.g., premature drop-out from school, insufficient [peer] relationships) play a role in diagnostics. To prevent a stigma, many mental health workers choose to delay a formal diagnosis and to label separate symptoms or clusters of symptoms (like emotional instability, or affect dysregulation) instead. However, early recognition and assessment is important in order to facilitate early interventions, and to prevent the long-term consequences (Chanen et al., 2008a). Moreover, it is not likely that BPD symptoms suddenly appear at one's 18th birthday.

Though deliberate self-harm is quite common in adolescents (Madge et al., 2008), a significant percentage of them will not develop BPD in adulthood. On the other hand, self-harm in childhood or adolescence has been identified as an early risk marker for BPD (Zanarini et al., 2006). It has been suggested that when an adolescent suffers from severe emotional dysregulation in combination with self-injurious behavior, suicidal behavior, and/or antisocial behavior, a spontaneous recovery is not to be expected (Meijer, 2000).

## THERAPEUTIC INTERVENTIONS FOR BPD SYMPTOMS IN ADOLESCENTS

Considering the high prevalence and the adverse consequences of BPD symptoms in adolescence, there is an urgent need for early interventions. However, as mentioned, few treatments have been developed for youth with BPD symptoms, and the few that are available are poorly evaluated. The scarce data that are available suggest that early intervention may lessen the burden, may prevent the development of full-blown BPD, and may reduce the negative psychosocial consequences in the long term (Chanen et al., 2008b; Miller, Muehlenkamp, & Jacobson, 2008).

Several therapeutic protocols have been developed for adult patients with BPD. Many have been evaluated in (randomized) clinical trials, and there is variable evidence for the effectiveness/efficacy of these treatments (Emmelkamp & Kamphuis, 2007). Evidence-based treatments for adults with BPD include dialectical behavior therapy (DBT; Linehan, et al., 1991; Linehan et al., 2006; Verheul et al., 2003), mentalization based therapy (MBT; Bateman & Fonagy, 1999, 2001), schema focused therapy (SFT; Giesen-Bloo et al., 2006), Systems Training for Emotional Predictability and Problem Solving (STEPPS; Blum et al., 2008), and transference focused psychotherapy (TFP; Clarkin et al., 2001; Giesen-Bloo et al., 2006).

Some of the aforementioned interventions have been adapted to adolescents, but little research has been done to investigate the effectiveness with this population. Four treatment protocols for adolescents with BPD symptoms have been described in the literature. As far as we know, none has been evaluated sufficiently. To give an overview of the current treatment modules for adolescents with BPD symptoms, the four protocols will be discussed briefly.

## Cognitive Analytic Therapy (CAT)

Cognitive Analytic Therapy (Ryle, 2004) has been developed for adult BPD patients, and has been adapted in Australia for a younger population (Chanen et al., 2008b). The protocol consists of 16-24 weekly individual sessions and uses elements of cognitive psychology and psychoanalytic object relations theory. The basic assumption in CAT is that patients with BPD (or BPD symptoms) have a history of insecure attachment early in life, combined with genetic vulnerability. The aim of the therapy is to identify and recognize dysfunctional patterns, especially in interpersonal relationships. The therapeutic alliance focuses on transference and countertransference. The central tenant is to link the past to present patterns of functioning in a collaborative relationship with the therapist, in order to reformulate old damaging patterns and develop more adaptive patterns (Ryle, 2004). CAT differs from more traditional psychodynamic therapies in using homework assignments and behavioral interventions (Bateman, Ryle, Fonagy, and Kerr, 2007). Moreover, CAT is a time-limited intervention. CAT was compared to manualized good clinical care in a randomized controlled trial with 86 adolescents aged 15–18 years (Chanen et al., 2008b). Both groups showed significant improvement in externalizing psychopathology as measured by the Child Behavior Checklist. There were no significant differences between the two conditions, in terms of borderline symptoms and parasuicidal behavior; however, the CAT-group improved more rapidly than the control group.

## Dialectical Behavioral Therapy for Adolescents (DBT-A)

Dialectical behavioral therapy is a treatment method for suicidal behavior and BPD, developed in the 1990s by Marsha Linehan (1996), and adapted to adolescents by Miller, Rathus, and Linehan (2007). Dialectics is the continuous process of unification (synthesis), proceeding from the tension between opposite poles (thesis and antithesis). In DBT the emphasis lies on the dialectical tension between acceptance and change. Emotional dysregulation is considered as the core symptom of the illness (Linehan, 1996).

DBT originally consists of weekly individual cognitive behavioral therapy, weekly group skills training, telephone consultation as needed, and weekly consultation meetings for the whole team. Adaptations for adolescents (DBT-A) are additional family therapy and participation of one of the parents in the skills training. Much attention is paid to the therapeutic alliance. Further, the intensive phase of the treatment is limited to 16 weeks. After the skills training, DBT-A often continues in a less intensive way. The adolescent version was originally developed for outpatient treatment, but has been applied to other settings as well.

Though DBT has frequently been evaluated in adult samples with good results (Emmelkamp & Kamphuis, 2007), the adolescent version has only been evaluated in non-randomized, small samples (Fleischhaker et al., 2011; Katz, Cox, Gunasekara, & Miller, 2004; Rathus & Miller, 2002). The results suggest that

DBT-A is equally effective in the treatment of adolescents as in adults with regard to suicidality, BPD symptoms and possibly depressive symptoms. Further, the number of hospitalizations decreased, and the dropout rate was reasonably low. The results up till now are promising, though randomized clinical trials are needed to confirm the preliminary findings to demonstrate that the specific treatment was indeed responsible for the change in symptomatology.

Most of the treatments developed for adults with BPD are intensive and require a long-term commitment by the patient (e.g., Emmelkamp & Kamphuis, 2007), including DBT (Linehan 1993a and 1993b). Yet DBT-A is even more intensive and time-consuming than is DBT for adults. In addition to individual therapy, skills training and telephone consultation (all components of DBT for adults), family members join the skills group and family therapy is embedded in the program (Miller et al., 2007).

## Mentalization Based Treatment for Adolescents (MBT-A)

Mentalization Based Treatment for adult BPD patients was developed by Bateman and Fonagy (2004). MBT is based on psychodynamic theory, attachment theory, and cognitive theory. Mentalizing is the capacity by which people can make sense of themselves and of each other, in the way that we are attentive to our own and others' feelings, thoughts, desires, and intentions. Mentalizing is insufficiently developed in patients with BPD which increases the risk of emotional regulation problems and interpersonal and impulsivity difficulties. The treatment aims to improve the capacity to mentalize, especially under stressful circumstances and in attachment relationships. The central focus of the treatment is to improve the capacity to mentalize in order to improve agency, reflection and interpersonal relationships, and to stimulate more effective ways to manage vulnerability and difficulties (Bleiberg, Rossouw, & Sharp, 2011).

The adolescent version of MBT (MBT-A) focuses on five targets: stimulate commitment, reduce psychiatric symptoms, decrease self-destructive behavior, improve interpersonal functioning, and resume age specific developmental tasks. The program usually consists of a combination of group therapy and individual therapy. Parents and other relatives are always intensely involved in the treatment. MBT-A has been evaluated in an RCT with 80 adolescents with self-harm and comorbid depression (not necessarily diagnosed with BPD or BPD symptoms; Rossouw & Fonagy, 2012). MBT-A showed more improvement in reducing self-harm and depression than treatment as usual.

## Emotion Regulation Training (ERT)

All the interventions described require extensive additional training for therapists Moreover, DBT-A and MBT-A are directed at adolescents with severe BPD symptoms, and are time-intensive. However, early intervention might prevent the adverse outcome in the long-term (Chanen et al., 2007; Winograd et al., 2008). Therefore, a low threshold care was developed, not only for full-syndrome BPD adolescents, but also for (referred) sub-syndromal cases, which is time-limited and easy to implement in general mental health care.

Emotion regulation training (ERT) is a group skills training model for adolescents with BPD symptoms, developed in 2002 by van Gemert, Ringrose, Schuppert, and Wiersma (2009a and 2009b), and is based on the STEPPS program, developed by Blum et al. (2008); Black, Blum, and St. John (2009). Age-specific adaptations are the duration of the program (17 weeks), the length of the sessions (105 minutes), and specific topics to meet the developmental stage of self-exploration (Steinberg and Morris, 2001). This course for adolescent BPD patients combines cognitive behavioral elements and skills training, and involves to some extent family members, partners and "important others" in the training. A more recent adaptation of STEPPS for adolescents is described by Renee Harvey in Chapter 4 of this book.

As in DBT-A, the core symptom addressed in ERT is emotional dysregulation (Putnam & Silk, 2005). ERT involves 17 weekly sessions and two booster sessions at 6 and 12 weeks post-treatment. The training involves three phases. The first phase provides psychoeducation combined with instruction on behavioral chain analyses and problem solving techniques. The second phase is focused on "knowing yourself." The adolescents are asked to take a close look at their character and temperament in relation to their emotions and behaviors. In the third phase participants learn to make better lifestyle choices including eating, sleeping, substance use, mental hygiene, and personal relationships. They learn to implement better coping mechanisms in their daily life. Improving "locus of control," i.e., getting a better handle on emotional dysregulation, is one of the main issues in the training.

Each session starts with a group discussion about the homework assigned the previous week. Participants use daily mood rating scales to obtain better insight into their mood swings and what triggers them. Next, the "topic of the day" is introduced and after a short break the group continues with their own illustrations of the current topic. After relaxation exercises, the session ends with homework assignments for the next week.

## Common Factors

Although the four treatment modules differ to some extent, they also have several common features. Recognition and realization of the psychological vulnerability (or emotional dysregulation) is the first phase in all treatments. Next, all four interventions focus on the therapeutic alliance, and aim to decrease treatment-interfering behavior and self-injurious behavior. Some kind of skills training is often applied. All treatment modules involve parents and relatives to some extent, though this is described less explicitly in CAT. While DBT-A and ERT use a clear manual, this is less explicit in MBT-A and CAT. DBT-A was specifically developed for severe BPD problems in adolescence, while CAT and ERT are also intended for milder cases as well.

The aim of these four interventions is to enhance balance in the life of the adolescent with BPD symptoms, to diminish the all-or-nothing thinking, and to improve the locus of control on emotions and behavior. The basic assumption of these interventions is that expectation of improvement is reasonable, and that early interventions are needed to prevent the adverse consequences in the long term. Early interventions could lessen the suffering of both patients and their environment, and may prevent the development of full-blown BPD in adulthood and the lower (social) functioning related to BPD symptoms in adolescence (Chanen, Jovev, and Jackson, 2007; Miller, Muehlenkamp, and Jacobson, 2008).

In the next section we will report on two multi-center randomized controlled trials on the treatment of BPD symptoms in adolescence, with ERT as the treatment module. ERT has been implemented in the outpatient departments of six mental health centers in The Netherlands.

## EMOTION REGULATION TRAINING

The main goal of the training is to introduce alternative ways of coping with affective instability, daily stressors, and psychological vulnerability. Reducing self-harm or harm to others is another important issue. The adolescents learn that they can take more responsibility for their behavior, and to realize they have a choice in how to (re)act when emotionally distressed. After four sessions, there is a meeting for important system members (e.g., parents, partner, mentor, friends). The meeting involves psychoeducation about emotion dysregulation, and provides a brief summary of the therapy program with instructions on how to deal best with their emotionally volatile relative/friend.

ERT groups consist of six to nine adolescents, 14 to 19 years old. The group meets for 17 weekly sessions of 105 minutes. The group is facilitated by two therapists, neither of whom provides individual therapy to the adolescents. We required that at least one facilitator have experience in the treatment of emotion dysregulation disorders and in group therapy. The ERT manual consists of a workbook for the subjects and the facilitators. The program requires little additional training for mental health professionals who represent different disciplines. In our setting we provided a one-day course and monthly supervision during the training.

Each session begins with a discussion about the homework assignments made the previous week and using the newly learned skills is emphasized (Table 8.1). Subjects are asked to fill out a mood rating scale daily to achieve better insight into their mood swings and their triggers. The topic of the current session is then introduced; after a brief break the session resumes and the topic for the current session is illustrated with an example. A relaxation exercise follows. Each session ends with the homework assignment for the next week.

The first phase of training involves psychoeducation about emotional dysregulation and increasing the awareness of patterns of behavior and emotion.

*Table 8.1.* A SESSION-BY-SESSION OUTLINE OF THE ERT PROGRAM

| Session | Content |
| --- | --- |
| 1 | Introduction, psychoeducation |
| 2 | The cognitive model |
| 3 | Automatic thoughts and dysfunctional patterns of thinking |
| 4 | How to recognize an emotional storm |
| Systems meeting | Psychoeducation, information about the training |
| 5 | Knowing yourself |
| 6 | Using your self-knowledge |
| 7 | Emotional storms and time out |
| 8 | How to recognize, prevent, and/or stop an emotional storm |
| 9 | Introduction to behavior modification plans |
| 10 | Behavior modification plans |
| 11 | Sleeping and eating |
| 12 | Balancing school, work, free time |
| 13 | Taking care of your body (including how to deal with self-harm) |
| 14 | Money |
| 15 | Relationships—introduction |
| 16 | Relationships |
| 17 | Evaluation and goodbyes |
| Booster sessions | |

Behavioral principles are taught and subjects learn to make a behavioral chain analysis (Figure 8.1). This begins with the self-monitoring of thoughts and feelings to better understand the patterns of their emotional storms. The term "emotional storm" describes the feeling of being swept away in an avalanche of emotions.

The second phase is characterized by "knowing yourself." Adolescents are invited to explore their temperament and character, to have a closer look at past experiences, present circumstances, and personal plans for the future. "Knowing yourself" aims at improving one's locus of control and gaining better insight regarding one's personal strengths and vulnerabilities.

The third phase involves learning emotion regulation skills (e.g., gaining distance and stepping back, or challenging negative and distorted basic assumptions), followed by attention to lifestyle. An important component of this phase is learning how to avoid deliberate self-harm and other forms of self-destructive behavior. Adolescents learn to make "behavior modification plans," in which they describe a lifestyle problem, pros and cons of changing, and then develop a plan to attack the problem.

The training ends with a final evaluation meeting and two booster sessions at six and twelve weeks posttreatment. A letter with a brief summary of the training, the progress, and specific areas addressed is sent to the adolescent's individual therapist.

| Date time | What happened? | Thoughts | Feelings | What did you do? | What were the consequences? |
|---|---|---|---|---|---|
| | | | | | |
| | What are helping thoughts in this situation? | | What feeling do you get from the helping thoughts? | | What else could you do? In that case, what would have been the consequences? |

**Figure 8.1** Behavioral Chain Analysis

## EMOTION REGULATION GROUP TRAINING FOR ADOLESCENTS: A PILOT STUDY

The effectiveness of ERT was examined in a randomized controlled pilot study with 43 youth (aged 14–19 years) in five mental health centers in The Netherlands (Schuppert et al., 2009). Subjects were assessed before and after random assignment to ERT plus treatment as usual (TAU; $n = 23$) or to TAU alone ($n = 20$). Outcome measures included assessment of BPD symptoms, locus of control, and internalizing and externalizing behavior.

## METHOD

Adolescents age 14 to 19 years were referred for treatment of emotion dysregulation problems or borderline personality symptoms and underwent a standard intake in which the Borderline Personality Severity Index (BPDSI-IV; Giesen-Bloo, et al., 2010) was administered to confirm the presence of either BPD or subclinical BPD. Subjects had to meet the criterion of mood instability in combination with at least one other BPD symptom. The two treatment conditions were ERT combined with TAU (ERT + TAU) and TAU alone. Components of TAU included medication, individual psychotherapy, systems-based therapy, in-patient psychiatric care, and emergency services in case of self-harm or suicidal behavior.

Baseline assessment was made after inclusion and prior to randomization. Follow-up assessments took place post-treatment. Three independent research psychologists completed the ratings. They had no contact with the therapists and were blind with respect to treatment allocation.

Forty-six patients entered the study between July 2005 and October 2005; three withdrew after baseline assessment and before randomization. Inclusion criteria were: age between 14 and 19 years and meeting the following (DSM-IV) criteria based on the concurrent sections of the BPDSI-IV:

A. *Mood instability due to a marked reactivity of mood (e.g., intense episodic dysphoria, irritability, or anxiety usually lasting a few hours and only rarely more than a few days).*
B. *At least one of the following criteria (1-3):*
   1. Impulsivity in at least two areas that are potentially self-damaging (e.g., spending, sex, substance abuse, reckless driving, binge eating).
   2. Recurrent suicidal behavior, gestures, or threats, or self-mutilating behavior.
   3. Inappropriate, intense anger or difficulty controlling anger (e.g., frequent displays of temper, constant anger, recurrent physical fights).

When the adolescent met the inclusion criteria, the adolescents as well as the parent(s) were informed about the training and about the research project. Participating adolescents and their legal representatives signed an informed consent.

## ASSESSMENT

We used the *Borderline Personality Disorder Severity Index—IV* (BPDSI-IV; Arntz et al., 2003; Giesen-Bloo et al., 2010) to assess current severity and frequency of the DSM-IV BPD manifestations. The total score on the interview and the sub-score on mood instability were used as primary outcome measures.

The *Multidimensional Emotion Regulation Locus of Control* (MERLC) was developed by our team (Nauta & Plat, 2005) based on the Multidimensional Health Locus of Control (MHLC; Wallston, Wallston and DeVellis, 1978; Wallston, 2005). The measure has 18 items in four subscales: Intern (6 items; e.g., "it is mainly due to myself how long it takes to handle an emotional storm"), Coincidence (6 items; e.g., "whatever I do, I will have emotional storms anyway"), Medication (3 items; e.g., "when an emotional storm fades away, this is mainly due to medication"), Others (3 items; e.g., "when I have an emotional storm, I can only do what others tell me to do"). The report of the subscale "Intern" was included as a primary outcome measure in this study.

The *Youth Self Report* (YSR; Achenbach, 1991) is a commonly used and well-established measure. It consists of 112 items. Scores on both internalizing and externalizing subscales were included as secondary outcome measures.

## RESULTS AND DISCUSSION

Both groups showed equal reductions in BPD symptoms over time. The group receiving ERT plus TAU (and not the TAU only-group) had a significant increase in internal locus of control: ERT participants reported more sense of control over their own mood swings, and did not attribute changes in mood swings to external factors only. Contrary to our expectations, we found no differential effect with regard to our primary measures of mood regulation (BPDSI-IV subscale affect regulation) and BPDSI-IV total. Adolescents in both treatment conditions had less severe borderline symptoms after six months, regardless of whether they received ERT. One explanation for this finding is that the adolescents had relatively low scores on the BPDSI-IV at base-line, leaving little room for improvement. Their mean score was 19.8 (SD 8.4; Range 7.0–44.2) while in treatment outcome studies for adult BPD patients, a cut-off score of 20 is often set as an inclusion criterion.

Given that both groups showed improvement over time in their borderline symptoms with no differences on the BPDSI-IV, TAU alone might be more powerful than previously thought. Psychiatric treatment for children and adolescents is easily available in The Netherlands, usually combines family and individual therapy, and is covered by all insurance plans.

In line with our expectations, the adolescents reported higher levels of internal locus of control after ERT + TAU, and lower levels of internal locus of control after TAU alone. Gaining control over one's emotions and thoughts and taking responsibility for one's behavior are the main goals of ERT.

The study was complicated by a high attrition rate; 39% of the adolescents in the experimental condition were lost to second assessment. In other studies with adolescents more than one third of participants also dropped out of treatment (Chanen et al., 2008b; Rathus and Miller, 2002). The non-completers in our study differed from the completers in pre-treatment internalizing behavior: completers reported significantly higher levels of internalizing behavior than the adolescents who did not participate in the second assessment. This suggests that the adolescents who fail to complete treatment are not the ones with more severe borderline pathology, but rather the ones with fewer internalizing complaints.

In sum, the results of our pilot study were less powerful than we hoped. This could be due to the program itself, to the quality of TAU in The Netherlands, or to the lack of reliable and valid assessments for adolescents with borderline symptoms. Therefore we conducted a larger RCT after making some modifications in the program based on our work in the pilot study.

## EMOTION REGULATION TRAINING: A RANDOMIZED CONTROLLED TRIAL

Our following treatment study (Schuppert et al., 2012c) aimed to evaluate the effectiveness of ERT on a larger scale. Adolescents were randomized to either TAU, or to ERT + TAU. We hypothesized that the adolescents in the ERT + TAU condition would improve more on borderline symptoms, general psychopathology, and quality of life than those in the TAU condition. There is a paucity of studies that address the identification of predictors in the treatment of BPD in adolescents (Barnicot, Katsakou, Marougka, and Priebe, 2011). Therefore, we explored the predictive value of a history of abuse and/or trauma, depressive, and externalizing symptoms. In the current study, we hypothesized that ERT would be particularly beneficial for adolescents with higher symptom severity at baseline, and for completers (defined as attending nine or more sessions).

### METHOD

Participants were 109 adolescents aged 14 to 19 years, who were referred for emotion regulation problems and/or BPD features to one of four mental health centers in the North of The Netherlands. Recruitment took place between November 2007 and February 2010. In case of emotion regulation problems or BPD symptomatology as the main problem area, adolescents were referred to trained clinicians for complementary screening. To participate in the study, subjects had to meet at least two BPD criteria (according to SCID-II) (Weertman, Arntz, and Kerkhofs, 2000). Exclusion criteria were: psychotic disorders, conduct disorder, and substance dependence, as assessed by the K-SADS (Kaufman et al., 1997), and IQ below 80, as estimated on the basis of educational level. Anxiety disorders, mood disorders, or ADHD could be present as co-morbid disorders, but were not the primary diagnosis.

    To improve the representativeness of the sample, stratified sampling was applied by first randomizing the adolescents with a score of 15 or more on the total scale of a structured interview on BPD severity (BPDSI-IV-ado, Schuppert, Bloo, Minderaa, Emmelkamp, and Nauta, 2012a) and subsequently the adolescents with a lower score. Assessments were accomplished at baseline and posttreatment (i.e., after ending the ERT, or after a comparable period), and at 6 months' follow-up (for the ERT + TAU condition only). Adolescents in the TAU condition were not assessed at follow-up, since they were allowed to enter ERT after posttreatment assessment.

### Emotion Regulation Training

The ERT protocol has been adapted according to the findings of the pilot study. The training consisted of 17 weekly sessions of 105 minutes, followed by two booster sessions at 6 and 12 weeks. A "network" meeting takes place between session 4 and 5, where parents, caretakers, partners, and close friends are informed about the background and contents of ERT. Treatment as Usual (TAU) consisted of (a combination of) pharmacotherapy, individual psychotherapy, counseling, family therapy, inpatient psychiatric care, and emergency care in case of self-mutilation or suicidal behavior.

All therapists had previous therapy experience in psychiatry (mean: 12.4 years; range 3–34 years), which included at least 2 years of experience with adolescents with borderline features. At least one of the two therapists per ERT group was a licensed cognitive behavioral therapist or clinical psychologist. To keep the study as naturalistic as possible, there were no specific criteria for the therapists in the TAU condition. To enhance treatment adherence and comparability between centers, the manuals were highly structured. Treatment integrity of a random sample of 10 audio-taped sessions was checked by an independent rater. On average, sessions covered 93% of the ERT manual.

## Measures

The assessments were conducted by research psychologists who were blind to treatment condition and included the *Structured Clinical Interview for DSM-IV Personality Disorders—borderline personality disorder section* (SCID-II-BPD; Weertman, Arntz, and Kerkhofs, 2000), the *Kiddie-Schedule for Affective Disorders and Schizophrenia for School-Age Children—Present and Lifetime version* (K-SADS-PL) (Kaufman et al., 1997), and the *Borderline Personality Disorder Severity Index-IV–adolescent version* (BPDSI-IV-ado) (Schuppert et al., 2012a), the *Symptom Checklist–90–R* (SCL-90-R) (Derogatis, Lipman, and Covi, 1973), the *Youth Quality of Life—research version* (YQOL-R, 2002), the *Children's Depression Inventory* (CDI) (Kovacs, 1981), and the *SNAP-IV Rating Scale* (Swanson, Sandman, Deutsch, and Baren, 1983), which addresses ADHD and ODD symptoms. We used the total score as a moderator.

## Results and Discussion

To our knowledge, this study reports data on the largest sample in a treatment outcome study of adolescents with BPD features, and is the second published RCT for this group (Chanen et al. 2008b). The study was conducted in general mental health institutes, with few exclusion criteria, thus enhancing external validity. The majority of adolescents (73%) fulfilled full BPD criteria according to DSM-IV. The attrition rate was relatively low, and those who dropped out had fewer symptoms at pre-treatment. Attrition was defined as attending less than half of the training (nine sessions); the attrition rate was 19%.

Participants were free to use mental health care services, and the frequency of contacts between baseline and postintervention was equal across conditions.

The mean number of individual contacts was 5.1 and 3.2 for family contacts. The number of participants admitted to inpatient care or day-care was equal (six adolescents in the ERT-group, and eight in the control-group).

There were no significant differences between conditions on any of the measures. Both groups improved from baseline to postintervention on all measures but quality-of-life. The ERT group improved significantly from postintervention to follow-up.

We investigated whether depressive symptoms (CDI), symptoms of ADHD (SNAP-IV), and a history of physical and/or sexual abuse were associated with improvement on the outcome measures. More depressive symptoms at baseline were found to be associated with less reduction in borderline severity and general psychopathology at postintervention, but this was unrelated to condition. Adolescents with a history of physical and/or sexual abuse reported a lower reduction in complaints. Further, having more ADHD symptoms was associated with poorer quality-of-life at follow-up. This appeared once again to be unrelated to treatment condition and may merely reflect predictors of the course of symptoms rather than moderators of treatment outcome.

As to the clinical significance of the results described, a minority of participants in both groups reached an end-point within the normative range of the BPDSI-IV-ado total score (cut-off at 6): 19% of youth in the ERT condition versus 12% in the control condition were remitted as a function of the cut-off at posttreatment. At six months follow-up, 67% of youth still fell in the normative range of borderline symptomatology (see Figure 8.2).

The current findings that a relatively short intervention does not seem to have substantial additional benefits, are similar to the results of our pilot study (Schuppert et al., 2009), but also are in agreement with Chanen et al. (2008b), who found no added value of cognitive analytic therapy above good clinical care. The disappointing results may be explained at least partially by the following: we hypothesized that a brief, time-limited intervention for BPD symptoms in adolescence might prevent the development of the full syndrome, based on the assumption that symptoms

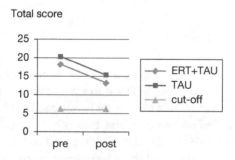

Total score

ERT = Emotion Regulation Training
TAU = Treatment as Usual
BPDSI-IV-ado = Borderline Personality Disorder
      Severity Index IV-adolescent version

Figure 8.2  BPDSI-IV-ado Means (Total Score) Pre- and Postintervention

would not yet be as severe as in adults. However, it is possible that BPD symptoms are already persistent and serious, and require intensive treatment (as in BPD treatment of adult patients). Our brief module might be too limited for such a complex disorder. Recovery from BPD symptoms might require a more intensive intervention, such as the evidence-based interventions developed for adult BPD patients (Emmelkamp and Kamphuis, 2007). Secondly, ERT is not grounded in a particular theory. Elements of different therapies have been used, such as elements of dialectical behavior therapy (DBT; Linehan, 1996), and cognitive behavioral therapy, with STEPPS (Blum et al., 2008; Bos, van Wel, Appelo, & Verbraak, 2010) as the starting point. ERT may be too fragmented, just barely touching the core symptoms (such as emotional dysregulation), and not producing fundamental changes. Third, the group format leaves little room for individual tailoring. Finally, it is conceivable that some of the adolescents might have received greater benefit from specific treatment for depression or abuse and trauma.

The low attrition rate (19%) in our study is remarkable: Chanen et al. (2008b) found attrition as high as 54% after six months of therapy. In a study with a quasi-experimental design with DBT-A for adolescents with BPD symptoms, an attrition of 38% in the DBT-A condition was reported (Rathus & Miller, 2002). The low attrition rate in our study can be explained in part by peer contact, as mentioned by the adolescents.

## CONCLUSION

Despite the growing body of evidence for effective interventions for adult patients with BPD, research in this field for adolescents is still in its teens. Despite the poor results, our studies may encourage clinicians to recognize the necessity for early intervention in adolescents with BPD symptoms:. A majority of adolescents in our study still suffered from borderline symptomatology, even after 12 months of TAU (with or without ERT). Outcome was especially negative for adolescents with a history of abuse, and with more severe comorbid symptoms including symptoms of depression and ADHD/ODD. The low attrition rate in the Schuppert et al. (2012c) RCT demonstrates that the treatment was feasible, while the response and the enthusiasm of therapists and parents can be viewed as an indication of the clinical need for specific treatment modules for these adolescents.

Considering the modest level of motivation often seen in adolescents, we hoped that ERT could possibly function as a first step in a stepped care model. It has the advantage of being brief, easy to implement in everyday care, and it can assist therapists to pioneer in a poorly developed area. During the training for therapists, we experienced their enthusiasm and relief that an intervention for adolescents with BPD symptoms was developed. In our studies, we found all the therapists eager to get a better understanding of BPD symptoms in adolescence and to apply a more specific treatment for this group. However, we found no additional effect of ERT when added to TAU. Even though these negative results are disappointing, the findings are of great importance for the further development of

BPD treatment protocols in adolescence. The current RCTs have demonstrated a need for age-specific treatment protocols for adolescents with borderline features.

Treatment of BPD in adolescence is still in its early stages. A few treatment protocols have been investigated, but none have shown sufficient evidence of additional effectiveness (Chanen et al., 2008b; Ougrin et al., 2012; Schuppert et al., 2009; 2012c). However, since more is known about the serious adverse outcomes in the long-term, "wait and see" is not a viable option. Future research should aim not only at demonstrating effectiveness of the treatment module as a whole, but should also identify the active ingredients. In this regard, it would also be interesting to examine differences in effectiveness between different countries. The standard of psychiatric care for children and adolescents in The Netherlands is rather high. It is conceivable that the additional effect of treatment interventions such as ERT might be greater than TAU in countries where standard psychiatric care is less developed and/or accessible.

In general, future research on treatment of BPD in adolescence should investigate contributing and confounding factors. For instance, what is the additional effect of parent involvement in treatment? What are the important characteristics of the therapist? What is the optimal duration for treatment? Based on the results of our treatment studies, we believe that a relatively small and time-limited intervention is insufficient to produce significant changes. Development and/or improvement of age-specific treatment protocols for adolescents with BPD symptoms should include family interventions, and should take into account axis I disorders, e.g., depressive symptoms, anxiety, and PTSD.

Finally, longitudinal studies are needed to examine the effect of treatment over time. As is often the case in developmental processes, the effect of an intervention might not be obvious in the short term. It is possible that the effects of treatment in adolescence will become apparent perhaps a few years later. Long-term follow-up studies will be needed to unravel the course of BPD after treatment.

## REFERENCES

Achenbach, T. M. (1991). *Manual for the Child Behaviour Checklist 4–18, YSR, and TRF profiles*. Burlington, VT: University of Vermont, Department of Psychiatry.

Arntz, A., van den Hoorn, M., Cornelis, J., Verheul, R., van den Bosch, W.M., & de Bie, A.J. (2003). Reliability and validity of the borderline personality disorder severity index. *Journal of Personality Disorders, 17*, 45–59.

Barnicot, K., Katsakou, C., Marougka, S., & Priebe, S. (2011). Treatment completion in psychotherapy for borderline personality disorder: A systematic review and meta-analysis. *Acta Psychiatrica Scandinavica, 123*, 327–338.

Bateman, A. W., & Fonagy, P. (1999). Effectiveness of partial hospitalisation in the treatment of borderline personality disorder: A randomised controlled trial. *American Journal of Psychotherapy, 156*, 1563–1569.

Bateman, A. W., & Fonagy, P. (2001). Treatment of borderline personality disorder with psycho analytically oriented partial hospitalization: An 18-month follow-up. *American Journal of Psychotherapy, 158*, 36–42.

Bateman, A. W., & Fonagy, P. (2004). *Psychotherapy for borderline personality disorder.* Oxford, United Kingdom: Oxford Medical Publications.

Bateman, A. W., Ryle, A., Fonagy, P., & Kerr, I. B. (2007). Mentalization based therapy and cognitive analytic therapy compared. *International Review of Psychiatry, 19*, 51–62.

Bernstein, D. P., Cohen, P., Velez, C.N., Schwab-Stone, M., Siever, L.J., & Shinsato, L. (1993). Prevalence and stability of the DSM-III-R personality disorders in a community-based survey of adolescents. *American Journal of Psychiatry, 150,* 1237–1243.

Bezirganian, S., Cohen, P., & Brook, J. S. (1993). The impact of mother-child interaction on the development of borderline personality disorder. *American Journal of Psychiatry, 150,* 1836–1842.

Black, D. W., Blum, N., & St John, D. (2009). Borderline personality disorder: STEPPS is practical, evidence-based, easier to use. *Current Psychiatry, 8,* 18–37.

Bleiberg, E., Rossouw, T., & Sharp, C. (2011). *Mentalization based treatment for adolescents: A framework to treat adolescent breakdown and emerging personality disorders.* In P. Fonagy, & A.W. Bateman (Eds.), Handbook of mentalizing in mental health practice. Washington DC: American Psychiatric Publishing Press.

Blum, N., St. John, D., Pfohl, B., Stuart, S., McCormick, B., Allen, J., Arndt, S., & Black, D. W. (2008). Systems training for emotional predictability and problem solving (STEPPS) for outpatients with borderline personality disorder: A randomized controlled trial and 1-year follow-up. *American Journal of Psychiatry, 165,* 468–478.

Bornovalova, M. A., Hicks, B. M., Iacono, W. G., & McGue, M. (2009). Stability, change, and heritability of borderline personality disorder traits from adolescence to adulthood: A longitudinal twin study. *Development and Psychopathology, 21,* 1335–1353.

Bos, E. H., van Wel, B., Appelo, M. T., & Verbraak, J. P. M. (2010). A randomized controlled trial of a Dutch version of Systems Training for Emotional Predictability and Problem Solving for borderline personality disorder. *The Journal of Nervous and Mental Disease, 198,* 299–304.

Bradley, R., Jenei, J., & Westen, D. (2005). Aetiology of borderline personality disorder: Disentangling the contributions of intercorrelated antecedents. *Journal of Nervous and Mental Disorders, 193,* 24–31.

Carlson, E. A., Egeland, B., & Sroufe, L. A. (2009). A prospective investigation of the development of borderline personality symptoms. *Development and Psychopathology, 21,* 1311–1334.

Chabrol, H., Montovany, A., Duconge, E., Kallmeyer, A., Mullet, E., & Leichsenring, F. (2004). Factor structure of the borderline personality inventory in adolescents. *European Journal of Psychological Assessment, 20,* 59–65.

Chanen, A. M., Jackson, H. J., McCutcheon, L. K., Jovev, M., Dudgeon, P., Yuen, H. P., Germano, . . . McGorry, P. D. (2008b). Early intervention for adolescents with borderline personality disorder using cognitive analytic therapy: Randomised controlled trial. *The British Journal of Psychiatry, 193,* 477–484.

Chanen, A. M., Jovev, M., & Jackson, H. J. (2007). Adaptive functioning and psychiatric symptoms in adolescents with Borderline Personality Disorder. *Journal of Clinical Psychiatry, 68,* 297–306.

Chanen, A. M., Jovev, M., McCutcheon, L. K., Jackson, H. J., & McGorry, P. D. (2008a). Borderline personality disorder in young people and the prospects for prevention and early intervention. *Current Psychiatry Reviews, 4,* 48–57.

Chanen, A. M., & Kaess, M. (2012). Developmental pathways to borderline personality disorder. *Current psychiatry reports, 14*, 45–53.

Cheng, H. G., Huang, Y., Liu, Z., & Liu, B. (2011). Associations linking parenting styles and offspring personality disorder are moderated by parental personality disorder, evidence from China. *Psychiatry Research, 189*, 105–109.

Clarkin, J. F., Foelsch P. A., Levy K. N., Hull J. W., Delaney J. C., & Kernberg O. F. (2001). The development of a psychodynamic treatment for patients with borderline personality disorder: A preliminary study of behavioral change. *Journal of Personality Disorders, 15*, 487–495.

Crawford, T. N., Cohen, P., First, M. B., Skodol, A. E., Johnson, J. G., & Kasen, S. (2008). Comorbid axis I and axis II disorders in early adolescence: Prognosis 20 years later. *Archives of General Psychiatry, 65*, 641–648.

Crone, E. H., Bullens, L., van der Plas, E. A. A., Kijkuit, E., & Zelazo, P. D. (2008). Developmental changes and individual differences in risk and perspective taking in adolescence. *Development and Psychopathology, 20*, 1213–1229.

Derogatis, L. R., Lipman R. S., & Covi, L. (1973). SCL-90: An outpatient psychiatric rating scale: Preliminary report. *Psychopharmacological Bulletin, 9*(1), 13–28.

Distel, M. A., Middeldorp, C. M., Trull, T. J., Derom, C. A., Willemsen, G., & Boomsma, D. I. (2011). Life events and borderline personality features: The influence of gene-environment interaction and gene-environment correlation. *Psychological Medicine, 41*, 849–860.

Emmelkamp, P. M. G., & Kamphuis, J. H. (2007). *Personality disorders.* Hoove: Taylor & Francis/Psychology Press.

Fleischhaker, C., Böhme, R., Sixt, B., Brück, C., Schneider, C., & Schulz, E. (2011). Dialectical behavioral therapy for adolescents (DBT-A): A clinical trial for patients with suicidal and self-injurious behavior and borderline symptoms with a one-year follow-up. *Child and Adolescent Psychiatry and Mental Health, 28*, 5(1), 3.

Giesen-Bloo, J., van Dyck, R., Spinhoven, P., van Tilburg, W., Dirksen, C., van Asselt, T., Kremers, I., . . . Arntz, A. (2006). Outpatient psychotherapy for borderline personality disorder: Randomized trial of schema-focused therapy vs. transference-focused psychotherapy. *Archives of General Psychiatry, 63*, 649–658.

Giesen-Bloo, J., Wachters, L., Schouten, E., & Arntz, A. (2010). The Borderline Personality Disorder Severity Index-IV: Psychometric evaluation and dimensional structure. *Personality and Individual Differences, 49*, 136–141.

Gunderson, J. G., Zanarini, M. C., Choi-Kain, L. W., Mitchell, K. S., Jang, K. L., & Hudson, J. I. (2011). Family study of borderline personality disorder and its sectors of psychopathology. *Archives of General Psychiatry, 68*, 753–762.

Haan, A. D., Dekovic, M., & Prinzie, P. (2012). Longitudinal impact of parental and adolescent personality on parenting. *Journal of Personality and Social Psychology, 102*, 189–199.

Hovens, J. G., Giltay, E. J., Wiersma, J. E., Spinhoven, P., Penninx, B. W., Zitman, F. G. (2012). Impact of childhood life events and trauma on the course of depression and anxiety disorders. *Acta Psychiatrica Scandinavica, 23*, e-pub ahead of print.

Hufford, M. R., & Shiffman, S. (2003). Assessment methods for patient-reported outcomes. *Disease Management and Health Outcomes, 11*, 77–86.

Johnson, J. G., Cohen, P., Brown, J., Smailes, E. M., & Bernstein, D. P. (1999). Childhood maltreatment increases risk for personality disorders during early adulthood. *Archives of General Psychiatry, 56*, 600–606.

Johnson, J. G., Cohen, P., Chen, H., Kasen, S., & Brook, J. S. (2006). Parenting behaviours associated with risk for offspring personality disorder during adulthood. *Archives of General Psychiatry, 63*, 579–587.

Katz, L. Y., Cox, B. J., Gunasekara, S. M. D., & Miller, A. L. (2004). Feasibility of dialectical behavior therapy for suicidal adolescent inpatients. *Journal of the American Academy for Child and Adolescent Psychiatry, 43*, 276–283.

Kaufman, J., Birmaher, B., Brent, D., Rao, U., Flynn, C., Moreci, P., Williamson, D., & Ryan, N. (1997). Schedule for affective disorders and schizophrenia for school-aged children–present and life-time version (K-SADS-PL): Initial reliability and validity data. *Journal of the American Academy for Child and Adolescent Psychiatry, 36*, 980–988.

Kendler, K.S., Aggen, S.H., Czajkowski, N., Roysamb, E., Tambs, K., Torgersen, S., Neale, M.C., & Reichborn-Kjennerud, T. (2008). The structure of genetic and environmental risk factors for DSM-IV personality disorders: A multivariate twin study. *Archives of General Psychiatry, 65*, 1438–1446.

Kovacs, M. (1981). Rating scales to assess depression in school-aged children. *Acta Paedopsychiatrica, 46*, 305–315.

Lewinsohn, P. M., Rohde, P., & Seeley, J. R. (1996). Adolescent suicidal ideation and attempts: Prevalence, risk factors and clinical implications. *Clinical Psychology: Science and practice, 3*, 25–46.

Lewinsohn, P. M., Rohde, P., Seeley, J. R., & Klein, D. N. (1997). Axis II psychopathology as a function of axis I disorders in childhood and adolescence. *Journal of the American Academy for Child and Adolescent Psychiatry, 36*, 1752–1759.

Linehan, M. M. (1993a). *Cognitive-behavioral treatment of borderline personality disorder.* New York, NY: The Guilford Press.

Linehan, M. M. (1993b). *The skills training manual for treating borderline personality disorder.* New York, NY: The Guilford Press.

Linehan, M. M. (1996). *Borderline-persoonlijkheidsstoornis. Handleiding voor training en therapie.* Lisse, Netherlands: Swets & Zeitlinger.

Linehan, M. M., Armstrong, H. E., Suarez, A., Allmon, D., & Heard, H. L. (1991). Cognitive-behavioral treatment of chronically parasuicidal borderline patients. *Archives of General Psychiatry, 48*, 1060–1064.

Linehan, M.M., Comtois, K.A., Murray, A.M., Brown, M.Z., Gallop, R.J., Heard, H.L., Korslund, K.E., . . . Lindenboim, N. (2006). Two year randomized controlled trial and follow up of dialectical behavior therapy vs. therapy by experts for suicidal behaviors and borderline personality disorder. *Archives of General Psychiatry, 63*, 757–766.

Madge, N., Hewitt, A., Hawton, K., de Wilde, E.J., Corcoran, P., Fekete, S., van Heeringen, K., de Leo, D., & Ystgaard, M. (2008). Deliberate self-harm within an international community sample of young people: Comparative findings from the Child & Adolescent Self-harm in Europe (CASE) Study. *Journal of Child Psychology and Psychiatry, 49*, 667–677.

Materson, J., & Rinsley, D. (1975). The borderline syndrome: Role of the mother in the genesis and psychic structure of the borderline personality. *The International Journal of Psychoanalysis, 56*, 163–177.

Meijer, M. (2000). Borderline persoonlijkheidsstoornis. In F. C. Verhulst and F. Verheij (Eds.), *Adolescentenpsychiatrie.* Assen: Van Gorcum & Comp. B.V.

Miller, A. L., Rathus, J. H., & Linehan, M. M. (2007). *Dialectical behaviour therapy with suicidal adolescents.* New York, NY: The Guilford Press.

Miller, A. L., Muehlenkamp, J. J., & Jacobson, C. M. (2008). Fact or fiction: Diagnosing borderline personality disorder in adolescents. *Clinical Psychology Review, 28,* 969–981.

Nauta, M. H., & Plat, M. (2005). Multidimensional Anxiety Locus of Control: Emotion Regulation Problems. Groningen, Accare: Unpublished manual.

Ougrin, D., Tranah, T., Leigh, E., Taylor, L., & Rosenbaum Asarnow, J. (2012). Practitioner review: Self-harm in adolescents. *Journal of Child Psychology and Psychiatry, 53,* 337–350.

Paris, J. (2003). *Personality disorders over time: Precursors, course and outcome.* Washington DC: American Psychiatric Publishing, Inc.

Paris, J. (2008). *Treatment of borderline personality disorder. A guide to evidence-based practice.* New York, NY; London, England: The Guilford Press.

Putnam, K. E., & Silk, K. R. (2005). Emotion dysregulation and the development of borderline personality disorder. *Development and Psychpathology, 17,* 899–925.

Rathus, J. H., & Miller, A. L. (2002). Dialectical behavior therapy adapted for suicidal adolescents. *Suicide Life Threatening Behavior, 32,* 146–157.

Roberts, B. W., Walton K. E., & Viechtbauer, W. (2006). Patterns of mean-level change in personality traits across the life course: A meta-analysis of longitudinal studies. *Psychological Bulletin, 132,* 1–25.

Rossouw, T., Fonagy, P. (2012). Mentalization-based treatment for self-harm in adolescents: A randomized controlled trial. *Journal of the American Academy for Child and Adolescent Psychiatry, 51,* 1304–1313.e3.

Ryle, A. (2004). The contribution of cognitive analytic therapy to the treatment of borderline personality disorder. *Journal of Personality Disorders, 18,* 3–35.

Sartor, C. E., Grant, J. D., Lynskey, M. T., McCutcheon, V. V., Waldron, M., Statham, D. J., Bucholz, K. K. . . . Nelson, E.C. (2012). Common heritable contributions to low-risk trauma, high-risk trauma, post-traumatic stress disorder, and major depression. *Archives of General Psychiatry, 69,* 293–299.

Schuppert, H. M., Albers, C. J., Minderaa, R. B., Emmelkamp, P. M. G., & Nauta, M. H. (2012b). Parental rearing and psychopathology in mothers of adolescents with and without borderline personality symptoms. *Child and Adolescent Psychiatry and Mental Health, 6,* 29.

Schuppert, H. M., Bloo, J., Minderaa, R. B., Emmelkamp, P. M. G., & Nauta, M. H. (2012a). Psychometric evaluation of the Borderline Personality Disorder Severity Index-IV adolescent and parent version. *Journal of Personality Disorders, 26,* 628–640.

Schuppert, H. M., Giesen-Bloo, J., van Gemert, T. G., Wiersema, H. M., Minderaa, R. B., Emmelkamp, P. M. G., & Nauta, M. H. (2009). Effectiveness of an emotion-regulation group training for adolescents: A randomized controlled pilot study. *Clinical Psychology and Psychotherapy, 16,* 467–478.

Schuppert, H. M., Timmerman, M. E., Bloo, J., van Gemert, T. G., Wiersema, H. M., Minderaa, R. B., Emmelkamp, P. M. G., & Nauta, M. H. (2012c). Emotion regulation training for adolescents with borderline personality disorder traits: A randomized controlled trial. *Journal of the American Academy for Child and Adolescent Psychiatry, 51,* 1314–1323.e2.

Silk, K. R., Lee, S., Hill, E. M., & Lohr, N. E. (1995). Borderline personality disorder symptoms and severity of sexual abuse. *American Journal of Psychiatry, 152,* 1059–1064.

Stanley, B., & Siever, L. J. (2010). The interpersonal dimension of borderline personality disorder: Toward a neuropeptide model. *American Journal of Psychiatry, 167,* 24–39.

Steinberg, L., & Morris, A. S. (2001). Adolescent development. *Annual Review of Psychology*, *52*, 83–110.

Stepp, S. D., Whalen, D. J., Pilkonis, P. A., Hipwell, A. E., & Levine, M. D. (2011). Children of mothers with borderline personality disorder: Identifying parenting behaviors as potential targets for intervention. *Personality Disorders: Theory, Research, and Treatment*, *3*, 76–91.

Swanson, J. M., Sandman, C. A., Deutsch, C., & Baren, M. (1983). Methylphenidate hydrochloride given with or before breakfast: I. Behavioral, cognitive, and electrophysiological effects. *Pediatrics*, *72*, 49–55.

Torgersen, S., Czajkowski, N., Jacobson, K., Reichborn-Kjennerud, T., Roysamb, E., Neale, M. C., & Kendler, K. S. (2008). Dimensional representations of DSM-IV cluster B personality disorders in a population-based sample of Norwegian twins: A multivariate study. *Psychological Medicine*, *38*, 1617–1625.

Torgersen, S., Lygren, S., Oien, P. A., Skre, I., Onstad, S., Edvardsen, J., Tambs, K., & Kringlen, E. (2000). A twin study of personality disorders. *Comprehensive Psychiatry*, *41*, 416–425.

van Gemert, T. G., Ringrose, H. J., Schuppert, H. M., & Wiersema, H. M. (2009a). *Emotieregulatietraining (ERT), een programma voor adolescenten met emotieregulatie problemen*. Amsterdam, Netherlands: Boom.

van Gemert, T. G., Schuppert, H. M., & Wiersema, H. M. (2009b). *Emotieregulatietraining (ERT), een programma voor adolescenten met emotieregulatie problemen: handleiding voor therapeuten*. Amsterdam, Netherlands: Boom.

Verheul, R., van den Bosch, L. M. C., Koeter, W. J., de Ridder, M. A., Stijnen, T., & van den Brink, W. (2003). Dialectical behaviour therapy with women with borderline personality disorder: 12-Month, randomised clinical trial in the Netherlands. *British Journal of Psychiatry*, *182*, 135–140.

Wallston, K. A., Wallston, B.S., & DeVellis, R. (1978). Development of the Multidimensional Health Locus of Control (MHLC) scales. *Health Education Monographs*, *6*, 160–170.

Wallston, K. A. (2005). The validity of the Multidimensional Health Locus of Control scales. *Journal of Health Psychology*, *10*, 623–631.

Weertman, A., Arntz, A., & Kerkhofs, M. L. M. (2000). *Gestructureerd klinisch interview voor DSM-IV persoonlijkheidsstoornissen (SCID-II)*. Lisse, Netherlands: Swets & Zeitlinger.

Winograd, G., Cohen, P., & Chen, H. (2008). Adolescent borderline symptoms in the community: Prognosis for functioning over 20 years. *The Journal of Child Psychology and Psychiatry*, *49*, 933–941.

Youth Quality of Life instrument: Research Version (YQOL-R). (2002). Seattle, WA: University of Washington.

Zanarini, M. C., Frankenburg, F. R., Hennen, J., Reich, D. B., & Silk, K. R. (2006). Prediction of the 10-year course of borderline personality disorder. *American Journal of Psychiatry*, *163*, 827–832.

Zanarini, M. C., Williams, A. A., Lewis, R. E., Reich, R. B., Vera S. C., Marino, M. F., Levin, A., . . . Frankenburg, F. R. (1997). Reported pathological childhood experiences associated with the development of borderline personality disorder. *American Journal of Psychiatry*, *154*, 1101–1106.

# 9

# Alternatives to Self-Harm Program

*A Skills-Based Approach to Complement STEPPS*

DIANE CLARE ∎

This chapter describes the Alternatives to Self-Harm program (ASH) and its follow-up program, PHOENIX. These programs complement STEPPS and STAIRWAYS. Data supportive of ASH are presented and show that the program leads to a reduction of self-harm risk for people with emotional dysregulation. ASH can stand alone or be adjunctive to STEPPS. ASH is an approach that reduces risk and increases confidence for participants in maintaining more effective coping strategies as well as progressing to other therapies as needed.

## A JOURNEY TO A HOPE PLUS APPROACH

In order to understand how ASH developed, it is first important to go back to the history of my personal and professional journey. A series of significant life experiences led me to become interested in the field of psychology at a relatively later stage in life, such that much of what I have brought to my work has come first from personal experience, then my academic and professional training, and finally by my professional experience. The most significant event in my young adult years was the birth of my second son, whose disabilities and later death led to my deepening interest in human development, grief, and issues of identity. I emigrated from the United Kingdom to New Zealand in 1981, where I continued to raise my other son and two daughters in the South Island of this beautiful country, which quickly came to be home. That year became etched in New Zealand history as the "Year of the Springbok Tour" where the country was split between supporting the South African Rugby team as a sporting endeavor versus seeing this as condoning apartheid by allowing the Spring Boks to tour. This was significant in the history of Aotearoa/New Zealand and the events that followed helped to form my understandings of biculturalism and a keen interest in applying my learning to the New Zealand context.

I trained in New Zealand first as a grief and relationship counsellor, then as a psychotherapist and clinical psychologist. I worked mainly in adult mental health and in intellectual disabilities services and developed specialist knowledge about the effects of trauma, including that of sexual and physical abuse. I regularly worked with people who coped with their distress through a range of self-harming methods and the themes that emerged began to direct my interest in this area.

An employment opportunity led me to return to the United Kingdom, where I took up senior roles in forensic and general mental health services. This was a period in which I developed the ASH Program, initially on an individual basis and then adapted it to a group-based approach. In particular I drew on my experience with people whose distress was alleviated through self-harming. Within the forensic setting, a high number of residents had histories of abuse and major trauma: sexual, physical, and emotional with extreme neglect. The ASH program drew on what I refer to as a HOPE Plus approach:

History of working in mental health services

Observed no models that specifically target self-harm

Practical approach needed for clients and staff

Evidence based & effective approach

Plus practice-based insider knowledge—an "experience consultant" assisted in the design and delivery of the initial program.

ASH is influenced by my strong interest in narrative therapy, in that it takes a position of curious and respectful enquiry to the stories of those who consult with us, developing a re-authoring approach to stories about their lives and the role self-harm has played. The program also includes cognitive-behavioral coping strategies as well as some art therapy ideas, where a less verbal approach has proved valuable for expressing feelings and telling stories in meaningful ways.

## A FIRST LINK TO STEPPS

Around the time I was creating ASH, I came across Systems Training in Emotional Predictability & Problem Solving (STEPPS), which offered a new approach to working with people with emotional intensity difficulties, developed by Nancee Blum and her colleagues at the University of Iowa (2002 www.steppsforbpd.com; 2012). I later met Nancee Blum in London in 2006, and we have maintained a strong collegial relationship since that chance meeting. I invited her to England to provide training to staff in the Kent & Medway National Health Service (NHS)

Trust where I worked. This Trust is the largest Mental Health Trust in England and Wales. This training led our service to roll out the STEPPS program concurrently with ASH in Kent, England from 2005 onward. As part of the roll-out of the STEPPS approach, I met Renee Harvey, a colleague in Sussex, who was pivotal in the development of STEPPS, when we gave feedback to assist Nancee in the creation of a United Kingdom version of her program (STEPPS-UK).

This was to be a parallel journey in my learning about STEPPS and using ASH to complement STEPPS. As part of this work, I led a range of developments to raise greater awareness of the evidence base. The National Institute for Clinical Excellence (NICE) produced guidelines drawing on the international evidence base, and this includes an early version (2004 www.nice.org.uk) and a later version (2011 www.nice.org.uk) for working with people who self-harm. They also produced guidelines in 2009 for people with borderline personality disorder (BPD), which in STEPPS terminology is reframed to emotional intensity disorder (EID) and more recently as emotional intensity difficulties.

Dialectical behavior therapy (DBT; Linehan, 1993) has long been recognized for demonstrating strong evidence in the reduction of self-harm and in developing skills for coping with emotional dysregulation and distress tolerance. DBT combines cognitive-behavioral elements with mindfulness and is usually offered as a group-based approach with supporting individual DBT psychotherapy. In many services where I worked, it was seen as being too costly and somewhat inaccessible for the wider multidisciplinary team.

STEPPS, like DBT, is a skills-based approach for managing emotional intensity and distress rather than focusing specifically on self-harm. STEPPS, however, is relatively inexpensive and very much more accessible for staff with little or no psychological training, and is therefore more easily shared with the participants in a consistent way across the service. We found in Kent that this enabled a very rapid roll out of the STEPPS program and some initial clinical trials for ASH, with excellent outcomes, discussed later in this chapter. STEPPS was found to be invaluable and a quiet revolution took place. Gradually over time the approach has been implemented widely across the United Kingdom, where much credit goes to Renee Harvey and her colleagues for their persistence in enabling this process to unfold.

After returning to New Zealand in 2010, I noted that DBT was strongly supported by the mental health services. It had taken on something of a mystique across the wider services, such that it was mainly the domain of psychology staff. There was less of the joint ownership of the approach as I had seen it practiced in Europe and some resistance to considering anything different, given the amount of investment of resources in a relatively small country. There was little opportunity within this culture to concurrently run other programs such as STEPPS or ASH despite these being inexpensive as well as evidence-based. I therefore provided elements of STEPPS and ASH to a number of individuals here in New Zealand (in much the way I had started this work many years earlier in the United Kingdom) and found this approach worked well for a wide range of people.

Interestingly, at a meeting of the European Society for the Study of Personality Disorder in Amsterdam in 2012, Linehan commented that we do not really sufficiently know the precise components of DBT that make the difference for people. She suggested that perhaps there are many such components that are less than necessary and that more research is desirable to clarify this point. This, and feedback from clients, encouraged me to persist with using what fits for the person, as we are all aware now that the therapeutic approach is not the significant issue, but the relationship between the therapist and the person consulting them (Miller et al., 2004).

Drawing on the literature and consulting with service users, NICE Guidelines for Self-Harm were first published in 2004, but their focus was mainly on the initial 48 hours' treatment in the emergency room. Though useful in developing consistent care, a thorough biopsychosocial assessment and a more appropriate attitude of compassion toward the people who self-harm, it did not focus on general interventions or on the vast number of the population of those who self-harm but do not attend the emergency room. It was not until late 2011, that the revised NICE Guidelines on Self-Harm outlined what was psychologically useful in terms of interventions. Here is a summary of these guidelines:

- Target self-harm specifically
- Use a psychological approach
- 3–12 weeks to be focused on this work, preferably the longer option
- Group-based approaches are considered most effective
- Problem-solving approaches should be included in this work
- Service user consultations should influence the design of such approaches

It was heartening to see this, as all of these recommendations have been part of the success of the ASH Program since 2005.


## DESCRIPTION OF ASH AND ITS RELATIONSHIP TO STEPPS

I have seen a large number of clients in community mental health services as well as in a medium security forensic service where self-harm was a predominant feature of their difficulties. A thematic analysis of my work across these settings in terms of treatment as usual (TAU), led me to identify what I have coined as the "AILS" approach, which is cyclic in its nature, as follows:

- Attitude that harming is behavior to simply stop and just "attention seeking"
- Inadequate understanding of how harming "helps" with no concept of the purpose or needs met by the harming
- Lack of effective coping skills identified to meet the individual needs differently

- Struggle for control resulting in poor outcomes with poor attitude by the professionals leading to the repeat of this cycle

The AILS approach does little if anything to reduce self-harm behavior, and revolving door admissions continue while emergency room data showed that risk increased while hope decreased. Hope was minimal in the staff in terms of their attitude remaining one of resistance, and an inaccurate belief that people who self-harmed did this for "attention." In some practices there is a rule that if a patient self-harms between sessions, they are not allowed contact for 24 hours following a self-harm episode—based on the presumption that giving support in this time will behaviorally reinforce the self-harming. At the Bethlem Unit in South London and Maudsley's specialist unit for self-harm treatment, they advise against engaging in such a power struggle as it *increases* risk due to the riskier behavior becoming more covert.

## ASH APPROACH—APEX MODEL

Although STEPPS offers many useful strategies for managing emotional intensity, this does not target self-harm specifically. I devised the APEX model to underpin the approach used in the ASH Program. Each element of APEX draws on the evidence based knowledge which has emerged in the years intervening that of the development of DBT, whereby we now know that the attitude of the caring staff is more helpful if accepting that the harming provides a means of coping in the first instance (NICE, 2011). This stance is captured well in the position of curious enquiry that is the basis of a Narrative Therapy approach (White & Epston, 1990). Although such a stance is not the sole domain of Narrative Therapy, it is a style which is clearly helpful according to the evidence base (NICE, 2011).

Such an attitude de-centers the professional and the centering of the client becomes possible. Narrative therapy takes a position whereby the person is not the problem; the problem is the problem (White, 1995; Wingard, 1996). If a person is deemed as the problem, consider how this might pan out in terms of the risk of self-harm. By externalizing the problem of the effects of harming, this enables some curiosity and the possibility of generating alternatives. It is also worth considering that the purposes of harming can change and are not all the same.

We have found using the ASH program that clients have a number of reasons why they harm, and these are supported in the literature by Sutton (2007) who found eight common themes all beginning with C.
*Sutton's 8 reasons that people self-harm:*

- Coping and crisis intervention
- Calming and comforting
- Control
- Cleansing
- Confirmation of existence

- Creating comfortable numbness
- Chastisement
- Communication

The ASH Program has confirmed all these and also identified a ninth reason or theme: *Compliance*. This is a common theme described by those working with youth and may be influenced by a need to be acceptable to one's peers. The phenomenon of compliance also arose in my work in forensic services where self-harming became a means of connection and identity, and where materials with which to self-harm became currency within the unit. If we identify that the main purpose being met by such forms of harming is to be acceptable or part of the group, then other ways of being part of the group might be possible.

Once any purpose for the harming is clarified, then it becomes possible to generate alternatives to match those needs, in much the same way as Michael White developed an approach of deconstruction of meaning in his work (White, 1995). Adopting an open attitude enables this enquiry into purpose or purposes of the actions of harming, to lead to generating a range of other options in the form of an emotional first aid kit tailored to the person.

The emotional first aid kit must be tailored to fit the purpose and it is here where many errors occur, due to presumptions about what will work. For example, I have come across a number of ideas being applied without consideration of how these strategies may or may not fit the purpose that harming is meeting for the individual. I was due to see "Jenny," a woman in a hospital ward, and in her notes there were several pages of red pen scribbles. The nurse explained that they had heard that a red pen was known to be helpful sometimes so without any discussion with Jenny, she was provided with a red pen and paper when she requested it as an alternative to self-harming. The nurse was unsure if it had made a difference for Jenny, so when I met with her I asked her about the red pen drawings:

> Diane: *Your notes contain several pages of red pen drawings, can you tell me about these?*
> Jenny: *Oh that is something the nurses suggested I do whenever I have the urge to self-harm. I have to ask for the paper and a red pen and then draw my feelings in red on the paper.*
> Diane: *Does that help you and if so how?*
> Jenny: *No, not at all, but it seems to make the nurses less anxious!*

In this example we then looked at the purpose of harming for Jenny so that more meaningful emotional first aid ideas could be generated. Once an attitude of enquiry had identified the purpose or purposes of the harming and some alternatives had been tailored for an emotional first aid kit, it was possible for Jenny to take charge of her difficulties in more constructive ways.

There was another occasion in my practice when a male self-harmer told me that he needed to "see the red" in order to feel alive (part of the ongoing effects of early trauma where he had created numbness to the impact by dissociation). When we considered the possibility of substituting a soft felt pen using red ink on such occasions, he found this helpful. This illustrates how matching the need and the method is a useful means of reducing the risk and increasing a sense of control.

When the attitude, purpose, and emotional first aid kit have been worked on, the final part of the APEX model is the X Factor. The X Factor is something I have adapted to pull all this together into a self-contract. In the AILS approach, contracts have notoriously been about professionals demanding that the person complies with their rules. I liken this to Nancy Reagan who, as First Lady, adopted the stance that the answer to the drug problem among the youth of America was to "Just say no to drugs." We are all aware that the United States and other countries worldwide have not reduced drug addiction this way!

The XYZ contract is a self-contract, whereby the person identifies the purpose or purposes of the harming. They then identify three things which they consider would generally meet that need as an alternative to self-harming. For each purpose they then create a list of three alternatives: X, Y and Z. These are three matched alternatives they are prepared to do first prior to harming (e.g., before I self-harm to feel in control I will do X, Y & Z or before I self-harm, I will do X, Y and Z to calm down). This acts as a delay tactic and enables a greater sense of personal agency for the person in managing the urge to harm. The three choices (X, Y and Z) must be linked to the purpose of the harming at the time and must be SMART (specific, measurable, achievable, realistic and timely). For example, calling a friend might help, but only if that person is available 24/7, such that one of the choices might be better named as, "call someone like my friend or a 24/7 crisis line," so that it covers all time frames.

In summary, here is the APEX approach:

- Attitude: self-harm is a coping strategy to be understood
- Purpose of harming is clarified with the person (each time)
- Emotional First Aid kit of matched needs is developed
- X factor is the XYZ self-contract that emerges from this process

*Outcome: Hope increases & risk decreases* (a general theme in the ASH program findings to date).

## COMPONENTS OF ASH

- 12 structured sessions (weather report* check-in, review of home task, the new topic and practice, set new home task, weather report check-out)
- Focus on skills development
- Narrative therapy ideas: the person is not the problem, outsider witness use of the group's reflections

- Cognitive-behavioral ideas: STEPPS Emotional Intensity Continuum and other Problem Solving Strategies, including Stop & Think
- Art therapy: group based sharing & learning through art work
- Brief homework tasks between sessions e.g., 1 square centimeter, Yes/No exercises

## *Weather report

This is a brief way of engaging the group without going into details and where attendees are encouraged to provide a weather metaphor to describe their mood at the start and end of each session. Attendees find this a way to get used to speaking briefly without feeling pressure to "unpack" what they say. There is no analysis of these metaphors but we have found it helpful to keep track of them and establish with the individual if there are any problems in follow up if necessary. The idea to end the session with a weather report came at the session of one of the earlier participants and has been incorporated into the design since that time.

## Homework tasks

Some people like using traditional diary methods and other CBT type approaches as a form of homework but the majority of those attending the ASH Program to date have found it helpful to engage in exploratory exercises such as the following examples:

The **1 square centimeter task** asks for all participants to choose one small area of skin they will aim to care for during the intervening week, even if they persist in harming other parts. They are asked to keep this area warm if the weather is cold or cold if it is a warm season, and perhaps use some moisturizer on it. They are invited to notice what they are thinking and feeling and any ideas that arise, and come back to discuss this. Invariably some remarkable new awareness arises from this simple mindful exercise.

The **Yes/No exercise** is a similar mindful approach: notice how often you say no when you mean yes and yes when you mean no. Maybe consider the contexts where this happens more or less often. Be curious about it rather than blaming yourself. Simply acknowledge this is a time when you are saying the opposite of what you feel. There is the option to choose one small thing where you say yes and mean it or you say no and mean it. Provided it is something small, we guarantee two things: the world does not end and nobody dies! Issues in the feedback are often about being more assertive, paying more attention to the self and generally being more authentic.

**Key aspects of the ASH approach:**

- Developing a trusting group-based learning space
- Clarifying the purposes of harming

- Alternatives matched to purposes
- Creating an emotional first aid kit of strategies
- Encouraging self-contracts (XYZ Contracts that draw on these kits)
- Individual plans for the future beyond attending the group
- Providing a supportive ending experience

## WHY USE ASH WHEN THERE IS THE OPTION TO USE STEPPS?

ASH has been helpful to many people in whom self-harming is not only a risk, but where it is also likely to increase if they enter therapy due to the individuals finding therapy or the prospect of it too emotionally challenging at first. Similarities between STEPPS and ASH have been identified as being skills-based and involving a support team, as well as being low-cost and clinically effective. Differences are that ASH is a 12-week and STEPPS a 20-week program. A more important distinction is that with ASH, the focus is on self-harm while STEPPS provides a more general range of skills for managing emotional distress and learning to tolerate this distress. As follow-up support programs, PHOENIX is to ASH what STAIRWAYS (Blum et al., 2009) is to STEPPS and can be offered for those who find this helpful.

Linehan made a clear contribution to our understanding about the reduction of self-harm risk, although she has acknowledged the limits of DBT and the need for more research in order to learn what actually makes the difference (Linehan, 2012). It could well be that the success of programs such as STEPPS is due to it being relatively more accessible, understandable, and less costly than DBT for example, and ASH has similar benefits for those who are not psychologically or psychotherapeutically trained. My work in a specialist DBT service in New Zealand in 2015 confirmed for me how important it is to the success of a program that participants are adequately skilled in managing urges to self-harm. This experience highlighted how much ASH could be used as an entry-level group for programs such as DBT or STEPPS where the self-harm is a potential barrier to successful outcomes.

ASH acts as a complement to STEPPS and is not necessarily a replacement. It can be run alongside STEPPS for those who need it, or run separately. As with all these options, no one size fits all, and given the complexity of those who have emotional intensity difficulties, this variety of options is clearly useful.

## DISSEMINATION OF ASH

The ASH Program has been honed over the years, based on participant and professional feedback, such that it originally was designed as a set of session plans with accompanying handouts. Over time this has been developed to a full manual. In 2012, ASH was presented alongside STEPPS at the European Congress for the Study of Personality Disorder in Amsterdam (Clare, 2012) followed by the International Congress for the study of Personality Disorder in Copenhagen in

2013 (Clare, 2013), and the European Congress in Rome in 2014 (Clare, 2014). By this stage ASH was adapted to a tertiary education setting and trialled at the University of Auckland from July 2014. In 2015 ASH was presented at the International Congress for the study of Personality Disorder in Montreal (Clare, 2015) where it was noted as offering a means of reducing the shame so prevalent in the borderline population.

## EXPERIENCE WITH ASH (INCLUDING TRAINING)

Originally ASH was offered as an on-the-job training, whereby non-psychologically trained staff worked alongside the author to deliver the group based approach. Feedback from these staff was extremely positive and a considerable amount of cross over learning was applied to a range of service users with or without emotional intensity difficulties or self-harming. Through international presentations, ASH has been co-presented alongside STEPPS to demonstrate how well they complement each other.

In the past 5 years, training has been offered in New Zealand with an initial two-day workshop to establish an understanding of the APEX Model, followed by a further two day workshop to take participants through the program itself. The content may be adapted to fit a tertiary setting or any institution where there are brief terms or semesters. This has led to an adjustment to the format such that it is split into two six-session modules with an initial screening session and an adjustment to outcome measures as detailed later.

Some of those who completed the ASH training in New Zealand have begun to adapt it to school settings for children age 8 through to teenage years. This two module approach lends itself well to school settings and would also be suitable within a prison or correctional environment.

## RESEARCH CONDUCTED AND IN PROGRESS

Initial trials in the United Kingdom as well as individual-based outcomes in New Zealand are encouraging. The years 2005-2010 saw the first 6 groups run in the United Kingdom. Each group had 4 to 6 participants and usually had an equal number of men and women. We considered issues around gender and whether an all-female or all-male group would be preferable, but client feedback showed this was not generally an issue. They commented how valuable it was to have mixed groups even though they had been a little nervous about it at first.

### Experts by Experience

Isobel Elliot was an invaluable resource as an "expert by experience" who advised on the content of the original groups and she was involved in co-leading these.

Participant feedback showed how much they valued her support and how inspired they were by her. Sadly she died of natural causes and it is hoped in the future for graduates of the ASH Program to be included in ongoing service delivery. So the "Isobel effect" is something to aim for as part of future plans for ASH.

## Outcomes

Outcomes (by participants' self-report) repeatedly showed that participants found greater hope for the future and their risky behavior decreased (see Table 9.1). In addition, staff that supported them have been encouraged by the simplicity of the strategies as well as their efficacy. There have been some who only needed this group based approach and were discharged from the service, although many found it a means for going forward to other therapies.

The following themes have been identified from initial United Kingdom based trials of ASH (evaluation tool for each of the points in brackets):

- Increased understanding of the purpose of harming (evaluation questionnaire)
- Enhanced confidence and hope (SCQ-22, BHS)
- Wider range of coping strategies as alternatives (evaluation questionnaire)
- Reduction in risky behavior (evaluation questionnaire)
- Benefit from focus on the harming (evaluation questionnaire)
- More engaged in other programs e.g., STEPPS or DBT approaches (staff feedback)

A very small group in 2008 was maintained at the request of all attendees, who made a commitment to attend every session to make it sustainable. It is considered helpful to aim for 6-8 in the group, and to avoid having only one male if it is a mixed-gender group. The groups run in the United Kingdom were generally a gender mix, although there was one all-female group. All outcomes are by self-report.

## Outcome Measures

The Beck Hopelessness Scale (BHS) was used pre- and post-group to measure risk of suicide. It is of note because it has stronger predictive value in terms of future suicide risk than other measures of its kind.

The Self-Harm Questionnaire (SHQ-8) is used to obtain a history of self-harming. It is an 8 question current behavior screen evaluating: a person's readiness to address self-harm, their capability to seek alternatives and the frequency and likelihood of continued self-harm. These latter components were missing from the original SHQ-5 and are considered a means of capturing the key information

Table 9.1. DATA FROM ASH GROUPS RUN IN THE UNITED KINGDOM, 2005–2010

| Date | # | Finishers | Improved Confidence | Reduced Self-Harm | Improved skills | Sustained at 6-months | Reason for drop out | Comment |
|---|---|---|---|---|---|---|---|---|
| 2005 | 6 | 6 | 100% | 100% | 100% | 100% | n/a | – |
| 2006 | 6 | 5 | 100% | 100% | 100% | 100% | Knew someone in group | Attended another group |
| 2007 | 5 | 4 | 100% | 100% | 100% | 100% | Hospital surgery | Attended another group |
| 2008 | 3 | 3 | 100% | 100% | 100% | 100% | n/a | All 3 agreed to 100% attendance |
| 2009 | 5 | 4 | 100% | 100% | 100% | 100% | Wanted 1:1 | Offered 1:1 |
| 2010 | 6 | 6 | 100% | 100% | 100% | 100% | n/a | – |
| TOTAL | 31 | 28 | 100% | 100% | 100% | 100% | n/a | – |

which the previous longer measures did not capture in early trials. The SHQ-8 can be used as a pre- and post-measure to establish whether frequency and likelihood as well as confidence in a range of alternative options are sustained over time.

An ASH Adherence Rating Scale has been developed that is similar to the STEPPS Adherence Rating Scale which Blum and colleagues have devised (Blum et al., 2008).

In 2014 an initial 30 minute screening session was provided by the co-leaders with each individual participant which means there is a stronger focus on engagement in the first session as all the measures are completed beforehand.


## ACCEPTANCE BY PARTICIPANTS AND THERAPISTS

### Participants

Since implementation of the first group based approach using ASH in 2005, evaluations by participants have indicated strong themes: gaining then retaining confidence over time; a wider range of coping strategies; a reduction in risk from self-harm or a reduction in the riskier type self-harming behaviors.

Qualitative feedback included comments from a 54-year-old woman when she began the ASH program. She had a 30-year pattern of stockpiling her prescription medication and then overdosing on it when she found life too difficult, but never with the intention to die. At the conclusion of the ASH program she said that, "*When I started I was stockpiling pills, but now I am stockpiling good ideas.*" At 6 month review she had sustained this achievement and had been discharged from mental health services.

An 18-year-old male participant had a history of sexual abuse and found that suggestions offered to him by well-intended professionals were frequently unhelpful, as they seldom matched the purpose of harming. Using the Emotional First Aid kit to match his purposes was a major change for him. For example, a professional advised him to have a warm bath to help him relax (a sensation achieved for him by harming). This professional failed to check whether this strategy fitted for him. As the majority of his childhood abuse had occurred in the bathroom, this was one of the least helpful suggestions that could have been made to him. He said that by using the ASH Program he was able to select coping methods that truly fitted his need at the time.

A New Zealand woman in her forties, who had a history of rotating among community mental health and inpatient services, used the approach on an individual basis. She learned the ASH skills and this enabled her to remain out of hospital. She said that the skills gave her confidence and hope, and she found the XYZ Contract to be pivotal in this change for her.

The ASH program has also been offered to a variety of individuals across the age range (from children as young as 9 years to adults and older adults both in the United Kingdom and New Zealand) with similar outcomes.

## Therapists

During the early years in the United Kingdom many mental health staff expressed an interest in the new ideas generated by ASH and there was a theme in feedback from these staff that they found it much easier to work with the person when there was a clear and detailed emotional first aid kit to use with them. Colleagues, who learned the methods used in ASH by working alongside the author in delivering these early ASH groups, noted how the skills had a value for a range of different clients, whether or not they self-harmed. A key element of this was the A in APEX: Attitude of curious inquiry and respectful interpersonal discussions about the purpose of harming enabled a more useful set of strategies to be generated by way of the Emotional First Aid Kit and the XYZ Contract.

In the past few years, training workshops have been offered in New Zealand using the ASH approach and evaluations have been positive. Therapists commonly report that they use the ideas with other clients who have problems with impulse control or with various addictions, even if they do not self-harm.

## Support from Others

As part of the approach, attention to the members of the ASH participant's support system team is recommended. Each participant is encouraged to involve supportive others in their recovery process, in much the same way that the STEPPS program describes the concept of the "Reinforcement Team." This support system helps to maintain the progress made, and to reduce a sense of isolation that many participants have described when they leave the group situation. Work is in progress to include some additional sessions for professional support people and family members, and is included in the ASH program guidelines. In Maori culture and in other Pacific Island cultures, the collective is extremely important, such that individualized programs are less valued. Maori consider the *whanau* or extended family to be crucial in a recovery approach. STEPPS and ASH offer this collective approach, which augurs well for the future of such programs within such a cultural context. Indeed, where the ASH Program has been presented to Australian audiences, the use of ASH and STEPPS within an Australian Aboriginal context have been considered very helpful.

## PHOENIX

Follow-up support can be offered as a peer-support approach with a similar stance to that used in the STAIRWAYS program (Blum et al., 2009) which follows on from STEPPS. For ASH this has also been designed as a review of skills used in the ASH Program and it is called PHOENIX, which has yet to be studied. PHOENIX stands for the key elements of learning from the original ASH program and allows the person time to consolidate skills learned with others who have been through the ASH program. PHOENIX is therefore a peer group for maintenance plus support.

The components of the PHOENIX Program are

- Purpose of harming review
- Helpful links and hints
- Only what works for me
- Emotional first aid kit revisited
- New ideas developed and shared
- Involving support network
- XYZ contracts refreshed

A guideline for PHOENIX will be published once ASH has been published.

## CURRENT STATE OF ASH

ASH continues to be provided in the United Kingdom, drawing on the 2010 version of the approach. The prototype was studied successfully with professional colleagues in the United Kingdom. This was achieved by offering the groups with colleagues working alongside the presenter and thus learning on the job; then they were given a copy of the manual to guide them to run it themselves. Feedback to date is very positive. A longer 20 session version was studied but found to be less helpful than consideration of the PHOENIX follow-up program which is also being finalized. Part of this was a lack of clear guidelines on the exclusions or inclusions, which is also addressed in the manual. Training continues to be offered to other professionals in New Zealand about the APEX model together with training on a session by session guide to the program itself.

Once the adapted manual was completed in 2014, it was strongly recommended that this more polished version is used consistently. A tool to evaluate therapist fidelity to the program has been included to assist in providing a consistent approach. Adjustments have been made based on feedback from earlier groups and to training provided in the past 5 years, which has indicated an adjustment to the order of different components to improve the flow of the program and to enhance learning. The adapted outcome measures and the use of a briefer screening method are now included.

ASH is being offered in New Zealand, mainly in tertiary and secondary educational settings at this time but could be offered in other settings such as forensic services and adult mental health given that it was originally designed based on these settings. Presentations were offered for those providing support in tertiary settings in Wellington (Clare, 2013) and Auckland (Clare, 2014a) as well as published in a related journal (Clare, 2014b ANZJSSA).

## FUTURE OF ASH

Work to date has been within adult mental health and forensic settings and ASH has been adapted for working within a tertiary educational setting. The development of PHOENIX could be adapted as a peer-led follow up program for participants who find it helpful without the necessity for professional intervention, other than occasional consultations perhaps. With more complex needs such as in mental health and forensic settings, it may be appropriate to offer PHOENIX as a professionally-facilitated option.

Within a university setting, the possibility of including trainee psychologists and trainee counsellors is being considered for assisting in the delivery of ASH in the future. It is hoped that the promising outcomes from initial trials with relatively small numbers of participants can be replicated in larger numbers of participants across a range of settings.

The ASH Guidelines (a preferred term to "manual" more in keeping with a Narrative Therapy approach) is being finalized as a resource in 2016 and PHOENIX will follow. The promising outcomes from initial trials have been replicated in the individual work of my clients over the past 15 years. As part of the provision of the guidelines, it is a requisite for all future purchasers to submit anonymous data about their outcomes so that larger numbers can be studied. Expressions of interest to purchase the Alternative to Self Harm Guidelines can be made through www.mindbusinessconsultancy.com.

## REFERENCES

Blum, N. S., Bartels, N. E., St. John, D., & Pfohl, B. (2002). *Systems Training for Emotional Predictability and Problem Solving (STEPPS): Group treatment program for borderline personality disorder*. Level One Publishing (www.steppsforbpd.com).

Blum, N. S., & St. John, D. (2009). *STAIRWAYS: The next step in group treatment for borderline personality disorder*. Available on CD-ROM from Level One Publishing (www.steppsforbpd.com).

Blum, N. S., Bartels, N. E., St. John, D., & Pfohl, B. (2012). *Systems Training for Emotional Predictability and Problem Solving* (STEPPS 2nd Ed). Available on CD-ROM from Level One Publishing (www.steppsforbpd.com).

Blum, N., St. John, D., Pfohl, B., Stuart, S., McCormick, B., Allen, J., Arndt, S., & Black, D.W. (2008). Systems Training for Emotional Predictability and Problem Solving (STEPPS) for outpatients with borderline personality disorder: A randomized controlled trial and 1-year follow-up. *American Journal of Psychiatry, 165*, 468–478.

Clare, D. (2012). *ASH:A skills-based approach*, paper presented as part of STEPPS across the Globe Symposium by Blum, N. S., Black, D. ESSPD Conference, Amsterdam, 2012.

Clare, D. (2013a) . *ASH: A skills-based approach,* as part of STEPPS across the Globe Symposium by Blum, N. S., Black, D. ISSPD Conference, Copenhagen, 2013.

Clare, D. (2013b). *Alternatives to Self-Harm: A skills-based approach in a tertiary setting?* Paper presented at ANZSSA Conference, Wellington, New Zealand, 2013.

Clare, D. (2014a). Alternatives to Self-Harm: A skills-based approach in a tertiary set-ting? Journal *of Australian and New Zealand Student Services Association, Special Conference Edition.*

Clare, D. (2014b). *Alternatives to Self-Harm: A skills-based approach in a tertiary setting.* Paper presented at ANZSSA Conference, Auckland New Zealand, 2014.

Clare, D. (2014). *ASH: A skills-based approach in a tertiary setting* as part of STEPPS across the Globe Symposium by Blum, N. S., Black, D. ESSPD Conference, Rome, 2014.

Clare, D. (2015). *Is there an alternative to self-harm? ASH, a skills-based approach.* ISSPD Conference, Montreal, 2015.

Linehan, M. (1993). *Cognitive behavioural treatment of borderline personality disorder.* New York, NY: Guilford Press.

Linehan, M. (2012), an unpublished personal address to the ESSPD Conference Amsterdam 2012.

Miller, Scott D., Duncan, B. L. & Hubble, M. 2004. Beyond Integration: the Triumph of Outcome Over Process in Clinical Practice. Psychotherapy in Australia Vol 10. No 2 February, pp. 1–20.

National Institute for Health & Clinical Excellence (2004). Self-harm: The short-term physical and psychological management and secondary prevention of self-harm in primary and secondary care. *Clinical Guidance,* 16. Downloadable from www. nice.org.uk

National Institute for Health & Clinical Excellence (2011). *Self-harm: Longer term man-agement. Clinical Guidance,* 133. London, England: British Psychological Society & Royal College of Psychiatrists.

Sutton, J. (2007). *Healing the hurt within: Understand self-injury and self-harm, and heal the emotional wounds* (revised, updated 3rd ed.). Oxford, England: How To Books.

White, M., & Epson, D. (1990). *Narrative means to therapeutic ends.* New York, NY: Norton.

White, M. (1995). *Re-authoring Lives: Interviews and Essays.* Adelaide: Dulwich Centre Publications.

White, M. (2000). *Reflections on narrative practice, essays and interviews.* Adelaide, Australia: Dulwich Centre Publications.

Wingard, B. (1996). Introducing 'Sugar' Adelaide. *Dulwich Centre Newsletter* No. 3, pp. 25–29.

# Appendix: STEPPS Forms

Form 1. BEST© *(Borderline Evaluation of Severity over Time)*

Name: _____ ID#_____

Total Score: _____ Date: _____

For the first 12 items, the highest rating (5) means that the item caused extreme distress, severe difficulties with relationships, and/or kept you from getting things done. The lowest rating (1) means it caused little or no problems. Rate items 13–15 (positive behaviors) according to frequency.

| Circle the period you have been asked to rate: | Last 7 Days | Last 30 Days | Other _____ |
|---|---|---|---|

*Circle the number that indicates how much the item has caused distress, relationship problems, or difficulty with getting things done.*

A. Thoughts and Feelings [    ]

| | None/slight | Mild | Moderate | Severe | Extreme |
|---|---|---|---|---|---|
| 1. Worrying that someone important in your life is tired of you or is planning to leave you | 1 | 2 | 3 | 4 | 5 |
| 2. Major shifts in your opinions about others such as switching from believing someone is a loyal friend or partner to believing that the person is untrustworthy and hurtful | 1 | 2 | 3 | 4 | 5 |
| 3. Extreme changes in how you see yourself. Shifting from feeling confident about who you are to feeling like you are evil or that you don't even exist | 1 | 2 | 3 | 4 | 5 |
| 4. Severe mood swings several times a day. Minor events cause major shifts in mood | 1 | 2 | 3 | 4 | 5 |
| 5. Feeling paranoid or like you are losing touch with reality | 1 | 2 | 3 | 4 | 5 |
| 6. Feeling angry | 1 | 2 | 3 | 4 | 5 |
| 7. Feelings of emptiness | 1 | 2 | 3 | 4 | 5 |
| 8. Feeling suicidal | 1 | 2 | 3 | 4 | 5 |

**To the clinician:** the total for each section (A, B, and C) should be recorded in the brackets following the section titles. At the top of the page record the total composite score (15 + A + B − C)

## B. Behaviors (Negative) [   ]

| | None/slight | Mild | Moderate | Severe | Extreme |
|---|---|---|---|---|---|
| 9. Going to extremes to try to keep someone from leaving you | 1 | 2 | 3 | 4 | 5 |
| 10. Purposely doing something to injure yourself or making a suicide attempt | 1 | 2 | 3 | 4 | 5 |
| 11. Problems with impulsive behavior (<u>not</u> including suicide attempts or injuring yourself on purpose) Examples are overspending, risky sexual behavior, substance abuse, reckless driving, binge eating, other _____(*circle those that apply*) | 1 | 2 | 3 | 4 | 5 |
| 12. Temper outbursts or problems with anger leading to relationship problems, physical fights, or destruction of property | 1 | 2 | 3 | 4 | 5 |

*Circle the number that indicates how often you used the following positive behaviors*

## C. Behaviors (Positive) [   ]

| | Almost always | Most of the time | Half of the time | Sometimes | Almost never |
|---|---|---|---|---|---|
| 13. Choosing to use a positive activity in circumstances where you felt tempted to do something destructive or self-defeating | 5 | 4 | 3 | 2 | 1 |
| 14. Noticing ahead of time that something could cause you emotional difficulties and taking reasonable steps to avoid/prevent the problem | 5 | 4 | 3 | 2 | 1 |
| 15. Following through with therapy plans to which you agreed (e.g., talk therapy, "homework" assignments, coming to appointments, medications, etc.) | 5 | 4 | 3 | 2 | 1 |

Excerpted from STEPPS™: Group Treatment Program for Borderline Personality Disorder
www.steppsforbpd.com

## Form 2. QuEST© *(Quick Evaluation of Severity over Time)*

Name: _____ ID# _____

Total Score: _____ Date: _____

For the first 12 items, the highest rating (5) means that the item caused extreme distress, severe difficulties with relationships, and/or kept you from getting things done. The lowest rating (1) means it caused little or no problems. Rate items 13–15 (positive behaviors) according to frequency.

| Circle the period you have been asked to rate: | Last 7 Days | Last 30 Days | Other _____ |
|---|---|---|---|

*Circle the number that indicates how much the item has caused distress, relationship problems, or difficulty with getting things done.*

A. Thoughts and Feelings [   ]

| | None/slight | Mild | Moderate | Severe | Extreme |
|---|---|---|---|---|---|
| 1. Worrying that someone important in your life is tired of you or is planning to leave you | 1 | 2 | 3 | 4 | 5 |
| 2. Quickly changing your opinions about others such as switching from believing someone is a loyal, caring friend to believing that the person is completely untrustworthy and hurtful | 1 | 2 | 3 | 4 | 5 |
| 3. Extreme changes in how you see yourself. Shifting from feeling confident about who you are to feeling like you are evil, or that you don't even exist | 1 | 2 | 3 | 4 | 5 |
| 4. Severe mood swings several times a day. Minor events cause major shifts in mood | 1 | 2 | 3 | 4 | 5 |
| 5. Feeling paranoid or like you are losing touch with reality | 1 | 2 | 3 | 4 | 5 |
| 6. Feeling extremely angry | 1 | 2 | 3 | 4 | 5 |
| 7. Feeling very empty | 1 | 2 | 3 | 4 | 5 |
| 8. Feeling suicidal | 1 | 2 | 3 | 4 | 5 |

**To the clinician**: the total for each section (A, B, and C) should be recorded in the brackets following the section titles. At the top of the page record the total composite score (15 + A + B − C)

## B. Behaviors (Negative) [    ]

| | None/slight | Mild | Moderate | Severe | Extreme |
|---|---|---|---|---|---|
| 9. Going to extremes to try to keep someone from leaving you | 1 | 2 | 3 | 4 | 5 |
| 10. Purposely doing something to injure yourself or making a suicide attempt | 1 | 2 | 3 | 4 | 5 |
| 11. Problems with impulsive behavior (<u>not</u> including suicide attempts or injuring yourself on purpose) Examples are: over-spending, risky sexual behavior, substance abuse, reckless driving, binge eating, other _____ (*circle those that apply*) | 1 | 2 | 3 | 4 | 5 |
| 12. Temper outbursts or problems with anger leading to relationship problems, physical fights, or destruction of property | 1 | 2 | 3 | 4 | 5 |

*Circle the number that indicates how often you used the following positive behaviors*

## C. Behaviors (Positive) [    ]

| | Almost always | Most of the time | Half of the time | Sometimes | Almost never |
|---|---|---|---|---|---|
| 13. Choosing to use a positive activity in circumstances where you felt tempted to do something destructive or self-defeating | 5 | 4 | 3 | 2 | 1 |
| 14. Noticing ahead of time that something could cause you emotional difficulties and taking reasonable steps to avoid/prevent the problem | 5 | 4 | 3 | 2 | 1 |
| 15. Following through with therapy plans to which you agreed (e.g., talk therapy, "homework" assignments, coming to appointments, medications, etc.) | 5 | 4 | 3 | 2 | 1 |

© 1997, 2012 Bruce Pfohl, MD & Nancee Blum, MSW.

Adapted from STEPPS™: Group Treatment Program.

Reprinted from Blum, N. S., Bartels, N. E, St. John, D., & Pfohl, B. (with Harvey, R., Henley-Cragg, P., Burgess, J., Parrott, M.) (2015). *Managing Emotional Intensity: A STEPPS Resource for Younger People.* Iowa City, IA: Level One Publishing, www.steppsforbpd.com

## Form 3. What Do We Mean by "Emotional Intensity Difficulties?"

Levels of emotional intensity that may cause difficulties could include some of the following feelings, thoughts, or behaviors. The difficulties might affect your relationships, how you view yourself, how you experience various moods, or whether you can control urges to act impulsively.

1. Fear and worry that someone important in your life is tired of you or planning to leave you. You may go to extremes to keep someone from leaving you.
2. Unstable and stormy relationships and friendships because of quickly changing your opinions about others, such as thinking someone is completely wonderful and just as quickly deciding they are the worst person you've ever known.
3. Frequent or extreme changes in how you see yourself, such as shifting from feeling confident about who you are to being very unsure of who you are or what your goals and values are.
4. Being impulsive and engaging in risky behaviors (such as risky sexual behavior, using drugs or alcohol, driving recklessly) without thinking of the consequences.
5. Feeling very sad and/or hopeless, purposely doing something to injure yourself, or making a suicide attempt.
6. Experiencing very rapid mood changes several times a day, often going from feeling depressed to normal to angry or anxious very quickly. Minor events seem to cause major shifts in mood.
7. Feeling very empty.
8. Temper outbursts or problems with anger leading to relationship problems, physically hurting other people, or breaking things (your own or other people's).
9. When you are stressed, feeling paranoid or distrustful of people you usually trust. Having brief blackouts or periods when you forget what has happened (not due to using drugs or alcohol).

Such characteristics should be a long-term feature of your personality and not the result of a physical illness, use of substances, or only relating to one or two specific situations.

Based on American Psychiatric Association (2013), DSM-5, and BEST/QuEST, STEPPS Group Treatment Programme (2002, 2012). Reprinted from Blum, N. S., Bartels, N. E., St. John, D., & Pfohl, B. (with Harvey, R., Henley-Cragg, P., Burgess, J., Parrott, M.) (2015). *Managing emotional intensity: A STEPPS resource for younger people.* Iowa City, IA: Level One Publishing, www.steppsforbpd.com

Form 4. Emotional Intensity Continuum

**Event:** *What happened?*

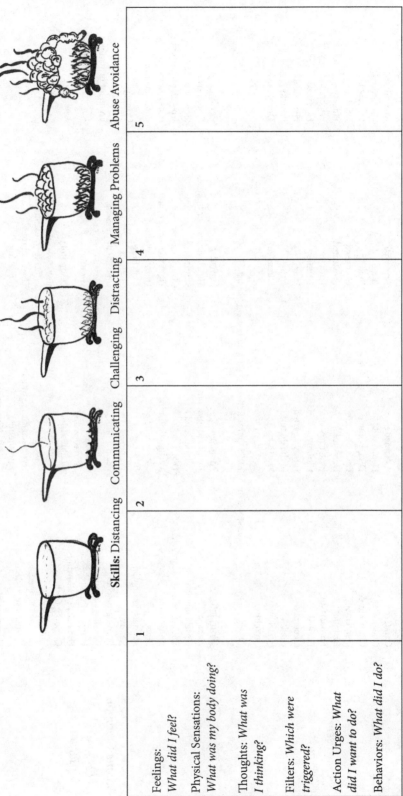

| | **Skills:** Distancing | Communicating | Challenging | Distracting | Managing Problems | Abuse Avoidance |
|---|---|---|---|---|---|---|
| | 1 | 2 | 3 | 4 | 5 | |
| Feelings: *What did I feel?* | | | | | | |
| Physical Sensations: *What was my body doing?* | | | | | | |
| Thoughts: *What was I thinking?* | | | | | | |
| Filters: *Which were triggered?* | | | | | | |
| Action Urges: *What did I want to do?* | | | | | | |
| Behaviors: *What did I do?* | | | | | | |

**Filters:** Abandonment  Emotional deprivation  Subjugation  Mistrust  Failure to achieve  Unrelenting standards  Vulnerable to harm
Defectiveness  Self-sacrifice  Entitlement

| | Happy | Sad | Angry | Afraid |
|---|---|---|---|---|
| **Some Feeling Words** | Carefree | Ashamed | Annoyed | Anxious |
| | Cheerful | Depressed | Bitter | Cowardly |
| | Comfortable | Disappointed | Boiling | Defeated |
| | Contented | Discontented | Confused | Fearful |
| | Ecstatic | Dreadful | Frustrated | Fidgety |
| | Enthusiastic | Embarrassed | Furious | Frightened |
| | Excited | Gloomy | Grumpy | Horrified |
| | Generous | Heavy-hearted | Irate | Hysterical |
| | Glad | In the dumps | Irritated | Panicky |
| | Hilarious | Worthless | Offended | Threatened |
| | Grateful | | | |

Please see the STEPPS Quick Reference for a more complete list.

| | Happy | Sad | Angry | Afraid |
|---|---|---|---|---|
| **Some Common Physical Sensations** | Gastrointestinal | Numbness | Muscular | Cardiac |
| | Nausea | Burning sensations in hands and feet | Muscle tension or tightness | Fast heart rate |
| | Upset stomach | Dizziness | Stiffness | Slow heart rate |
| | Butterflies in the stomach | Vertigo (spinning sensation) | Clenching jaw | Irregular heartbeat |
| | Indigestion | In-a-fog | Tight facial expression | Palpitations |
| | Bloating | Weakness | Tremor/shaking | Pounding heart |
| | Stomach cramping | Feeling faint | Twitching | |
| | Reflux | Sensory | Chills | Urinary |
| | Burping/belching | Blurred vision | Unusual movements | Urinary urgency |
| | Burning sensation | Double vision | Closed posture | Frequent urination |
| | Lump in throat | Photophobia (sensitivity to light) | Sweating | |
| | Difficulty swallowing | Hyperacusis (sensitivity to sounds) | Respiratory | |
| | Grinding teeth | Tinnitus (ringing ears) | Shortness-of-breath | |
| | Choking | Unusual taste(s) | Difficulty breathing | |
| | Change in appetite (increase or decrease) | Unusual smell(s) | Chest tightness | |
| | Neurological | | Wheezing | |
| | Headache | | | |
| | Tingling | | | |

Reprinted from Blum, N. S., Bartels, N. E, St. John, D., & Pfohl, B. (2012). *Systems Training for Emotional Predictability and Problem Solving (Second Edition): Group Treatment Program for Borderline Personality Disorder.* Iowa City, IA: Level One Publishing, www.steppsforbpd.com

Form 5. Emotional Intensity Continuum (Example 1)

Event: Boyfriend late

What did happened?

**Skills:** Distancing　Communication　Challenging　Distracting　Managing Problems　Abuse Avoidance

| | 1 | 2 | 3 | 4 | 5 |
|---|---|---|---|---|---|
| **Feelings** *What did I feel?* | Relaxed Happy Calm | Anxious Irritable Annoyed | Frustrated Angry | Fuming Suicidal | Boiling Abandoned Desperate Hopeless |
| **Physical Sensations** *What was my body doing?* | Muscles relaxed | Muscles tense | Butterflies in stomach, hands shaking, jaw clenching | Sweating, nauseated | Heart pounding, trembling |
| **Thoughts** *What was I thinking?* | Things are going well. This is a great relationship. | He's late ... again! Why does he do this to me?! | He's never coming back. He wants to break up! | He's found someone else. I can't stand this! | I'll never have another boyfriend. Everyone leaves me. |
| **Filters** *Which were triggered?* | Positive: caring, relationship stability | Negative: abandonment | Abandonment | Abandonment | Abandonment, defectiveness |
| **Action Urges** *What did I want to do?* | Do something enjoyable. | Call him at work | Go to his work-place | Self-harm, overdose | Self-harm, cut, overdose |
| **Behaviors** *What did I do?* | Listening to music, Reading watching TV | Pacing Calling his cell phone | Calling his work-place, friends, family | Crying, looking for a razor | Screaming, throwing things, cutting |

**Filters:** Abandonment　Emotional deprivation　Subjugation　Mistrust　Failure to achieve　Unrelenting standards　Vulnerable to harm
Defectiveness　Self-sacrifice　Entitlement

## Some Feeling Words

| Happy | Sad | Angry | Afraid |
|---|---|---|---|
| Carefree | Ashamed | Annoyed | Anxious |
| Cheerful | Depressed | Bitter | Cowardly |
| Comfortable | Disappointed | Boiling | Defeated |
| Contented | Discontented | Confused | Fearful |
| Ecstatic | Dreadful | Frustrated | Fidgety |
| Enthusiastic | Embarrassed | Furious | Frightened |
| Excited | Gloomy | Grumpy | Horrified |
| Generous | Heavy-hearted | Irate | Hysterical |
| Glad | In the dumps | Irritated | Panicky |
| Hilarious | Worthless | Offended | Threatened |
| Grateful | | | |

Please see the STEPPS Quick Reference for a more complete list.

## Some Common Physical Sensations

**Gastrointestinal**
Nausea
Upset stomach
Butterflies in the stomach
Indigestion
Bloating
Stomach cramping
Reflux
Burping/belching
Burning sensation
Lump in throat
Difficulty swallowing
Grinding teeth
Choking
Change in appetite (increase or decrease)

**Neurological**
Headache
Tingling
Numbness
Burning sensations in hands and feet
Dizziness
Vertigo (spinning sensation)
In-a-fog
Weakness
Feeling faint

**Sensory**
Blurred vision
Double vision
Photophobia (sensitivity to light)

**Hyperaccusis** (sensitivity to sounds)
Tinnitus (ringing ears)
Unusual taste(s)
Unusual smell(s)

**Muscular**
Muscle tension or tightness
Stiffness
Clenching jaw
Tight facial expression
Tremor/shaking
Twitching
Chills
Unusual movements
Closed posture
Sweating

**Respiratory**
Shortness-of-breath
Difficulty breathing
Chest tightness
Wheezing

**Cardiac**
Fast heart rate
Slow heart rate
Irregular heartbeat
Palpitations
Pounding heart

**Urinary**
Urinary urgency
Frequent urination

Reprinted from Blum, N. S., Bartels, N. E, St. John, D., & Pfohl, B. (2012). *Systems Training for Emotional Predictability and Problem Solving (Second Edition): Group Treatment Program for Borderline Personality Disorder.* Iowa City, IA: Level One Publishing, www.steppsforbpd.com

Form 6. Emotional Intensity Continuum (*Example 2*)

**Event:** Person on cell phone rams into you at supermarket—no apology

*What happened?*

**Skills:** Distancing   Communicating   Challenging   Distracting   Managing Problems   Abuse Avoidance

| | 1 | 2 | 3 | 4 | 5 |
|---|---|---|---|---|---|
| **Feelings:** *What did I feel?* | Calm | Anxious Irritated | Upset/angry | very angry | Furious — in a rage |
| **Physical Sensations:** *What was my body doing?* | Muscles relaxed | Restless | Startled Stomach churning | Muscles tensed Flushed Sweating | Heart pounding Clenched jaw Fists clenched |
| **Thoughts:** *What was I thinking?* | This is fine. I can do the shopping, no worries | It's getting busy. There are too many people | What! that guy just ran into me | He did that on purpose, that @%£$% | He started it. He deserves to be punished. Disrespected me! |
| **Filters:** *Which were triggered?* | Self-control Positive | Vulnerability to harm | Vulnerability to harm Defectiveness | Vulnerability to harm. Defectiveness Entitlement | Entitlement |
| **Action Urges** *What did I want to do?* | Get on with the shopping | Speed up the shopping | React defensively, then move after him | Run after him and tell him people don't treat me like that & get away with it | Shout at him and/or punch him |
| **Behaviors** *What did I do?* | Walking around supermarket | Looking around nervously | Looking around checking for danger, moving fast | Clenched fists, staring, moving quickly towards him | Shout at him, shove or hit him |

**Filters:** Abandonment   Entitlement   Emotional deprivation   Subjugation   Mistrust   Failure to achieve   Unrelenting standards   Vulnerable to harm   Defectiveness   Self-sacrifice

|  | Happy | Sad | Angry | Afraid |
|---|---|---|---|---|
| **Some Feeling Words** | Carefree | Ashamed | Annoyed | Anxious |
|  | Cheerful | Depressed | Bitter | Cowardly |
|  | Comfortable | Disappointed | Boiling | Defeated |
|  | Contented | Discontented | Confused | Fearful |
|  | Ecstatic | Dreadful | Frustrated | Fidgety |
|  | Enthusiastic | Embarrassed | Furious | Frightened |
|  | Excited | Gloomy | Grumpy | Horrified |
|  | Generous | Heavy-hearted | Irate | Hysterical |
|  | Glad | In the dumps | Irritated | Panicky |
|  | Hilarious | Worthless | Offended | Threatened |
|  | Grateful |  |  |  |

Please see the STEPPS Quick Reference for a more complete list.

|  | Happy | Sad | Angry | Afraid |
|---|---|---|---|---|
| **Some Common Physical Sensations** | <u>Gastrointestinal</u> | <u>Numbness</u> | <u>Muscular</u> | <u>Cardiac</u> |
|  | Nausea | Burning sensations in hands and feet | Muscle tension or tightness | Fast heart rate |
|  | Upset stomach | Dizziness | Stiffness | Slow heart rate |
|  | Butterflies in the stomach | Vertigo (spinning sensation) | Clenching jaw | Irregular heartbeat |
|  | Indigestion | In-a-fog | Tight facial expression | Palpitations |
|  | Bloating | Weakness | Tremor/shaking | Pounding heart |
|  | Stomach cramping | Feeling faint | Twitching |  |
|  | Reflux |  | Chills | <u>Urinary</u> |
|  | Burping/belching | <u>Sensory</u> | Unusual movements | Urinary urgency |
|  | Burning sensation | Blurred vision | Closed posture | Frequent urination |
|  | Lump in throat | Double vision | Sweating |  |
|  | Difficulty swallowing | Photophobia (sensitivity to light) |  |  |
|  | Grinding teeth | Hyperaccusis (sensitivity to sounds) | <u>Respiratory</u> |  |
|  | Choking | Tinnitus (ringing ears) | Shortness-of-breath |  |
|  | Change in appetite (increase or decrease) | Unusual taste(s) | Difficulty breathing |  |
|  |  | Unusual smell(s) | Chest tightness |  |
|  | <u>Neurological</u> |  | Wheezing |  |
|  | Headache |  |  |  |
|  | Tingling |  |  |  |

Reprinted from Blum, N.S., Bartels, N. E. St. John, D., & Pfohl, B. (2012). *Systems Training for Emotional Predictability and Problem Solving (Second Edition): Group Treatment Program for Borderline Personality Disorder*. Iowa City, IA: Level One Publishing, www.steppsforbpd.com

Form 7. Skills Monitoring Card

## Instructions: Check The Skills You Practiced This Week

Dates

| Emotion Management Skills | / | / | / | / | / | / | / |
|---|---|---|---|---|---|---|---|
| Distance: step back | | | | | | | |
| Communicate: put words on it | | | | | | | |
| Challenge: think about it differently | | | | | | | |
| Distract: get involved | | | | | | | |
| Manage problem | | | | | | | |

Dates

| Behavior Management Skills | / | / | / | / | / | / | / |
|---|---|---|---|---|---|---|---|
| Took medications as prescribed | | | | | | | |
| Used relaxation technique | | | | | | | |
| Used self-soothing activity | | | | | | | |
| Used distraction activity | | | | | | | |
| Used Emotional Intensity Continuum | | | | | | | |
| Used reinforcement team member | | | | | | | |
| Balanced eating | | | | | | | |
| Regular sleeping | | | | | | | |
| Regular exercise | | | | | | | |
| Physical health | | | | | | | |
| Leisure activities | | | | | | | |
| Avoided abusive behaviors | | | | | | | |
| Used relationship skills | | | | | | | |

Reprinted from Blum, N. S., Bartels, N. E., St. John, D., & Pfohl, B. (2012). *Systems Training for Emotional Predictability and Problem Solving (Second Edition): Group treatment program for borderline personality disorder.* Iowa City, IA: Level One Publishing. www.steppsforbpd.com

## Form 8.  Responding to the Person with Emotional Intensity Disorder

1. Where are you on your *Emotional Intensity Continuum* (1–5)?
2. Have you used your binder/folder?
3. What skill can you use in this situation? How will you use it?
4. If the person cannot think of what skill to use, ask about each skill on the list.

| Emotion Regulation Skills |
|---|
| Distance: step back |
| Communicate: put words on it |
| Challenge: think about it differently |
| Distract: get involved |
| Manage problem |

| Behavior Skills |
|---|
| Take medications as prescribed |
| Use relaxation technique |
| Use self-soothing activity |
| Use distraction activity |
| Use Emotional Intensity Continuum |
| Use reinforcement team member |
| Eating |
| Sleeping |
| Regular exercise |
| Physical health |
| Relaxation/leisure activities |
| Avoid abusive behaviors |
| Use relationship skills |

Reprinted from Blum, N. S., Bartels, N. E., St. John, D., & Pfohl, B. (2012). *Systems Training for Emotional Predictability and Problem Solving (Second Edition): Group treatment program for borderline personality disorder.* Iowa City, IA: Level One Publishing, www.steppsforbpd.com

Therapists _____

Date of Session ___/___/___     Session #_____

Date of Rating ___/___/___      Rater _____

**INSTRUCTIONS:** For each item assess the therapists on a scale from 1 to 5 by circling the rating next to the item number. When rating each item, the following should be taken into account: (1) stage of therapy and (2) difficulty of patients in therapy. In addition, the ratings should take into account both the presence of the intervention (adherence) and the quality with which it is delivered (competence).

1 = Poor   2 = Barely adequate   3 = Satisfactory   4 = Good   5 = Excellent
n/a = Not Applicable

**STEPPS Framework**

1. BPD conceptualized as a disorder of behavior & emotion regulation............................................................... 1 2 3 4 5 n/a

2. A specific agenda was set at the beginning of each session.................................................................................. 1 2 3 4 5 n/a

3. The BEST questionnaire was reviewed ............................ 1 2 3 4 5 n/a

4. A relaxation exercise was conducted near the beginning of the session*.................................................... 1 2 3 4 5 n/a

5. Efforts were made to involve clients in reviewing the Emotional Intensity Continuum* ..................................... 1 2 3 4 5 n/a

6. Skills to manage cognitive & emotional effects of BPD were discussed*................................................................... 1 2 3 4 5 n/a

7. Behavioral management skills were discussed*................................................................................. 1 2 3 4 5 n/a

8. Homework for the previous week was reviewed ............. 1 2 3 4 5 n/a

9. Therapists followed facilitator guidelines..................... ..... 1 2 3 4 5 n/a

10. Individual goals were reviewed (after lesson on goal setting).................................................................................. 1 2 3 4 5 n/a

11. Clients were encouraged to seek individual therapy or to speak with their individual therapist when appropriate.......................................................................... 1 2 3 4 5 n/a

12. Clients were encouraged to utilize their reinforcement team when appropriate...................................................... 1 2 3 4 5 n/a

13. Homework was assigned at the end of the session.......... 1 2 3 4 5 n/a

14. Crises were addressed that may require departure from session guidelines (e.g., suicidality, imminent self-harm, etc)................................................................... 1 2 3 4 5 n/a

    *If included in lesson plan for that session

## Specific STEPPS Techniques

15. Schemas (referred to as filters) underlying thoughts and behaviors were addressed (after 2nd session)............................................................ 1  2  3  4  5  n/a

16. Distorted cognitions were addressed in the group (after 6th session).................................................. 1  2  3  4  5  n/a

17. Difficulty applying the skills was normalized ................... 1  2  3  4  5  n/a

18. Discussions focus on the here and now............................ 1  2  3  4  5  n/a

## Group Dynamics

19. A psychoeducational format was utilized.......................... 1  2  3  4  5  n/a

20. Therapists avoided allowing one person to monopolize session.................................................................. 1  2  3  4  5  n/a

21. Group members were encouraged to participate ............. 1  2  3  4  5  n/a

22. Group cohesiveness was fostered....................................... 1  2  3  4  5  n/a

## Non-Specific Therapy Techniques

23. Therapists worked collaboratively with patients................ 1  2  3  4  5  n/a

24. Therapists were responsive to patients' feedback............... 1  2  3  4  5  n/a

25. Therapists were non-judgemental....................................... 1  2  3  4  5  n/a

26. Therapists conveyed a sense of warmth............................. 1  2  3  4  5  n/a

27. Therapists displayed empathy............................................. 1  2  3  4  5  n/a

## Summary

Therapists' overall adherence in delivering the STEPPS intervention in this session............................................. 1  2  3  4  5  n/a

Reprinted from Blum, N. S., Bartels, N. E., St. John, D., & Pfohl, B. (2012). *Systems Training for Emotional Predictability and Problem Solving (Second Edition): Group treatment program for borderline personality disorder.* Iowa City, IA: Level One Publishing, www.steppsforbpd.com

Page references for tables are indicated by *t*, for figures by *f*, and for boxes by *b*.